STRUGGLE IN BABYLON

THE AUTHOR

Kenneth Leech is a graduate of King's College, London and Trinity College, Oxford. He trained for the priesthood at St Stephen's House, Oxford and was ordained in 1964. He worked for several years in the East End of London and in Soho among drug addicts, and wrote *A Practical Guide to the Drug Scene*, which has been acclaimed as the best book written on the problems of drug dependence. He is also the author of *Youthquake*, a study of the 1950s and 1960s, *Soul Friend*, a study of Christian spirituality, and its successors *True Prayer* and *True God*, and *Spirituality and Pastoral Care*, which examines personal spiritual growth and his own influences. He has written for many journals, and broadcasts frequently on television and radio. From 1971–74 he was chaplain of St Augustine's College, Canterbury, and from 1974–80 he was Rector of St Matthew's, Bethnal Green. He was Race Relations Field Officer for the Board for Social Responsibility from 1981 to 1987, and he is presently Director of the Runymede Trust, an information and research unit on race relations.

STRUGGLE IN BABYLON

Racism in the Cities and Churches of Britain

KENNETH LEECH

SHELDON PRESS · LONDON

First published in Great Britain in 1988 by
Sheldon Press, SPCK, Marylebone Road, London NW1 4DU

British Library Cataloguing in Publication Data

Leech, Kenneth, *1939–*
Struggle in Babylon: racism in the cities and churches of Britain.
1. Great Britain. Racism, to 1987.
Attitudes of Christian church
I. Title
261.8'348'0941

ISBN 0–85969–577–8

Typeset by Deltatype, Ellesmere Port
Printed in Great Britain by Anchor Brendon Ltd, Tiptree, Essex

In memory of
MARTIN LUTHER KING, JR.
and
THOMAS MERTON
two prophets of the twentieth-century Church
who died during 1968.

Contents

Introduction

This is a book about race, racism and the churches within English cities. But in order to locate it both within the wider urban social context and within my own personal context as a pastor who has always lived in or on the edges of big cities, I need to begin with some reflections which may seem very far from the subject of racism.

I was born and brought up in a street in Greater Manchester in the years during and after the Second World War. The district, traditionally known as 'the cotton towns', is now called Tameside. Very few people in our street went to church and the church played little or no part in our lives. I attended a church primary school, but the church itself seemed a distant and alien institution. Sunday School was an accepted part of working-class children's lives; the church itself was something else, and only a small percentage of us effected the transition from Sunday School to church. From quite an early age I was conscious not only of a class division between my own working-class culture and what I saw, from a distance, as the culture of the Church of England, but also of a kind of class structure within the churches themselves. This class structure was visibly displayed every year at the 'Whit Walks' when Sunday School children, augmented by numbers of others, showed off their new clothes in the Whitsun processions. The buying of new clothes at Whitsun was a major headache, and if your parents were poor or unemployed, there were no new clothes and no participation in 'the walks'.

My earliest consciousness of 'class', in fact, was connected with clothes, indoor lavatories, telephones and books. The poor children – of whom I was one – whose parents could not afford new clothes at Whitsun, had no part in the processions. Anglican church life in particular was associated with respectable clothing. Again, the possession of an indoor lavatory was a major feature which distinguished the upper working class and the middle class from the rest of us, who either had lavatories (without chains) in the back yard, or shared them with four or five other houses. Telephones in our area and in this period were mainly restricted to professionals – clergy, doctors and the like – while the presence of books in the home marked you off as somehow 'different'. My first memories of going into a vicarage were of a house which was so much bigger than anything I had ever seen, very much 'posher' than my own home, and of the presence of large numbers of books.

So from an early age I was conscious of the Church of England as a middle-class presence within a mainly working-class community. To become an Anglican involved, in varying degrees, a break with your culture. My own first encounters with the Church of England were, as I recall them now, associated with a sense of 'going up in the world', of entering a new, middle-class world. One of my Sunday School teachers in the late 1940s was Kathy Staff, who now plays Nora Batty in *Last of the Summer Wine* on TV. Her name then was Minnie Higginbottom, and she and her sister Connie and their parents lived a few doors from us. For her, and for the relatively small number of upwardly mobile folk in our street, the Church of England and the Tory Party went together. They were both part of 'making it'. But neither Church nor party belonged to, or spoke to, the experience of the majority of working people. I shall never forget the mixture of hurt and disgust on my father's face when I told him that I wanted to be a priest. It seemed a kind of betrayal. In becoming an Anglican I was conscious, as a white, working-class person, of leaving behind something of my own culture, something of myself, in order to effect the transition. There was a deep sense of loss, and I think that many working-class people who have 'entered the Church' have felt it, and continue to feel it.

In 1954, at the time when, for various reasons, I was becoming interested in Christianity, I discovered the phenomenon – a strange one in our area – known as Anglo-Catholicism; not, fortunately, in its 'gin and lace', high-camp form which is so common in London, but in a back-street, working-class, very earthy form. It was in this small, fairly ugly church, tucked away in a side street, that I discovered it was possible to be an Anglican, albeit of a fairly marginal type, without completely taking on the trappings of bourgeois culture. For one of the byproducts of the Anglo-Catholic revival had been the emergence of poor parishes of ritualistic bent within the Church of England. They formed a kind of alternative rebel tradition. On a world scale it is a tradition with more black adherents than white. I did not know this in 1954, although I was becoming aware of the South African situation and of the work of such people as Michael Scott and Trevor Huddleston. Huddleston's return from South Africa in the mid-1950s and the publication of his *Naught for Your Comfort* were important in strengthening my belief that I had encountered a form of Christian discipleship which was compatible with, and which provided inspiration and resources for, my growing concern with social justice.

In fact, since the mid 1950s most of my experience of Anglicanism has been of its Anglo-Catholic back-street version. In 1958, as a student at the University of London, I lived in Cable Street, Stepney, in the parish of St George in the East, where the first riots over ritual had taken place in the mid-nineteenth century. Cable Street was my first real experience of living in a multi-racial community, and my first direct encounter with organized racism (though the word 'racism' was not much used in this period). My first curacy after ordination in 1964 was a few miles north at Holy Trinity, Hoxton, an old-fashioned working-class papalist parish. Built in 1848, it had been at the heart of the 'Romanizing' movement within the Church of England, and the *English Missal*, an English translation of the *Missale Romanum*, was compiled there, the original copy being still in the parish chest. In 1974, after some years working outside London, I became Rector of St Matthew's, Bethnal Green, another East End working-class parish. Built in 1748, St Matthew's had for many years had a 'civic' character, and its rectors were 'gentlemen'. None of them ever lived in the district until the late nineteenth century. The modern urban neighbourhood of Bethnal Green grew up around the old church, and although it has never been attended by more than a tiny fraction of the population, it is held in affectionate regard by the older inhabitants. Since 1981, in addition to working for six years as a national officer for the Church of England in the field of race relations, I have also held a part-time post as an assistant priest in the parish of St Clement, Notting Dale, in West London. St Clement's is another example of a nineteenth-century Anglo-Catholic church, built in a very run-down urban neighbourhood, dominated today by the Lancaster West Estate and other post-war developments. It was here, in the streets around the church, that the first 'race riots' in post-war Britain took place in 1958. I draw on the experience in these districts in the following chapters.

I have begun in this personal way in order to locate myself within the framework of the subject matter of the book. It was through working within an urban church that I first encountered racism. The incompatibility between racial hatred and prejudice and the claims of the Christian faith hit me at quite an early age. I felt that it was because I was a Christian that I was compelled to fight racial hatred and discrimination wherever, and in whatever form, it appeared. It was years later that I came to see the complex structural character of racism, the degree to which the Church itself was a racist institution, and the importance of working in solidarity with others who did not share the Christian basis on which I was acting.

The material in this book represents my thinking as it has developed over the years. Although I have written numerous articles, reports and pamphlets on the subject, this is the first full-scale book I have written on race and racism. It is also one of the very few books published in Britain on these issues as they specifically affect the Christian Church and Christian theology. Because of this, I have assumed that many of those who read it will be people who are not familiar with the enormous literature on race relations, and I have therefore included a good deal of material which is available in more detail in other studies. On the other hand, I have not assumed that all my readers are Christians or familiar with Christian theology or the workings of the Christian Church. My aim has been twofold: to introduce Christians to the serious study of race and racism, and to provide some insight for students of the British racial scene into the role of the Christian Church within the total context. My hope would be that the book might become a resource for people working for racial justice within British society.

Some of the material in this book has appeared elsewhere,

though in every case there has been substantial rewriting and expansion. Chapter Two grew out of an article in *Crucible* in 1982, Chapter Three out of an article in *Race* in 1967, and Chapters Four and Seven out of articles in *Third Way* in 1985 and 1982 respectively. Chapter Five draws on material in my pamphlet *Brick Lane 1978: The Events and Their Significance,* published by AFFOR of Birmingham in 1980. Chapter Nine was submitted as evidence to the Archbishop's Commission on Urban Priority Areas, and a shortened version of it was printed in *Crucible* in 1986. Chapter Ten was originally given as the Tawney Memorial Lecture for the Christian Socialist Movement in 1982. I am grateful to those who have given permission for the use of this material.

PART ONE

RACISM AND THE URBAN CONTEXT

1

Race, Class and the Church of England[1]

Black people who have come to Britain since the 1950s, and their children who were born here, have encountered British society and the churches within it in forms which have grown up over centuries, and which are intimately connected with the class structure of our society. They have also encountered, and continue to suffer, racism as an integral element of that society. But neither racism nor the Church can be understood without a sense of the historical class context in which they appear and function. In this first chapter, therefore, I want to consider the question of class in British society, and the place of the Church of England specifically within that class structure.

Is class obsolete?

Since the 1950s there has been a major debate among British socialists and others about the relevance of class language.[2] There has been much talk of the 'withering away of class', of class mobility, and of the growing irrelevance of class as a concept. Is the language of class, then, obsolete? Are we ceasing to be a class society? Are terms such as 'working class' no longer helpful, accurate or even meaningful? The language of class and of class conflict, some have argued, was valid in terms of nineteenth-century struggles when conflicts focused on income, and when it was possible to speak of the 'forgotten working class'. But such language is valid no more. It was, of course, during the nineteenth century that the term 'class' came to be widely used, replacing the earlier language of rank and order.[3] This change is often attributed to Marx, though Marx himself claimed that no credit was due to him for discovering the existence either of classes or of class struggle. Moreover, some of the key Marxist texts appeared (though not in English) during the 1840s, before the modern urban working class was fully established. However, Marx did see class divisions essentially in terms of two great classes directly facing each other: bourgeoisie and proletariat. His twofold division has dominated most thinking within the Marxist tradition down to the present day.

But in the 1950s many writers, including a number of former Marxists, began to argue that our society was experiencing a real shift towards equality and classlessness. Richard Hoggart in his major work *The Uses of Literacy* (1957) wrote of a 'bloodless revolution' which had taken place: 'It is often said that there are no working classes in England now, that a "bloodless revolution" has taken place which has reduced social difference, that already most of us inhabit an almost flat plain, the plain of the lower middle and middle classes.' Thus, Hoggart argued, 'a change towards a culturally "classless" society is being brought about'.[4]

The belief that there has been a significant shift towards greater equality was not peculiar to those who favoured such a shift. When the Thatcher government was elected in 1979, one of the key themes in its platform was the thesis that there had been too great a movement in the direction of equality within British society, and that this direction must be reversed. The belief in inequality, and the repudiation of egalitarianism as incompatible with freedom, is a central element in the thinking of the New Right.[5] But the belief that class divisions have been eroded, for good or ill, is held, too, by many who would claim no specific political allegiance, but who would assent to the general view that 'We are all middle class now.'

In this debate, great confusion has been caused by the use of the word 'class' in conflicting ways. Marx, correctly in my view, saw class as related primarily to the system of production. A class, in Marxist terms, is a group of people sharing the same relationship to that system, and thus sharing also in objective conditions of privilege or exploitation. Class is not, therefore, a subjective experience but a concrete reality. In this view, there are strictly only two classes within capitalist society: the capitalist ruling class, which controls the means of production, wealth and resources; and the working class, characterized by lack of wealth and property, dependence on wages and limited access to resources. The growth of new and 'transitional' classes – middle class, affluent working class, bureaucratic and managerial classes, and so on – has presented classical Marxism with some difficult problems. Nevertheless, the Marxist understanding of class is, I believe, correct in its essential features. Class can only be understood in relation to its economic base.

Central to the emergence of modern class society are the two processes of industrialization and urbanization. And so the question of the urban/suburban divide – about which I shall have more to say later in relation to the Church – is inseparably linked with a class analysis, and cannot be intelligently discussed apart from such an analysis. The growth of, and the commitment to, class society is one of the Victorian values. For, while the industrial working class began to emerge during the acute first stage of the Industrial Revolution (1760–1830), it was in the nineteenth century that segregation according to class developed within cities, and subsequent years have seen the intensifying of this process. The later growth of racially based concentrations must be viewed against the background of the earlier class segregation.

In recent years there have been two waves of 'class dissolution' theory. The first wave, associated with the 1950s included such writers as Anthony Crosland[6] and Douglas Jay.[7] Britain, it was argued, as a result of progressive direct taxation rather than the transfer of ownership, was moving towards a more egalitarian society, even a socialist society. Crosland even denied that contemporary society was any longer capitalist, and claimed that large-scale class conflict was a thing of the past. The alleged shift, it was claimed, was occurring gently, quietly, almost imperceptibly, not by revolution but by evolution. Today it is widely recognized that the transference of wealth and income from rich to poor on any significant scale cannot be achieved by taxation within an economy which is still based on the dominance of private business and profit. It could only be brought about through public appropriation of the means of production.

Linked with the view of 'creeping egalitarianism' was the doctrine of the 'affluent worker'. In 1961 Ferdinand Zweig studied 672 Sheffield workers, and concluded that there had been a marked decline in any sense of working-class solidarity, and a move towards 'middle-class values'. Zweig linked this movement with the increased access to consumer durables within a particularly hopeful phase of capitalism.[8] Other studies, however, cast doubt on the concept of the 'affluent worker'.[9] The period during which Zweig wrote was also the period when the theme of 'the end of ideology' was being promoted,[10] and when arguments were taking place among some younger socialists about the alleged 'classlessness' of the Left.[11]

The second, more recent wave of thinking about class has focused on the depressing condition of the Labour Party, traditionally seen as the party of the working class (although at parliamentary level it has for over fifty years been dominated by an Oxford-educated élite). Eric Hobsbawm has argued, in a famous article, that we have witnessed during the last few years a dissolution of 'the political expression of class consciousness'.[12] The debate is not simply one which concerns members of the Labour Party, or those interested in its fortunes, for it involves the wider issue of the changes which are occurring within the class structure of our society. Undoubtedly there is some evidence for Hobsbawm's view. While the Labour vote is still mainly a working-class vote, the majority of the working class is no longer committed to Labour.[13] The party's disastrous experience at the General Election of 1983 led writers such as Jeremy Seabrook to claim that its traditional class base had collapsed.[14] On the one hand, some have pointed to an alleged 'new class' or a new middle class which, they claim, now dominates the party, though paradoxically others have argued that a new radical intelligentsia has emerged which has so far found no political home.[15] On the other hand, there has been talk of a 'new working class', and some writers have argued that the Social Democratic Party held a particular attraction for professionals and white collar workers. Raphael Samuel, for example, has referred to a 'new political class', expressed through the SDP, a phenomenon which he sees as the political counterpart to gentrification.[16]

I believe that we should be careful to avoid simplistic parallels between class and political consciousness. Nevertheless, it is true that the Labour movement is most solid in areas where industrial decline is most evident, and weakest in areas of prosperity and new technology. It is in these areas that a figure such as Tony Benn, one of the few charismatic figures that the Labour Left has produced in recent years, may seem somewhat archaic. In Samuel's words:

> It is Mr Benn's tragedy that he espoused the cause of socialism at the very moment when, as it now appears, in Britain as in the rest of Europe (East as well as West), it was ceasing to be a working class faith . . . Benn found himself addressing an increasingly absentee constituency – those 'working people' who figure so prominently in his rhetoric, but who conspicuously fail to perform the part allotted to them, or even to listen to the socialist word.[17]

Some would argue that what had happened was that the working class, with some conspicuous exceptions in the traditional Labour areas in the north, Scotland and Wales, had forsaken the socialist path; others would claim that we were witnessing something more fundamental: the disappearance of the working class itself as an identifiable entity.[18]

In fact, the shift towards a more 'classless' and equal society is more apparent than real. That shift, praised by Crosland and Jay, feared by Thatcher and her friends, is actually far less advanced than either its protagonists or its critics believed. The Royal Commission on the Distribution of Income and Wealth (which was wound up by Margaret Thatcher in 1979 on the grounds that it encouraged the politics of envy) showed that there had been far less change in the pattern than was generally believed. The top 2–5 per cent of wealth holders had in fact stayed much the same since the 1920s.[19] Data from 1981 show that divisions based on wealth have actually increased in recent years. Tax cuts in 1979 led to a fivefold increase in the numbers of those with incomes of £20,000 and over after tax, and an elevenfold increase in the numbers of those with incomes of £50,000 and over.[20] In 1982 the relative earnings of the low paid were lower than in 1886 when the data were first collected.[21] In 1983 1 per cent of the population owned 23 per cent of total marketable wealth, and 5 per cent owned 43 per cent, while the bottom 50 per cent owned only 6 per cent of the total. Whatever trend towards equality had taken place, had been stopped by the mid-1970s.[22] Research suggests that by 1986 the number of people living in poverty or on the margins of poverty stood at over 16 million, an increase of 42 per cent on the 1970 figures.[23]

The framework of inequality is therefore very constant. It has not been significantly eroded as earlier commentators had suggested. Property, profit and the operation of the market remain the principal determinants of inequality. This is not, of course, to deny that significant changes *within* class society have taken place, or that the conditions of the poor have improved in many respects. For instance, there is now only one member of the traditional landed aristocracy – the Duke of Westminster – among the top ten wealth holders. At the other end of the spectrum, the conditions of life of working-class people have certainly improved in general. But the thesis of the 'withering away of class' is incorrect. Britain remains a class society, a society marked and disfigured by inequality and by the persistence of poverty. The recognition of this reality is a necessary preliminary to intelligent debate about the place of the Church within society.

The Church of England and class

The Church of England as an institution is an integral part of the ruling class, maintained and administered by the middle class and seeking to minister to the working class and the poor. Yet in spite of the fact that this is widely recognized, little serious attention to class issues is found in the thinking and writing which emanates from the Church and its leaders.

There have, of course, been many studies of Church and class, particularly in relation to the nineteenth century.[24] It was, many argued, during the process of urbanization which occurred then, that the churches 'lost the working class'. Nor was this belief peculiar to members of the Church of England. 'The greatest scandal of the church in the nineteenth century', claimed Pope Pius XI, 'was that it lost the working class.' On the other hand, Bishop Winnington Ingram in the early twentieth century argued that 'it is not that the Church of God has lost the great towns: it never had them'.[25] Disraeli had apparently believed that 'it will be in the great towns that the greatest triumphs of the church will be achieved',[26] and Bishop Blomfield, Bishop of London in the mid-nineteenth century, held the view that the working class did not attend churches because there were not enough churches for them to attend. So he initiated a period of promiscuous church building, building ten churches in Bethnal Green in ten years.

But the underlying problem was, and is, that the Church does not relate in any fundamental way to the needs of working-class people. It was, and for the most part remains, an alien institution, which seeks to minister to a community which it does not understand and with which it has never really identified. In 1898 a clergyman called Fry wrote:

> The church is mostly administered and officered by the classes; her influential laity belong almost wholly to the class; she is doing a great and growing work among the masses; but the deep sympathies of the clergy with the poor are largely obscured in the eyes of the masses by the fact that social rank and social position count for so much in her service, both among clergy and laity.[27]

His words remain as true today as they were in the nineteenth century.

The very presence of the Church in the new urban areas was an afterthought of the Industrial Revolution. Apart from the medieval churches and those built under an act passed in the reign of Queen Anne, there was no church building in the cities and new towns until the act of 1818. In 1843 the Church of England had seats for only 40.3 per cent of the population. So as the Victorian city grew up, healthier than its predecessors and less dependent on migrants, it grew up relatively churchless and, on the whole, irreligious. The Church of England in particular, as it grew in parochial terms during the nineteenth-century epoch of church building grew as a middle-class agency in areas which were entirely working class and poor. Areas such as the East End were virtually colonized by the Church of England in the mid-nineteenth century. And the pattern was repeated elsewhere. Between 1824 and 1880 over six hundred new churches were built in urban areas. But the model which dominated the growth was a model derived from an agrarian society, the parish based on territory within a mainly rural environment. The urban church grew up using a rural pattern of organization, and led by men with no real urban experience. Of 104 bishops between 1783 and 1852, only 17 had any experience in urban ministry.[28]

This is not to deny that the nineteenth-century Church, in its motivation and its pastoral zeal, both cared for the poor and often campaigned for social justice. There is considerable documentation of the contribution of church groups and individuals to the reform movements, and of the contribution of some of the heirs of the Tractarians to the emergence of Christian socialism as a powerful force.[29] Yet the overall impact of the Church's mission was to maintain and reinforce the class structure of which it was itself an integral part. The life, culture and spirituality of the Church of England in particular remained essentially alien to the working class, and so it is not surprising that 'in the modern urban environment, the act of worship did not become customary among most working class people'.[30] The 'rites of passage' were observed, though diminishing over the years, but the church as such never became part of working-class culture in the way that, for example, the Labour Party did. A study in Middlesborough in 1907 showed that more people went to the pub than to the church on Sundays: nearly seven times as many men, two-and-a-half times as many women, and twice as many children.[31] While, as is often pointed out, village communities often grew up around the church and the pub, in the cities it was the pub rather than the church which became the focal point of working-class neighbourhood life.

The general failure of the Church of England to make any profound impact on the urban scene is brought out in report after report from the later years of the nineteenth century. 'The church is nowhere in East London,' complained Bishop Walsham How of Stepney in 1897,[32] while south of the river a local newspaper announced: 'Christianity is not in possession in South London.'[33] A writer in *John Bull* described the East End as 'teeming with people who are almost as remote from Christian influences as savages in the wilds of Africa.'[34] At the turn of the century, both the Booth and Mudie Smith surveys bore witness to the weakness of all the churches in working-class areas of London.[35]

The period of what has been described as 'the Church condescending'[36] is manifested with particular visibility in the

East End of London. Here, apart from the medieval church of St Dunstan, Stepney, and a number of churches (Spitalfields, Bethnal Green, Limehouse, Poplar and St George's in the East) built in Queen Anne's reign, most of the parishes date from the nineteenth century. The ritualists concentrated much of their pastoral energy on East London, building great basilicas such as St Columba's Kingsland Road, and St Peter's, London Docks. The public schools and the universities established settlements: Toynbee Hall, Oxford House, St Hilda's East and the quaintly named St Mary of Eton, Hackney Wick, among many.

It is not my purpose here to condemn this upsurge of concern and goodwill, and there is no doubt that, in terms of benefit to individuals, the Church condescending has a great deal to its credit. But the whole enterprise was based on a refusal to question and attack the class system. Canon Barnett, the Warden of Toynbee Hall, was a fervent believer in the class organization of society.[37] Years later, George Lansbury wrote that the purpose of Toynbee Hall – and by implications of the other settlements – was 'to bridge the gulf between rich and poor by the use of smooth words and ambiguous phrases'.[38] The settlements, like the Church as a whole, sought to ameliorate the worst aspects of the system, to make it human and tolerable. The poor were worthy of care and compassion, but they had to be kept in their places. One of the motivating forces behind the Hoxton and Haggerston Church Extension Fund was the fear that something similar to the French Revolution might occur in London. The Church of England in the East End of London was first and foremost an instrument of social control.

The pattern of church life in the East End, where a powerful and wealthy Church sought to minister to the working class, was not unique, but it exposed the reality in an unusually stark form. This was because on the one hand, the East End was – and, in spite of some gentrification in the riverside areas, for the most part still is – an entirely working-class community, and on the other hand, because it was here that Oxbridge and the public schools put in so much effort over a century. But the reality which was so visibly portrayed in the East End was present in every city and town. Nowhere did the Church of England become an indigenous part of working-class culture. Those who sought to 'missionize' the East End in the nineteenth century made much of the fact that the population consisted exclusively of the working class or 'the poor'. Thus the Rector of Spitalfields informed the Ecclesiastical Commissioners in 1859 that the population of the new parish of St Stephen would be of this character: 'in the district there will *not* be *one* gentleman living, *not one* professional man of any description'.[39] A year later, the Rector of the nearby parish of St George in the East explained that his parish consisted entirely of 'those very classes who are alas! almost universally alienated from attendance upon the services of the Church'.[40] The history of that church, a Hawksmoor edifice of enormous proportions, rebuilt in the 1960s at great expense for a tiny congregation, shows that the population remained alienated down to the present. Its own essentially alien character was symbolized by a notice which remained on its main door until 1939: 'No dogs or women without hats allowed in.'[41] The attitude of benevolent (?) contempt indicated by such a notice is one which has characterized much of the Church's presence in working-class areas. The local people are seen as objects of the Church's care and concern – and as a pool of potential members. They are there to be done good to. But the Church does not belong to them. Its true home is elsewhere.

Its true home, in fact, has always been among the upper and middle classes in the wealthier parts of town, and more recently in the growth areas of suburbia. It is there that its interests lie, and where, in statistical terms, it is still largely 'successful'. The composition of the General Synod brings out very clearly the built-in bias of the Church towards the world of Oxbridge, the public schools and the professional middle class. In 1970–1, 49 per cent of the male lay members of the Synod had attended public schools, and 35 per cent had Oxbridge backgrounds.[42] A further study in 1975 showed that the composition of the Synod was 99 per cent middle class and 79 per cent upper middle class.[43] And the 1980 Synod, not surprisingly, was found to be 'still essentially a bastion of male, middle-aged and middle-class Anglicans'. By 1980 96 per cent of lay members had upper-middle-class professional or managerial backgrounds. There had in fact been 'a further entrenchment of the upper middle class within the Synod'.[44] The public school and Oxbridge backgrounds of the bishops are well known.[45] Of course, most of these men are more at home in the House of Lords, the Athenaeum Club and the homes of 'the great and the good' than they are in an East End pub. They represent the ethos and culture of a Church of the wealthy and the genteel. It was this Church of the wealthy and the genteel which was exported to the United States where, although the Episcopal Church accounts for only around 3 per cent of the population, a study in 1976 found that 48 per cent of its members had incomes over $20,000, 94 per cent were white, and 20 per cent of big business concerns and one third of the banks were run by Episcopalians.[46]

In the London borough of Tower Hamlets, however, one of the poorest and most deprived districts in Britain, and one with a long history of Anglican missionary activity, only 1 per cent of the population in 1973 were on electoral rolls of the Church of England. A report in that year, commissioned by the Bishop of Stepney, was still referring to the East End as a 'mission area'.[47] And there is no doubt that the Church has sent many devoted individuals as part of its mission into this and similar areas. But the people there know and realize that they come from elsewhere, they do not belong. The Church of England not only speaks the language of class; its interests clearly lie in the preservation of the present arrangement of society. Actions speak more loudly and more accurately than words, and nothing speaks more loudly in the inner urban areas than the concern of the Church, visibly represented in the property world by the Church Commissioners, to make as much money out of its land as possible. Thus the scandal of the sale of church property for luxury flats in areas of acute housing shortage, homelessness and deprivation is defended on the grounds that such commitment to the forces of the market enables the Church's mission to the poor to be maintained elsewhere.[48] Working-class people are unlikely to be convinced by arguments such as these.

It is difficult to see how this situation can become very different without so fundamental a restructuring of the Church of England that it could hardly be said to be the same body. For its entire ethos is bound up with the preservation of the stable order, with the monarchy, with the 'establishment' and with the structure of capitalism. In a class society, a racist society, a society rooted in hierachy and inequality, this is bound to mean that the Church of England will be a class Church, a racist Church, and a Church which, in its own life reflects and reinforces the inequalities of the dominant society. Yet most church documents seem not to be aware of this. They are filled with apparently 'radical' calls for an attack on inequality, for campaigns against racism and so on, but seem strangely blind to the structural reality of the position from which they themselves speak.

Nowhere is this more evident than in church utterances on the inner city. The commitment of the Church of England to the maintenance of its inner urban presence is not in doubt, at least in terms of what church leaders say. Thus the Archbishop of Canterbury has made his position very clear. 'There are, of course, temptations to withdraw from the inner cities . . . but as far as I have any influence, I am determined that we should maintain our presence in the most sensitive areas and allocate our resources accordingly.'[49] The warm reception which the report of his Commission on Urban Priority Areas (ACUPA) was given by the bishops and clergy (in marked contrast to the hostile reception from members of the Thatcher government) shows that his 'staying there' position commands a good deal of support within the leadership of the Church of England. But to maintain a presence without a serious attack on the nature and character of the body which is present will simply be to perpetuate the presence of a bourgeois Church among the poor. ACUPA itself recognized that the Church of England had 'traditionally been mainly middle class in character'.[50] This is not, of course, to say anything about the motivation or the goodwill of the Church and its representatives in working-class areas. Undoubtedly that Church will 'do good' there, and will even stand up for the rights of the poor. It will be represented in many of the poor areas by men and women of great prophetic and pastoral zeal and courage. Some of these individuals played important roles in the aftermath of the uprisings of 1981. But these uprisings (described by the media as 'riots') showed how detached the Churches as institutions were from what was going on.[51] For now the poor were no longer the passive recipients of ecclesiastical charity as in the nineteenth century: they were getting angry and standing up for themselves. And in spite of the witness and example of individual churchpeople, the Churches as institutions were not seen as being on their side. That perception was, in historical terms, correct. They never had been.

The Church of England and the black community

This is the history into which black immigrants to Britain and their children have entered. In the inner urban areas to which many of them moved, they encountered the Church of England as a body with which few of the indigenous white working-class inhabitants had any real relationship. Those who did relate, and who formed the hard core of the local churches' membership, were often very possessive of 'their' church, and resentful of the new black presence within it. The white working class had long experienced the Church of England as a middle-class presence within their communities; black people now experienced it as a racist presence.

For a variety of historical reasons, the Anglican Church had played a more significant role in the lives of the people of the Caribbean than it had done among white working-class people in the cities and towns of England. So immigrants from Jamaica, Antigua and particularly Barbados often came from solid Anglican backgrounds. The Church was more important to them than it had ever been to their white neighbours in England. So black Anglicans from the Caribbean came to fill the pews which had never been occupied by white working-class people in large numbers, and in parts of London, Birmingham and other cities, black people soon came to constitute the majority of worshipping Anglicans. Thus a recent study in the diocese of Birmingham showed that around 10 per cent of practising Anglicans were black, and that in six Birmingham churches they were the majority, while in 15 per cent of churches they formed between 40 and 85 per cent of the congregation.[52] But the presence of black people is not reflected in their place within the leadership and power structures of the Church, which are firmly in white hands. So the Church, whatever its conscious intentions, is experienced as a racist institution within a multiracial society.

As a result of the experience of white Christian racism, large numbers of black Christians have abandoned the Church of their upbringing and have moved into newer black-led churches, mainly (though not exclusively) of Pentecostal tradition. This movement is a post-immigration phenomenon and a response to racism. Thus, while in the West Indies the vast majority of practising Christians belong to the 'mainstream' Churches – Anglican, Roman Catholic, Methodist, Moravian, Baptist – and only a small percentage to the 'sideways' Churches, in Britain subsequent to immigration the position is almost the reverse. The majority of Afro-Caribbean Christians, it is now estimated, belong to black-led Churches, some of which originated not in Africa or the Caribbean but in the United States of America. The New Testament Church of God, the Church which has the largest growth rate among black people in Britain, has its headquarters in Cleveland, Tennessee. In the United States, where it is known simply as the Church of God, it is a mainly white Church. The members of this Church, and of other black-led Churches in Britain, include very large numbers of former Anglicans and members of other 'mainstream' Churches. As a result of their experience of racism, and of the cold and unwelcoming character of their sister Churches in Britain, black Christians are leaving the mainstream Churches in ever increasing numbers. A study by some British Methodists in 1983 noted that many of their black members were asking the question whether they belonged to 'the last generation of black Methodists'.[53]

And yet, when all that can be said has been said about the growth of the black-led Churches, the fact remains that the majority of black people in Britain, like the majority of white people, remain outside all the Churches. Black youth in particular have acted with their feet, and have rejected the Christian groups, whether black-led or white-led. If they have turned to any other religious community, it has been that of Ras Tafari. The majority have abandoned religion altogether. So while black-led congregations have grown in the inner urban areas, often using disused buildings abandoned by the Church of England, the gulf between the black underclass and organized religion of any kind has grown to be almost as wide as that between most white working-class people and religious groups.

Organized religion of mainstream type has in fact tended to leave the inner city for the more promising territory of suburbia. Since 1945 over half the churches in East London have closed. In

Newham, over half have gone since 1950, and eight in 1974 alone.[54] In the episcopal area of Stepney, where the Bishop has committed himself to the 'staying there' philosophy, twenty-eight churches have closed since 1969.[55] Meanwhile the Christian religion flourishes in suburbia, for the most part as a private pursuit which does little to increase solidarity with Christians in the inner city. It flourishes as a white religion, a religion of Englishness, of the status quo, of the stable order. It flourishes as a white institution within a multiracial society.

The general tendency within the Church of England is to accept that this is a deplorable state of affairs which can be remedied by the appropriate application of goodwill and good strategy. But if my analysis is correct, the problem is a much more serious and more intractable one. The Church has always been an alien institution within working-class areas. In multiracial working-class areas, it is now manifestly a racist institution. Perhaps the time is long overdue to accept the bitter reality of what is in fact the case. In the words of a former worker priest who, after thirty years, decided that the two worlds of Church and working-class society did not and could not meet:

> Perhaps after all, the church's separation from the poor is as much a judgment of God as a betrayal in itself, and who should try to reverse God's judgments? Perhaps the Gospel of Christ has nothing to do with the Christian church any more and is up for grabs by another 'nation' (Mt. 21:43). Certainly whenever I approach what I understand to be the meaning of the Gospel in conversation with my mates at work, whether it has to do with repentance or personal transformation, or justice and a new society, or indeed any of the crucial teachings of Christ, we seem as far as possible from the church and its concerns. And by the same token when the worker priest vests himself, as it were, to fulfil his functions among the faithful, he finds himself divested of the gospel.[56]

Perhaps, after all, the Church of England represents, within a class and racially divided society, the culture of the affluent white segment, of those who have most to gain by the preservation of the status quo. To recognize this truth is not necessarily to abandon hope, for hope is always rooted in realism. But it is to base our reflection and strategy on foundations of honesty rather than on the idealistic fantasy which is often mistaken for religion.

2

The Roots of Urban Conflict

The anti-urbanist tradition

Wordsworth once wrote of the

> Sorrow barricaded evermore
> Within the walls of cities.[1]

Since his time many people have seen the city as inevitably a zone of sorrow, a source of evil. In the nineteenth century the problems of cities were blamed on the 'riff raff' from the countryside who were moving in. (At the same time, there were complaints from the rural areas that the best people were leaving for the cities!) Earlier, in the seventeenth century, William Penn had claimed that it was in the countryside that the works of God were to be seen, while the cities only manifested the works of men. William Cowper in the eighteenth century called cities 'noisome sewers' through which flowed 'the dregs and feculence of every land'. The Liberal politician Lord Rosebery, Chairman of the London County Council at the end of the nineteenth century, wrote of London in disparaging terms:

> There is no thought of pride associated in my mind with the idea of London. I am always haunted by the awfulness of London: by the great appalling fact of these millions cast down, as it would appear by hazard, on the banks of this noble stream, working each in their own groove and their own cell, without regard or knowledge of each other, without heeding each other, without having the slightest idea how the other lives – the heedless casualty of outnumbered thousands of men. Sixty years ago, a great Englishman, Cobbett, called it a wen. If it was a wen then, what is it now? A tumour, an elephantiasis sucking into its gorged system half the life and the blood and the bone of the rural districts.[2]

His contemporary and fellow Liberal, Sir Edward Grey, spoke in similar vein of 'hideous cities' and expressed the hope that the urban civilization of the Victorian epoch would disappear.[3]

Anti-urbanism has a long history which some would date back even to Roman times.[4] The sense of the city as intrinsically evil and corrupting is well expressed in the words of a book of advice for young men issued in the nineteenth century:

> The city is a fearful place for temptation. Vices have an opportunity to thrive there as they cannot do in the country. In a rural village there are few openly vicious men to lead the young and unwary to ruin. But in a large metropolis there are great numbers of them on the look out at the corner of every street, and thousands falls into their webs of vice every year . . . Cities are the greatest centres of evil.[5]

The nineteenth-century anti-urbanists saw the city as a great monster. But they wanted also to maintain existing class divisions, and one way to do this was to break up the cities.

Ruth Glass, the founder of urban sociology in Britain, has claimed that there is a direct line of succession from the nineteenth-century thinkers to the contemporary exponents of 'urban doom'. According to these thinkers, cities are disintegrating, erupting, blowing up, exploding. Their language is a language of 'verbal incendiary devices' – exploding cities, the urban time bomb, and so on. At the same time, Professor Glass observes, we are told of immigrants 'flooding' into cities, though 'it is not quite clear how so much water can stoke so many fires'.[6] Much current writing on the 'inner city crisis' is preoccupied with issues to do with race and the black communities. Indeed the very term 'inner city' is, in origin, an American euphemism for 'black neighbourhood'. It is important, therefore, to see how the current demonology of inner cities connects with the long tradition of anti-urbanism which existed before the recent immigration of black people to the urban areas. The racial dimension has added to, and intensified, an already existing hostility directed at the poor.

Urbanization is a relatively modern phenomenon. In the mid-nineteenth century the population of the world was mainly rural. Today over 33 per cent of it is urban. In 1800 only a quarter of the population of England and Wales lived in settlements of over 5,000 people. The growth of the Victorian city is of central importance, for it was in the Victorian period that cities became healthier and self-sustaining.[7] In 1851, for the first time, half of the population of England and Wales lived in urban areas. The period from 1821–31 had been the fastest period for urban growth. By 1901, nearly four-fifths of the population were living in towns or cities of over 10,000. The population of London was 6.5 million, and over thirty other places had populations of over 100,000.

It was partly the problem of size which motivated anti-urbanists to look to the breaking up of cities and the development of smaller communities elsewhere. Ebenezer Howard (1850–1928) believed in the idea of the 'garden city', and his book *Garden Cities of Tomorrow* (1898) influenced town planning for many years.[8] It is from Howard that the idea of new towns surrounded by green belt derived and, as lasting monuments to his thought, he built Letchworth in 1903 and Welwyn Garden City in 1920. Later came Harlow New Town, designed by Sir Frederick Gibberd, author of *Town Design* (1953). Gibberd, too, was in no doubt about the intrinsic evils of city life:

> It is now generally agreed that the large city leads only to social evil. It monopolises the cultural life of the region and often the nation. Apart from its inherent evils, creating high death and low birth rates, and of breeding maladjusted social types such as gangsters and 'wide boys', it makes a full life impossible for the ordinary decent citizen.[9]

So the city became the scapegoat for all ills. Black people, who later entered into this tradition of urban demonology, experienced anti-urbanism in a specifically racial and racist form, in which their own presence came to be seen as intrinsically problematic. There is no doubt that anti-black prejudice and the operation of racism has introduced new and serious dimensions into the urban scene. Colour issues cannot be 'dissolved' into issues of class or poverty. They have their own reality. Nevertheless, the scapegoating of blacks cannot be understood apart from the more deeply historical rooted problem of the scapegoating of the urban poor.

Urban growth and urban decline

If one of the results of the growth of cities was the emergence of an anti-urbanist tradition, another was the development of an academic tradition: urban sociology. For years this was dominated by the Chicago School of Robert Park and Ernest Burgess.[10] From this school came Louis Wirth's seminal work *The Ghetto*, and his article (reprinted with regularity over the years) 'Urbanism as a Way of Life'.[11] It was Wirth's work which popularized the concepts of 'urbanism' and 'urban man' as identifiable entities. Wirth identified two major tendencies within the urban environment: the growth of social segregation, and the tendency for diverse groups to become similar ('urban man'). Later work, such as that of Willmott and Young in Bethnal Green, pointed to the existence of 'urban villages' and of closely knit kinship patterns within the urban context.[12]

While urbanization is a world phenomenon, Britain has a particularly rich urban history. Here 80 per cent of the population live in cities or towns of over 20,000, a ratio greater than that of the United States, Sweden and Denmark. 95 per cent of the British people depend on urban areas for their livelihood. It was the growth of cities and the problems associated with them which led to the developments initiated by the New Towns Act of 1946 and the Town and Country Planning Act of 1947. Within London, the Abercrombie Plan of 1943 tried to control the growth of the metropolitan area. This plan, rooted in 'a profoundly anti-urban vision',[13] was based on the assumption that, given the chance, most people would choose to move out of cities. So the notion of dispersal came to be an integral part of town-planning ideology.

Meanwhile, within the city itself there had developed centres of wealth and of poverty, the citadels of financial power and the dwellings of the urban poor. In London, the juxtaposition of the City and the East End symbolized the contrast. Into the City came vast numbers of commuters day by day. By the mid-1950s almost one million commuters travelled each day into the centre of London.[14] By 1954 articles were appearing on 'the parking problem in central London'.[15] Four years later *The Times* was attacking the concentration of offices in central London.[16] At the same time, the working-class areas of London were being rebuilt, often carelessly, in a period of urban population decline.

It is essential to grasp the absolute centrality of urban *decline* in the pattern of events which have led to the current 'urban crisis'. Between 1941 and 1981 inner cities lost one third of their population. London's population had been declining since the turn of the century, and by 1981 it was below seven million for the first time since 1900. In 1965 two leading urban sociologists emphasized that 'it has for long been perfectly clear that the more striking problems of inner London are the result of population decline rather than of population growth'.[17] Twenty years later, the report of the Archbishop's Commission on Urban Priority Areas pointed to the 'clear correlation between population decline and the social index':[18] that is, as the population declines, social deprivation increases. Yet much writing in the popular media, and much allegedly informed discussion, seems to be based on the entirely fallacious assumption that the problems of the inner city are the result of growth of population.

The areas of growth, in fact, have for years been outside the inner urban areas, in the suburbs and the new towns. Thus the population of Cheshire grew by 13 per cent between 1961–71, while in the area of Hazel Grove and Bramhall the growth rate was 85 per cent. Between 1971–81 East Anglia's population increased by 11.3 per cent. Milton Keynes has grown by 85 per cent. By contrast the metropolitan counties and Greater London have declined dramatically. The East End has lost population continuously since the Second World War. Kensington and Chelsea lost 26 per cent of its population in the inter-censal period 1971–81. As the better off have moved out, the populations left behind have become increasingly polarized, between the very rich and the growing numbers of the poor.

Polarization and maldistribution

So there has been a real and continuing sharpening of social inequalities within cities in recent years. This increased division within cities is paralleled by the wider division between north and south, and the division in terms of consciousness between the two parts of Britain. It is difficult to exaggerate the degree to which many working-class people in the north feel that the centres of power in London are out of touch with their needs and in fact do not care about them. To a great extent London and the south east are still shielded from the worst consequences of urban deprivation. Visitors from Glasgow and Liverpool often comment that what are called poor areas in London seem quite well off to them. In Glasgow, for instance, unemployment was twice the British average as long ago as 1968. The Easterhouse estate, the largest housing estate in western Europe, had at that time a population of 45,000, but no pub, no cinema, no library, no community centre and only four shops.

However, in London too, as long ago as 1965, it was possible to identify 'areas where a polarisation of society in inner London is visible: rich and poor directly confront one another'.[19] In 1985 the ACUPA Report returned to the word 'polarization' as a central concept of their study. 'The process is one of deprived people being left in the UPAs (Urban Priority Areas) as the successful move out to middle Britain. The former have decreasing wealth, health services, income, investment, and amenity. The latter have rising affluence, opportunity, power and advantage: in one ugly word – polarisation.'[20] The increased concentration of deprived groups has led to the growing use of the word 'ghetto', a word associated with the presence of black people. In fact, while black people are more heavily urbanized in general terms than the population as a whole, there has been little evidence in Britain of the emergence of racial ghettoes on American lines. Indeed, the most clear indication of 'ghettoization' in London in recent years has been the emergence of the new upper-class ghettoes and the ghettoes of the intelligentsia. This phenomenon is often called gentrification, a term first used by Ruth Glass in 1964. The term describes the process by which whole areas, previously occupied by working-class people, are taken over by the wealthy. The poor, who can no longer afford to live in these areas, are squeezed out into already deprived and overcrowded adjacent areas. So, in contrast to the upper-class ghetto, there develops also a ghetto of the deprived. This kind of ghetto, in Britain, is usually racially mixed.

Those who have worked in inner London over the past twenty years have witnessed this growing polarization, and the way in which neighbourhood populations have become increasingly unbalanced. Thus the centre of London has become almost childless, consisting of large numbers of one-person households.

In 1971, 70 per cent of the total of households in Westminster, Camden and Kensington were one- or two-person households. Other areas, often with a long history of overcrowding, have become more overcrowded. The Golborne Ward in North Kensington is a classic example. At the 1961 census it had the highest rate of overcrowding outside Glasgow. In Tower Hamlets, the population has declined but the percentage of elderly people has increased, and the ratio of those aged 25–34 is the lowest in London. Newham, an area of East London which grew rapidly at the end of the nineteenth century, has the largest number of houses without baths or indoor lavatories in London, and the highest perinatal mortality rate. Hackney, which showed the seventh-largest loss of population in London since 1971, also has the highest ratio of single-parent families, the second-highest ratio of overcrowding, the second-highest unemployment rate and the fifth-highest number of households without basic amenities.[21] Spitalfields, which for over a century has been a centre for the displaced and for outcasts of society has, in spite of some improvements, become more derelict and run down.[22]

Outside London a similar pattern is visible. Two of the areas which were shaken by uprisings in 1981 were Liverpool 8 ('Toxteth') and Moss Side, Manchester. In Liverpool, a social area analysis showed a clear concentration of extreme deprivation in an inner ring of some 70,000 people. Here 60 per cent of heads of households were semi-skilled or unskilled, and unemployment was twice the average for the city as a whole. In the Toxteth and Scotland Exchange constituencies, at the time of the 1981 uprisings, the male unemployment rate stood at 35 per cent.[23] In Moss Side, four Enumeration Districts (EDs) in 1981 showed a pattern of extreme deprivation, using the threefold category of stressful housing, large families and overcrowding. 22 per cent of families were one-parent ones, contrasted with just over 2 per cent for Greater Manchester as a whole. 80 per cent of households had no access to a car.[24]

All British cities show a gross maldistribution of resources, most evident in the area of housing. The housing problem of London is not new, nor is its documentation. In 1883 the chairman of the LCC Committee on the Housing of the Working Classes wrote: 'The housing problem indeed may be said to be the sum of all the social and economic problems which await solution, for it provokes the vexed question of the relation between rent and wages, which easily slide into that of capital and labour.'[25] A century later his words remain a relevant commentary on the London scene. Housing distress has increased as the population has declined and the number of households has risen. Yet the problem remains one of maldistribution and underinvestment rather than of objective shortage. At the 1961 census there were three million more rooms than persons in London.[26] However, during the course of the next ten years, the private rented sector declined by 24 per cent. Today there is a shortage of around 100,000 homes in London.[27]

Many of those who are not technically homeless are forced to live in conditions which are conducive to ill health, both physical and mental, as well as the breakdown of family life. A study of high-rise housing in one area of Manchester showed that there was a higher risk of suicide, of nervous illness, and of becoming a victim of crime.[28] And there is an abundance of evidence from all over the country that those who are deprived tend to become more deprived. The children of unskilled parents who live in overcrowded homes are invariably the recipients of poorer education and health care.[29] In health care, what has been termed the 'inverse care law'[30] tends to operate in the inner cities. The more in need the people are, the less care they get. The class basis of health and sickness is clear: cases of tuberculosis, stomach cancer, lung cancer, coronary heart conditions, bronchitis, duodenal ulcers and many other illnesses, are all commonest among the unskilled sections of the working class.[31] And the situation is not improving. Even government sources show that the deprived areas were served worse in terms of health care in 1985 than they had been the previous year.[32]

At the heart of the problem of maldistribution in the urban areas is the question of land ownership and control. In 1959, the Town and Country Planning Act initiated an era of permissiveness in land speculation. This act unfroze land values, and established market values as the determining factor in sales instead of current use values. It is from this period that the property speculation which has so defaced London and other cities, and which has made the conditions of the poor worse than ever, dates. Today office space in London is more expensive than anywhere in Europe. The ownership and use of property is determined not by human need but by profit. And only the large and powerful companies, or very rich individuals, can compete in the lunatic race for property in inner London.

One of the major landowners in London is the Church Commissioners, the Millbank-based organization which provides the public face of the Church of England. In 1955 the Church Commissioners sold sixty-seven acres of slum property in Paddington, and during the following decade they rid themselves of 36,000 out of 40,000 rented properties. Instead they moved into office blocks, and by 1972 they owned £80 million of them.[33] Perhaps more than any other group, the Church Commissioners provide the link between the old and new patterns of land ownership in London.[34]

But while, week by week, property is sold to the highest bidder, whole areas of the city lie derelict and unused. A Greater London Council survey in 1971 showed that 116,139 acres (4 per cent of the total area of London) was vacant, 2,076 acres being in inner London.[35] Six years later it was estimated that between 6–12 per cent of land within Britain's inner-city areas was vacant.[36] There is no way in which the social problems of the inner urban areas can be solved without a fundamental change in the system of land ownership and control.

Another major feature of the inner urban scene is the collapse of the manufacturing base in many cities. Between 1951 and 1981, urban areas lost two million manufacturing jobs, one million of which were from inner-city areas. London today has no real economic base. Ford's factory at Dagenham is the only big manufacturing centre in the London area. The city has come to be dominated by commerce and service industries. Manufacturing industry has left the inner city. In Tower Hamlets, for example, one-fifth of all jobs were lost between 1961 and 1971. Between 1971 and 1973, East London lost 10.5 per cent of jobs (compared with 2.7 per cent in Britain as a whole). The clothing trades, which had been so central to the life of the East End, declined during these two years by 19 per cent in Poplar, 9.2 per cent in Stepney and 10 per cent in Shoreditch.[37] In 1981, 39 per cent of all jobs in inner-city areas were filled by commuters. The further north one goes, the worse the situation gets. Unemployment in many districts affects 50 or even 80 per cent of the labour force. And, alongside the persistence of unemployment, there has grown up a profound hopelessness about the future for both communities and individuals.

Powerlessness, despair and conflict

Growing polarization between rich and poor, the growth of ghettoes of the disadvantaged, housing shortage, overcrowding and homelessness, ill health and inadequate health care, unemployment: there is no doubt that these are among the characteristics of inner urban areas. But they are not the whole story. Many commentators write as if these were the *only* features of inner-city life, ignoring the considerable evidence of vitality, community activity and happiness within urban neighbourhoods. The inhabitants of the inner city are often portrayed as helpless, inadequate, lacking in initiative and drive, incapable of 'getting on their bikes' and searching for work. The inner-city problem is thus described in terms of personal psychopathology. 'The problem of our inner cities', said the Conservative minister Peter Walker, 'is caused by the concentration of people living on the economic and social margins of poverty'.[38] But it would be more correct to say that the problem of the inner cities is *experienced* by these people: they are not its cause. The tendency to blame structural evils on personal inadequacy has run through much of the thinking of the 'cycles of deprivation' school. The problem of the inner city is seen basically as the problem of the 'wrong sort' of people, people who can't cope. The adequate and mature have moved out, leaving behind only the feckless and casualties.

> Isn't it a pity about the Inner City?
> People leave who shouldn't ought,
> And that affects the rate support.
> If only those who stayed behind
> Had left instead, no one would mind.[39]

In fact, the inner urban experience is marked by countless examples of people coping, surviving and flourishing in spite of overwhelming odds. It is marked by examples of tremendous courage and resilience. And yet, over all this, there hangs a sense of powerlessness, a sense that other people in other places are pulling the strings, that the power to effect change lies elsewhere. And this sense leads to despair in some, resignation in many, and from time to time it erupts in terrible anger. Often it is only when that eruption takes place that the powerful take notice.

The sense of powerlessness is one of the features of inner urban life which is most frequently mentioned. *Faith in the City* speaks of a 'pervading sense of powerlessness and despair'.[40] Margaret Simey, councillor for the Granby Ward in Liverpool, scene of the 1981 uprisings, has claimed that they were marked by despair and resentment rather than by protest.[41] A decade earlier, a study of poverty in Nottingham spoke of the hopelessness there.[42] And there are numerous other examples. People in the north feel cut off from the decision-making processes in London, and feel that the faceless people in Whitehall have little or no conception of their situation. Those of us who have had to talk with ministers within the Thatcher government about inner-city problems have been struck by the enormous gulf between us. At times it is as if one were describing conditions on Mars.

And yet Lord Scarman, who has been propelled into the position of custodian of inner-city compassion, has assured us that 'nobody living in the inner cities now could say that they were being neglected'.[43] He made that statement just after the abolition of the Greater London Council, a move which was opposed by 68 per cent of Londoners and even by 43 per cent of Conservatives.[44] If Scarman meant that the study of inner-city problems had become a profitable industry, he was certainly correct. Hardly a week goes by without some new research project being launched on behalf of the inner areas. Some areas, such as the East End of London, Notting Hill, Liverpool 8 and Moss Side, Manchester, have been experiencing the 'research syndrome' for years. Liverpool 8 (now known incorrectly, as Toxteth) is, perhaps next to Bethnal Green, the most over-researched piece of territory in the United Kingdom. And yet government minister Patrick Jenkin was 'visibly shaken' by his visit there, commenting that 'I have seen houses here the like of which I have never seen before.'[45] It is statements like these, about areas whose conditions have been fully documented for many years, which intensify the feeling of despair and hopelessness among residents of these well-studied areas.

And there have been inner-city programmes galore, one after the other, since the end of the 1960s: the original Urban Programme in 1968 after Enoch Powell's 'rivers of blood' speech, and its successor in 1978; the Community Development Programme in 1969 (abandoned when the workers became too radical in their analysis); the Home Office's Urban Deprivation Unit in 1973; and Peter Shore's White Paper, *Policy for the Inner Cities*, in 1977. This document contained an ominous warning about the consequences of continued neglect:

> The inner parts of our cities ought not to be left to decay. It would mean leaving large numbers of people to face a future of declining job opportunities, a squalid environment, deteriorating housing and declining public services. But without effective action, that could be the future for those who live in inner areas, bringing with it mounting social bitterness and an increasing sense of alienation. The hearts of our cities would suffer as the surrounding inner areas went further downhill.[46]

It is hard to envisage a more accurate account of what has in fact occurred. Declining job opportunities, squalid environments deteriorating housing and public services, lack of effective action, mounting social bitterness and increased alienation: this is precisely what has taken place. The weekly journal *New Society* in 1985 pointed to the present dangerous atmosphere.

> The writing on the wall of the inner cities was stencilled in the ghettoes of the United States before the first graffiti were daubed on the lift shaft of any British high-rise . . . But what has altered in this country in recent years is any clear hope that things can be changed; that the social injustices can be set right.[47]

Here lie the roots of urban conflict. Resentment and bitterness may simmer beneath the surface for many years. The existence of deprivation in itself does not mean that violent uprisings will occur. But the seeds have been sown. The combination of extreme social disadvantage and a specific set of local circumstances will lead to the kind of explosion which we have seen with increasing frequency since 1981. When these conditions occur within the framework of racism, the danger becomes more clear and more predictable. The depressing aspect of recent experience is the unfortunate truth that because something is predictable, and is indeed predicted, that is no guarantee that it will not take place.

3

London's Racial Crisis: The Early Years

'Racialism feeds on deep social discontents and translates them into prejudice. In doing so it obscures the real nature of the problems which confront the people of Britain and it distorts their political perspective.'[1] This comment, made over twenty years ago by a Pakistani academic based in London, is still an accurate description of the situation. The essential fact about racialist propaganda is that it confuses the issues, often using the housing problem as a way of making black people into scapegoats. This process was evident in a spectacular way in Britain in the 1960s, and it is this which I wish to examine in this chapter, looking specifically at London in these formative years in which racialism became respectable. It was 'racialism' rather than 'racism' which was the most frequently used term in this period. For some observers, the two terms are virtulaly synonymous, racism being merely a later usage. There are indeed many instances in which either word can be used, and there are points at which the distinctions become blurred. But in general I shall use racialism to refer to prejudice and its expression in discrimination and propaganda, and racism for the doctrine and the structural forms taken by racial disadvantage and discrimination.

During the 1960s I was working as a priest in the Hoxton (1964–7) and Soho (1967–71) districts of London. Hoxton, then part of the borough of Shoreditch and later of the new London Borough of Hackney, was – and for the most part still remains – a working-class urban village. In relation to London as a whole, its rate of population movement was very low, and still today many of the residents belong to families who have lived in Hoxton for generations. In the 1960s the population was almost wholly white, and there were individuals and groups who sought to exploit the fears of the white working class and direct them towards facism. Sir Oswald Mosley, who had gained considerable support in the area in the 1930s, stood as parliamentary candidate for Shoreditch in 1965, and two years later the newly formed National Front built up one of its first strongholds in the area. Soho, in the West End of London, was a multiracial neighbourhood, with restaurants of every nationality. As the recreational and music centre of London, it was a place to which vast numbers of black and white young people were drawn. As a priest in these two very different districts of London, I was day by day confronted by the challenges of a multiracial society and by the ominous growth of organized racism.

London: population and housing

In Chapter Two I showed the centrality of population decline in the emergence of the inner-city crisis. Early years had seen the growth of London as a residential area. Between 1841 and 1881, the London area doubled its population. By 1901 the population stood at 4.42 million, and by 1921 it had grown to 4.48 million. Since then the story became one of decline, combined with the continuing status of London as a commercial and, until recently, economic centre. Migration outwards went hand in hand with commerical concentration in the heart of the city. The 1881 census showed the existence of a strong tendency to move outwards and this process was to continue and intensify. But uncontrolled commercial development increased the movement of workers into the central area. Between 1948 and 1958 planning permission was given for 44.4 million square feet of office space in central London. Governments were not unaware of what was happening. A report presented by the Minister of Housing in February 1963 spoke of the 'government's firm determination to reduce the movement of population from Scotland and the North', admitting that 'the heavy growth and concentration of offices in central London is bringing formidable transport, housing and financial problems in its wake'.[2]

I argued in Chapter Two that no approach to urban problems would be adequate which did not deal with the crucial issue of land ownership and use. The centrality of the land question was evident in London in the 1960s in at least four areas.

(1) By the 1960s, one-sixteenth of the population of England and Wales was concentrated in one-sixtieth of the country: that is, 8,714,000 people were living in a space of 842 square miles, the area known as Greater London.

(2) Inner London was attracting an increasing flow of people from other parts of the country, a movement which had become known as a 'drift to the south'. This movement had been, and continues to be, presented in inaccurate and confusing terms as if it referred to an objective increase of population in the inner area. In fact the influx was occurring at a time of population decline. But the essential fact to grasp is that there was a movement of population away from the economically run-down areas in the north towards the more hopeful regions in the south, and towards London in particular.

(3) The land within London had for years been under the control of private corporations such as the Church Commissioners and the insurance companies. But by the early 1960s the property developers were assuming a key role.

(4) As a result of these developments – the concentration of population in Greater London, the movement of workers to inner London, and the growth of property speculation – the issue of land in London became a matter of urgency in the 1960s. The crucial factor in London's housing crisis was seen to be maldistribution. Two clusters of events in particular brought the matter to public attention: the Rachman scandal of 1963, and the growing problem of homelessness, publicised in the TV documentary *Cathy Come Home* and in the work of such groups as the Simon Community and Shelter. At the centre of the problem was the figure of the private landlord and the decline of the private sector.

Maldistribution was in fact characteristic of the pattern of wealth and property within Britain as a whole. The Report of the Commissioners for Inland Revenue for the year ending 31 March 1963, the year of the Rachman revelations, showed that 41.6 per cent of the population owned no property at all, while another 47.1 per cent owned an average of £987 per person. The remaining 11.3 per cent owned nearly three-quarters of the wealth of the country. The early 1960s were years when there was much talk of the 'property-owning democracy'. But a study of housing since the Rent Act of 1957 showed how far from the truth this was. There were, in 1958, 13.4 million occupied dwellings in England, of which about 5.3 million (39 per cent) were owner occupied; 2.7 million (20 per cent) belonged to local councils; 4.7 million (35 per cent) were let unfurnished; 0.3 million (2 per cent) were let furnished; and 0.4 million (3 per cent) were let in other ways. Of the unfurnished rooms, 53 per cent had no hot water supply, 63 per cent had no bath of their own, and 25 per cent had no unshared flush lavatory.[3]

In fact, as the 1960s began, only 19 per cent of houses in London were owner occupied, over three-quarters of all houses being rented. Even in Poplar, where over 45 per cent of property was in council hands, there were still 44 per cent rented from private landlords. The inner ring of east and south London had the lowest proportion of owner-occupied dwellings (0–5 per cent), while Paddington, St Marylebone, Westminster and Poplar came next (5–10 per cent). This was the situation into which immigrants from the Caribbean and Asia came at the end of the 1950s and early 1960s. Their arrival was greeted – as indeed it had been anticipated by some – with cries of alarm and warnings of a population crisis. Britain, and London in particular, were said to be overcrowded, and the overcrowding, it was claimed, was due to overpopulation.

But the population of London fell by 147,472 between 1951 and 1961, the period in which black immigration increased. Only four boroughs (Wandsworth, Hampstead, Stoke Newington and Kensington) showed population increases, while all the others declined; the most catastrophic decline taking place in St Pancras, where the population fell by 13,522. Population density and overcrowding showed an uneven pattern. Thus the average number of persons per acre in London at the 1961 census was 42.7. This fell in the City of London to 7, and in Poplar to 28.4, but rose to 86.2 in Paddington, 76.3 in Southwark and 74.7 in Kensington. Again, the average number of persons per room in London as a whole was 0.77. But 11.5 per cent of those living in private households were living at a density of 1.5 persons per room, and this rose to 17.7 per cent in Islington, 18.5 per cent in Kensington and 20.9 per cent in Paddington.

In 1965 the Milner Holland Report on Housing in Greater

London was published.[4] The report showed that London, which contained less than one-fifth of the total stock of dwellings in the country, contained well over half of all multi-occupied dwellings. There were at that time in the London conurbation around 26,000 dwellings containing four or more households, and the majority of these were in certain districts of inner London. Islington came top of the list with 8,500 dwellings containing three or more households. Kensington had 3,600, Paddington 3,500, Lambeth 3,400 and Hackney 3,300. In the Lancaster Gate West Ward of Paddington, there was one Enumeration District (ED) in which 26 dwellings contained 497 households, an average of 19 households per dwelling. Among the boroughs, Islington had 59 per cent of its households living in multi-occupation, while Hornsey had 54, Paddington 48, Hackney 48 and Willesden 42.

The 1961 census had shown that there were 31 local authority wards in which over one-fifth of the population was living at a level of more than one-and-a-half persons per room. The highest proportion was in the Golborne Ward of Kensington, which had also been the most overcrowded ward at the 1931 census. In 1961 40 per cent of the population lived at this density. The highest percentage of such overcrowded households in any one borough in 1961 was in Paddington (14 per cent), followed by Kensington (13 per cent) and Islington (11 per cent). A survey of the Walterton Road area of Paddington found that, while 29 per cent of the households on the estate were overcrowded, the proportion for black immigrant households was 64 per cent. On the wider front, the 1963 Tenant Inquiry showed that half of the heads of overcrowded households were born outside Britain. Thus, by the mid 1960s it was clear that black people were suffering the worst features of London's problem of overcrowding.

Black people and London housing

Black immigrants in these early years experienced two specific types of housing difficulty. First, as newcomers they tended to move about from one area to another during their early years of settlement. As a result they were allocated very low priority for local authority housing. A study of North Kensington reported:

> It is just these people on the move from places near and far who are required to meet local labour shortages in service and other industries; in all the unskilled and skilled occupations they keep the metropolitan machine running. Indeed, the very people who are not wanted on the local housing market are needed for the local labour market.[5]

Second, these newcomers were black, and they found very quickly that private landlords were reluctant and often entirely unwilling to let to black tenants. When they did, they imposed a 'colour tax': the rents went up. The combination of these two types of problem led to many black people buying large houses, often in bad condition, at outrageous prices, from unscrupulous 'agents'. In order to pay for these properties, high rents were charged, overcrowding spread, and so the spiral continued.

The reluctance of landlords to accept black tenants was well documented at the time; numerous surveys repeated the same miserable story. One tour of advertisement boards in Tottenham in 1964 produced a list of 105 addresses advertising rooms to let. Of these, 54 per cent laid down some conditions about the race of the prospective tenants. 33 per cent explicitly stated 'No Coloureds', many of them adding the word 'Sorry'. 18 per cent said 'Coloureds Only' or 'Coloureds Welcome', while 3 per cent specified Jews or Gentiles. Interviews with thirty-five people who advertised rooms to let in a Hackney newspaper showed that only three accepted responsibility for their refusal to accept black tenants, while the rest put the blame on others. A more intensive study of the same newspaper was made over a three-month period. This showed that, of 1,000 adverts studied, 546 (55 per cent) made some stipulation as to race or colour, and 454 (45 per cent) did not. Of the 546, 65 (12 per cent) did not object to black tenants, and 481 (88 per cent) did object. The survey by the Milner Holland Commission of 1,258 units of accommodation advertised, showed that 27 per cent clearly barred black people, while only 6 per cent indicated that they would be welcome.

Discrimination in the housing sector led to some exploitation by black landlords of both black and white tenants. Exploiting landlords are no new feature of the London scene. However, black landlords were easily noticed, and a few of them received exorbitant publicity. Moreover, in areas of high immigration, because of the existence of discrimination in white-controlled properties, a growing number of the landlords were black. Surveys of cases brought before rent tribunals in areas of high immigration showed, not surprisingly, that large numbers of cases related to persons not of UK origin (although not all of these were black, Rachman himself being the most outstanding example in this period). 90 per cent of applicants and landlords involved in cases before the North West London Rent Tribunal in the two years ending 31 March 1964 were born outside the United Kingdom. It would be wrong to assume that all these were cases of malicious landlords deliberately exploiting their tenants. As Milner Holland showed, most of the black landlords were inexperienced and ignorant of the legal security afforded by tenure legislation.

Nevertheless, a group of ruthless, exploiting black landlords quickly emerged. In Birmingham in 1963, out of 1,561 houses in the city known to be in multi-occupation and which had been inspected by the end of that year, 950 (61 per cent) were owned by Indian or Pakistani residents. Of these properties, 83 per cent were overcrowded, 75 per cent lacked adequate facilities, and 60 per cent were dirty and ill-managed. The tenants were often Irish or West Indian. The report of the Medical Officer of Health for Birmingham in 1963 noted that many Pakistanis and Indians were setting up in business as landlords and exploiting the housing shortage, and that their standards of management were lower than those required by British legislation. Taken in isolation from the wider context of landlord and tenant relationship, it was only too easy for these data to be used in racist propaganda.

It was during these early years of black immigration also that the use of the word 'ghetto' returned into popular usage after years of neglect since the Jewish settlements of the turn of the century. In fact, the ghettoes which began to emerge were not racial enclaves, 'coloured quarters', or anything resembling the North American pattern, but rather zones of stagnation in which the disadvantaged of all races lived because they had no alternative. Ruth Glass warned that the enforced crowding together of low-income groups and newcomers in inner London could well lead to the growth of 'ghettoes of "displaced persons" – of all kinds and shades . . . in the metropolitan area'.[6] In the same year, John Rex pointed to the developments in Birmingham's Sparkbrook, where black immigrants were becoming concentrated in old Victorian terraced houses within the 'secondary ring' of the city. Rex observed:

> In strict sociological terms what emerges is not a ghetto. For the immigrants will be of all races. And they will live alongside and above and below the flotsam and jetsam of the host society. But the fact is that the immigrants do, on the whole, live here. They do not belong to Birmingham as a whole. They belong to the marginal world of the twilight zone. The problem of integration is the problem of getting them out of it.[7]

What was true of Birmingham was true also of London. There were no 'coloured quarters' in London in spite of Michael Banton's book of that misleading title, a study of Cable Street where the black community was a very small section of the population.[8] Yet the belief that there were black ghettoes, and that the inhabitants of these ghettoes were responsible for the overcrowding and for the housing shortage (both at the same time!) was widespread and indeed was fostered. It was certainly true that the parts of London where the housing shortage was most acute were those with the highest numbers of immigrants. It was also true (though this was not usually reported in the mass media) that many black immigrants came in as builders, and many others who came under general permits entered the building industry. The Ministry of Labour study *Manpower in the Construction Industry* (1964) showed that in 1964, 600 entry vouchers were issued to building craftsmen from the Commonwealth. But in the previous year Britain had lost 900 building craftsmen through emigration. It is therefore worth pointing out that without black immigrant labour during this period, the housing problem in Britain would have been much worse. Black people probably built more houses than they occupied. Moreover, it is clear that the problems in the area of housing stress were not the result of black immigration. The Milner Holland Report put this clearly:

> If they did not come, either their place would be taken by migrants from other parts of the country, or a large number of essential jobs would remain unfilled. The plight of the immigrant is the outcome, and too often an extreme example, of London's housing difficulties; it is not their cause.[9]

This did not prevent Enoch Powell, several years later, from citing the Milner Holland Report in support of his own very different position.[10]

North Kensington, Paddington and the Rent Act

One of the areas of London with which Milner Holland was concerned was North Kensington, which includes Notting Hill. The term 'Notting Hill' became known throughout the country in August and September 1958 as the scene of anti-black violence, although in fact the disturbances covered a much wider area than Notting Hill. Chapter Four contains a more detailed discussion of the events which took place. They occurred, contrary to much media coverage, in an area with small numbers of black people. But it is important here to examine the background of social decay, and particularly of housing stress, which formed the wider context for the 'riots' and for the growth of what later became known, perhaps unfairly, as 'Rachmanism'.

North Kensington has a long history of deterioration. The Victorian houses in the area had long been the homes of the unsettled and the disadvantaged. Dickens described Notting Dale as 'a plague spot rarely equalled for insalubriety by any other in London',[11] while Booth, writing at the beginning of the twentieth century, described it as containing 'some of the worst patches of outcast life in London'.[12]

With some degree of exaggeration, the West London magistrate E. R. Guest, in 1958 called it 'the haunt of every drunkard in England',[13] while a study in 1964 referred to the whole area as exhibiting 'the sickness of a disintegrated society'.[14]

The area invited generalized comment of this type, and there had been no shortage of people prepared to offer instant social comment on the problems of Notting Hill before the advent of West Indian immigrants. When the immigrants did come, this was one of the main areas of settlement. Probably the first group of West Indians in the area had settled in Tavistock Road, and this was followed by a movement into Ladbroke Grove and then into the Colville/Powis Squares district.

Central to the problems confronting black people in the 1950s and 1960s, whether in Notting Hill or elsewhere, was the question of multi-occupation of property in very poor condition. Black immigrants were rarely in local authority housing, tended to be in worse housing than the average resident, and were likely to be blamed for the bad conditions which they suffered. Kensington manifested – and still manifests – the poles of affluence and misery. Thus unfurnished flats in South Kensington in the 1950s were let at £50 per week, while in North Kensington, 40.5 per cent of residents of Golborne Ward lived at a density of over one-and-a-half persons per room. An article in *The Observer* in 1967, referring to conditions in Golborne since 1961, noted:

> Six years ago this area in the part of London's North Kensington wrongly but evocatively known as Notting Hill had the highest degree of overcrowding outside Glasgow. Three-quarters of the households had no hot water, six out of ten no bath and a shared lavatory. Today rents are higher, overcrowding is probably worse, and it has become overwhelmingly a coloured area.[15]

The four wards in North Kensington (Golborne, Norland, Pembridge and St Charles) contained 45 per cent of the entire population of Kensington. An unpublished survey, written after the 1958 disturbances, described conditions in these four wards.

> Acres of desperation stand next to flourishing tree-lined crescents and private squares. There are four wards, whose boundaries are eccentric in the extreme. A rough division can be made along Portobello Road from north to south and along the Metropolitan railway from Westbourne Park to Latimer Road. St Charles Ward lies in the largest, north west corner, and is the most open area, with large flat-blocks and some playing-field space. There are also Nineteenth Century terraces and railway-type cottages. In the south western corner, Norland Ward has its expensive quarter near Holland

Park tube station, and deteriorates rapidly towards the north and west. There is an area of appalling, cramped little houses near Latimer Road, some fairly new flats and forbidding old ones. Pembridge Ward to the south east began life as imposing middle class housing on the South Kensington pattern; much of it has stayed that way, though there may be more flats and fewer servants' halls. But in the north there is a fairly compact area, around Powis and Colville Squares, where large terrace houses, tenancies with a key to the square, have declined even to half-room letting. Half a basement room, with a hardboard partition between you and the next two or three tenants, could cost you thirty shillings a week; a whole basement, seven pounds ten. Luckily the houses were solidly built: thirty people need to use the hallway over your head. Many of the people living here are coloured; nearly all are trying to keep out of 'trouble' with the landlord, his thugs or the neighbours, and moving on as soon as they can. The smallest, north east, corner contains almost the whole of Golborne Ward, and there is hardly a satisfactory house in it. There are three schools, two or three play streets, no youth club, and not one building that is actually pleasant to look at. The railways and the canal are the only 'open spaces' . . .[16]

This, then, was the area into which many of the early black immigrants to London moved. Their housing problems repeat in an extreme form a story which could be told of many run-down slum districts in other parts of London and other cities. A recurring factor was that rents were highest where essential domestic equipment was lacking.[17] One West Indian's story, reported by Pearl Jephcott in 1964, is not untypical.

In September 1957 I arrived in London. I was living in a house with Rats and Bed Bug. The wardrobe in the house the door was falling. The chesterdraw was meant to have three draws, only two was in use, no food cupbord, just one little wash basin for the whole house to use . . . In February I moved to S—— Street, W11. I was renting one room for £2.12s.6d. The Landlady gave me the key for the room. When I went in there I found the mattress on the bed, no pillow, no blanket, nothing on the line of comfort, the mattress half spent. When I ask her for bedclose she said I had to provide since she could not afford to give me any. Also there were rats I cold not sleep there I had to move again. In November I went to . . . W10 . . . another story of Rats again. This time I had my first child in his cradle. I couldn't let him sleep on his own they used to jump in his bed with him. One night I was awoke with a shock I felt something was crawling on me it was a Rat in my bed with me.

1958 September. I moved into a Basement flat. I had same rough stuff even worse I was nearly kiled there by Teddy Boys. My whole life was haunted there night and day. Eventually I had to move again. That Basement Room was wet, cold and all my silver used to grow green moss. I couldn't buy a bread and use it twice if I buy it today tomorrow I had to frow it away. April 1959, L—— Road, W12 when I moved in there I had to diposit £40 for one room empty and £2.10s a week. After 11 months I received notice to quit within four weeks. When I ask the landlord say either notice or pay more. Payment went up from £2.10s to £3.5s. No Bath room no kitchen there was one toilet for six separate tenants to use. In November we had complete Black out in the house the landlord refuse to pay the light bill. Every so often the gas metre is Broken in to no one knows who's doing it. Then in October 1962 there was inspector of health to the house. I find myself in real trouble. I was told that I am living overcrowd just myself and my three children. This time I had to look for flat I was offered one with £60 diposit. I had to let that go why I could not afford that amount. Backward and forward every day after a while I stop looking. Eventually the flat where I am living now came empty. I ask him meaning the landlord if he would let me have it. £5.10s for two rooms still no kitchen no Bathroom.[18]

There were many similar cases to this during this period. It took the disturbances of 1958 and, more important, the revelations of housing racketeering which were brought to public view as a byproduct of the Profumo affair of 1963, to arouse the 'conscience of the nation' to the reality of what was going on.

Perec (Peter) Rachman, the shadowy figure who was at the centre of the 1963 saga, had in fact been active and well known in the Notting Hill area for at least eight years. He had acquired property in Powis Square and Colville Road and Terrace in 1955 and 1956. Within the West Indian community, it has been claimed, 'everybody knew that he was the only person who would let to blacks'. The *Empire News* claimed that he was 'probably London's largest individual landlord for the coloured population'.[19] The black activist Michael Abdul Malik (Michael X) claimed that the real villains were those landlords, the majority, who refused to let to blacks. Rachman was a symptom of and, to some degree, a solution to the problem.[20] Shirley Green, Rachman's biographer, similarly claims that he became the scapegoat for a more pervasive and widespread evil.[21] It was discrimination in housing which created the phenomenon which was to become known as 'Rachmanism', and its growth was aided by the Rent Act of 1957 and the Street Offences Act of 1959.

The Rent Act divided rented dwellings into those which were 'decontrolled' (that is, outside the scope of the act) and those which were 'controlled' (that is, within the act). Decontrolled properties were those having a rateable value of £40 and upwards in London and Scotland or £30 and upwards in the rest of the country, and those, of whatever rateable value, which became vacant after the passing of the new act. This became known as 'creeping decontrol'. In effect, rent controls applied almost entirely to the unfurnished sector. Decontrol meant that the landlord could charge whatever he wished for rent, and could give notice to quit at any time. As a result of the act, any real security for tenants disappeared.

Out of an original stock of five-and-a-half million privately rented houses, not more than two-and-a-quarter million were still subject to control by the beginning of 1964. This had disastrous effects on impecunious newcomers, the very people who were needed, and indeed whose presence had been encouraged, to meet labour shortages. Many of these newcomers were black. Less than two years after the act was passed, a government inquiry showed that the rents of houses which were still controlled had risen by 60 per cent in the London area, and by 40 per cent outside London. But the rents of houses which had become subject to 'creeping decontrol' had risen by 145 per cent in London and 58 per cent outside London. In addition to the Rent Act, the Street Offences Act of 1959, passed to control street prostitution, led to the transfer of the trade to apartments and rented rooms, giving added incentive to the exploitation of prostitutes by landlords.

These were the years when Enoch Powell, at that time Parliamentary Secretary to the Ministry of Housing, was claiming that 'we are now within sight of, and should in twelve months' time or so be level with, an equation of the overall supply and demand for houses'.[22] Powell, who helped to draft the act, believed that it would 'halt the drain upon rented accommodation; it will release additional accommodation which is under-used or wasted; it will arrest the deterioration of millions of homes . . . and it will give to persons who are moving or setting up homes, opportunity to find accommodation in the market'.[23] Housing Minister Henry Brooke also promised that the act would make more accommodation available. The truth was otherwise, as a report from the South Kensington Tenants' Association in 1957 emphasized. The act, it pointed out, 'allows much real evil, encourages oppression of the poor and offers tenants bogus rights, no security of tenure, makes enforcement of repairs a farce, and will, unless repealed, surely lead to widespread civil disobedience'.[24]

Rachman recognized that the housing situation for black people in London's twilight areas was ripe for his activity to expand. He exploited both the desperate need for accommodation and the legalized insecurity of his tenants. The result of the first was an increase in the already serious problem of housing speculation; the result of the second was an increase in the numbers of the homeless in London.

In 1962 the London County Council's report of the Committee on Homelessness drew attention to 'the shrinking stock of privately rented houses' in London. 'The total number of privately rented dwellings is falling rapidly.'[25] Of the nineteen London boroughs which replied to the Council's request for information on the most frequent causes of homelessness, the reasons most often given were: Rent Act, 'creeping decontrol', eviction from furnished accommodation and insecurity of tenure. Rachman had cashed in on a situation which gave him vast scope, and upon legislation which was powerless to end his activities. But in 1963 the storm broke. The Profumo scandal, involving

John Profumo, the Minister of War, and his personal relationships, brought with it a scandal of far deeper significance.

However the Rachman story was not new, and this was perhaps the most scandalous aspect of it. In the debate in the House of Commmons on 22 July 1963, Harold Wilson claimed:

> My honourable friend the Member for Paddington South [Ben Parkin] has given the House details over the years of the way in which tenants have been treated in his constituency. He has given these details in the House with about as much impact on the complacency of the Treasury Bench as if he had been describing housing conditions in Nero's Rome.

Ben Parkin had, in fact, made seventeen major speeches since 1953. Nor was he alone. One MP from the provinces said that 'there are many of us who have been talking about these housing rackets for a long time before we heard of the Profumo affair'. The press, too, had not been entirely silent, although editors often wrote under threat of legal proceedings. When the *Kensington News* produced an article in its issue of 12 June 1959 entitled 'Where is Mr Rachman?', in which it suggested that he had avoided them at three addresses, he at once sent a solicitor's letter, and the following week the paper was forced to print a front-page apology. No more was said there about Rachman for several years. The *Kensington News* had probably done what it could in an atmosphere of parliamentary apathy, local authority paralysis, and racketeering which was quasi-legal.

The publicity of 1963 exposed the long-standing problems of North Kensington and Paddington to public view in the context of a sensational political scandal which soon was to bring the Labour Party to power. In a sense, the real heroines of the day were Christine Keeler and Mandy Rice-Davies. But for their sexual activities, the more fundamental social scandals might never have been brought to national attention in the mass media, although people in the affected areas had been trying to bring the issues into public debate for many years.

One depressing aspect of the whole saga is that the Church appears to have played no role at all. Yet North Kensington was an area in which churches were quite thick on the ground. Notting Hill was one of the great strongholds of Anglo-

Catholicism. But the priests did not seem to regard housing racketeering or racial hatred as coming within their sphere of activity. They belonged to the tradition described by a disillusioned Notting Dale curate as 'desiccated maiden aunt Catholicism'.[26] Here was none of the radical tradition which had marked the second phase of the Oxford Movement in parts of the East End, but rather an inward-looking, élitist pietism. Anglo-Catholicism in its most unhealthy and most reactionary form was particularly ill equipped to respond to the challenge of racism and racketeering. So as Rachman pursued his activity, and as blacks, many of them Anglicans, were attacked in the streets, the devotional guild at All Saints' Church recited 'the Living Rosary of Our Lady and St Dominic'.[27]

At the national level, the situation was little better. Those who looked to the church press for any kind of critical prophetic voice on 'Rachmanism' were disappointed. *The Church of England Newspaper* proclaimed in a leading article: 'The Labour Party blames the Rent Act. To this there are two answers: first, that Rachman's activities and others like them started before the Rent Act of 1957, and, secondly, Rachman's operations were only possible because premises were available not covered by the Rent Act and therefore very cheap.' It went on to claim that 'to impose rent restrictions might bring out other Rachmans', and proceeded to offer the comment: 'The Rent Act helped to make more accommodation available and this must continue. Safeguards are certainly necessary against intimidation and the coloured problem must be tackled.'[28] This was offered as serious social comment. Ben Parkin had observed in the Commons not long before that the claim that the Rent Act was not responsible for the situation would raise laughter in hell. When the church press were so distant from the problems of the housing stress areas that they simply repeated media platitudes, it must have caused tears in heaven.

In fact, whether in relation to housing or in relation to the growth of racial hatred, the record of the churches in North Kensington and Paddington was not good. There were some improvements as a result of changes in the Methodist presence in the area after 1960. But for the most part, during the period when black people were seeking to find a home within Britain and, in many cases, within the churches, the churches in this area were preoccupied with their own internal affairs.

Spitalfields and Cable Street

The housing situation was equally, if not more, desperate in London's East End. One of the most decayed areas of social breakdown in London, Spitalfields had inherited the social problems of other districts and of many generations. An entire volume of the London County Council's *Survey of London* was devoted to the property in this area, but much of it during the 1960s fell outside any development plans. In general, conditions in the East End had certainly improved during the twentieth century. But there was a dark side to the picture. Some districts had deteriorated, and in some of them social distress had reached alarming proportions. Spitalfields was one such district, rightly described as 'London's worst slum', the result of a prolonged policy of drift.[29] From the corner of one street, it was impossible to see any property which was less than two hundred years old. A study of the social history of the area – which has never been undertaken in the detail it deserves – would show that for generations it had been a refuge for the oppressed, the inadequate, the social outcast, the desperately poor and isolated. A pamphlet by William Hale in 1806 referred to the removal of the affluent and the consequent subdividing of properties, and a writer in a local newspaper in 1906 remarked that Hale's account related to 'circumstances closely akin to those existing in Spitalfields and its neighbourhood today'.[30] Sixty years later, his words were still applicable.

It is not unfair to say that the London County Council hardly ever drew attention to the terrible state of this part of the East End. Their admirable booklet *East End Housing*, which was much promoted in the 1960s, made virtually no reference to it. The redevelopment of this district, in fact, was not even programmed at the time, or was programmed for many years ahead. In 1962 the Revd Joseph Williamson, Vicar of St Paul's, Dock Street, a man who played a major role in the agitation for slum clearance in the East End, wrote to the Minister of Housing about the future of Spitalfields. On 31 July 1962 the Minister replied as follows: 'The position is that the Spitalfields part of Stepney, west of

Commercial Street, including the market, is zoned for commercial development in the development plan, but not programmed. The area east of Brick Lane, which is also zoned for industry, is however programmed from 1960 onwards.' A similar letter from the Ministry to me, dated 8 February 1963, also admitted that there was little immediate likelihood of change in the district. 'The area west of Brick Lane is outside any CDA [Comprehensive Development Area] proposals and is zoned part for light industrial, part (southern) residential . . . Only one patch of 2nd period programming well away from Brick Lane, the rest not programmed.' It was into this district that the new immigrants from East Pakistan, later Bangladesh, were moving. They encountered the East End in its most run-down aspect, in a district where hope of reconstruction was bleak.

An account from the early 1960s, written by the late Edith Ramsey, by then the oldest and most revered of Stepney's social workers, gives some indication of the kind of housing conditions in the area at this time.

> 'This is not a nightmare – it is stark truth,' gasped my companion as we emerged from a house in Spitalfields. He was right. This house, and many others like it, are not stage replicas of conditions described by Dickens more than a hundred years ago, but places where people are condemned to live in 1962.
>
> We had been visiting an old lady who with her daughter shares three rooms on the first floor of the house. Both the LCC and Stepney Borough Council now limit rehousing almost exclusively to those whose homes must be demolished under clearance schemes. But on the points system, needs, merit, and urgency of rehousing is supposed to be indicated by the number of points allotted to each application. With Stepney Borough Council this couple had no points, so clearly no priority. They had three rooms for their own occupation, I was told.
>
> What did we find? A flight of steep stairs, climbed in pitch darkness, led to the kitchen-living room. In this room a large wooden contraption was erected twelve years ago when the room – or was it the house? – was declared a 'dangerous

> structure'. It curtails the size of the small room, and makes cleaning more difficult. The lighting is gas, for 'it is too damp for electric wiring'. In the little scullery, the tap has been dripping for over ten years, and 'can't be put right'. The primitive WC is so heavily strutted that it is almost impenetrable. A daily battle is waged unsuccessfully with rust and mould, with cockroaches, beetles and other insects. The adjoining room is unusable, and to get to the bedroom entails descending and mounting five steep stairs. The window-ledge is bright with growing plants, but overlooks a yard of indescribable filth, and access to that yard is through a basement more filthy than the yard. Rats are said to live in the yard, but my friends are protected from them and from mice by their cat.
>
> 'Three rooms for their own occupation.' What rooms! But bombed out of Dron Buildings, excellent pre-war flats, this had been their home for twenty-one miserable years. Three years ago, the old lady, who cannot move without help, and whose legs often fail her, fell on the stairs and broke her wrist. Since then she has no power in one hand.
>
> The immediate area is scheduled for redevelopment (light industry) in the next five years. This house, according to present planning, is in the area to be 'reviewed' between 1972 and 2005.[31]

That description of property and conditions was not untypical of Spitalfields – and other parts of the East End – in the early 1960s, and indeed such conditions can still be found. It was in districts such as this that the housing and overcrowding problems of London were at their worst and most desperate. In the surrounding streets lived the homeless, the unwanted, the down and outs, the meths drinkers, the inhabitants of 'Itchy Park' and of the ruins of derelict buildings.

Many generations of immigrants had experienced the pain of these streets: Irish people fleeing from the potato famine, Ashkenazi Jews fleeing from persecution in Eastern Europe, black immigrants from Africa, Asia and the Caribbean. For the latter, the experience of the 1950s and 1960s (and, in the case of African immigrants, the 1940s) was a central element in shaping their view of, and response to, British society. It was these years which were to be of crucial importance for the future of race relations in Britain. And it was in these years that black people were subjected to the housing horrors of North Kensington and of the East End.

The conditions which they encountered in the East End are difficult to exaggerate. During the period 1960–5, for example, there were countless examples of housing decay of the most appalling kind. A roof of a derelict building collapsed, killing one child and injuring four others. The dead boy's parents had been on the housing list for thirteen years and had one living room and two cupboard-sized bedrooms. There had been many medical certificates about the health of the children, the dead boy having been asthmatic. In seven rooms nearby, ten adults and fifteen children were crowded together. Four more children had been put into a home. One of their rooms had a tap, the rest of the residents had to use a tap in the yard. Here, also, there were two WCs, both of them periodically out of action. To reach this yard, those who lived on the top floor had to struggle down forty-eight rickety steps. A few hundred yards away from this house was a once fashionable square where, in the early 1960s, the landlord created matchboarded boxrooms which lasted for two years inside the shell of a condemned and demolished factory and warehouse. Twelve or thirteen such rooms brought in weekly rents totalling about £37. Most of the families here were black, and they shared one tap and gas stove. There were many other examples with which those of us working in the area at the time were only too familiar. Fantastic rents for single rooms containing broken bits of furniture, damp basements surrounded by garbage and rats, squalor which can scarcely be described in sufficiently grotesque language: this was typical of much of the experience of urban Britain as encountered by the early black immigrants, who had been recruited for their labour but whose presence was not wanted.

Not far from Spitalfields is Cable Street. No street in Britain had received more hostile publicity than this street over the years. Much of the publicity was inaccurate and misleading. Cable Street is a long street which winds through the East End from near the Tower of London towards Limehouse. In the period under discussion, two-thirds of it was no different from other Stepney streets. It was the west extremity of the street to which people referred who spoke of it as 'the filthiest, dirtiest, most repellently odoured street in Christendom'. 'I have been in the Souks of Algeria and Tunis,' continued this writer, 'but some of these places in Cable Street are disgusting to me.'[32] Cable Street was the centre of the district described by Michael Banton in his book *The Coloured Quarter* (1955), based on research at the end of the 1940s.[33] From the final years of the Second World War, it had become a major social centre for the growing black community in East London, and for people from further afield. Almost the entire Somali community of London was concentrated here. The cafés and clubs catered for people from Sierra Leone, Aden, Gambia, Malta, Nigeria, Zanzibar, Somaliland and many other parts of the world. But many of the white residents of Stepney never entered Cable Street, and the dominant attitude of the ruling Labour Party was to ignore the existence of both the district and its black population.

By the 1960s, housing conditions in the western part of the street were terrible. Action was often in inverse relationship to the publicity. In August 1962 the local East End newspaper referred in an editorial to the housing policy of the LCC in relation to the area. 'The question is have they not turned a blind eye to the vice areas of Cable Street and Spitalfields, whilst demolishing and rebuilding the old but respectable areas whose need is by no means as great.'[34] The answer was clearly 'Yes'. The history of the proposed redevelopment of the Cable Street area is a tragic one. The area had been built around two of London's oldest squares, Wellclose Square and Swedenborg Square, and here a Scandinavian community had grown up at the end of the seventeenth century. The properties surrounding these squares had decayed over a century, and as a result there had been talk of demolition. But it was not until 1958 that the Housing Committee of the LCC recommended that the Swedenborg Square area should be designated as a clearance area under Section 42 of the Housing Act 1957. A report was produced in June 1961, and yet another in July 1964. In 1961, the Chairman of the Housing Committee was quoted as saying that 'large-scale demolition had started, and building would begin early next year'.[35] But this was not the case. In 1962 another LCC spokesman said, 'We want to see this area cleared very soon and the new homes built.'[36] It did not happen. In the same month, the Duke of Edinburgh observed that he had not realized how little progress was being made.[37] The Minister of Housing had described the area in 1961 as 'one of the worst examples of an area where many of the dwellings have been declared unfit'.[38] He said in the Commons in 1962 that no government could wish to pause when it was Cable Street which would be affected.[39] But his words were empty. Nothing happened.

I say nothing happened. Of course, there was some minor activity, and some more or less cosmetic changes. Several shops at the junction of Leman Street and Cable Street were demolished, and a few properties came down opposite the beginning of Christian Street. But for the most part the area between Swedenborg Square and Dock Street/Leman Street – Banton's 'coloured quarter' to the inch – remained essentially the same at the beginning of 1967 as it had been in 1947. The newspaper which, in 1964, announced 'Death sentence for Cable Street, E1, and they all rejoice',[40] overestimated both the sentence and the rejoicing. By the beginning of 1967 most of the property was still inhabited. The impression was given that great progress was being made, but this was not so. The slum zone of Cable Street in 1967 remained essentially the same. And it remained the same in spite of the fact that between 1958 and 1963 (in particular) an unparalleled campaign was waged by local clergy and others against the conditions of the district. The mass of correspondence with statutory bodies makes sad reading, and if it were published it would shock the country.[41] One was left, in the aftermath of the Cable Street campaign, with a feeling of acute paralysis. Unlike North Kensington, in Stepney the churches played a major role in the campaign for slum clearance. It is frightening to think, for example, how much worse the conditions would have been had it not been for the dramatic and prophetic, if at times irresponsible, zeal of Father Joe Williamson.

I have told this part of the East End story in some detail because it illustrates the way in which districts of housing crisis can deteriorate, and how the disadvantaged members of the community, especially its black members, can become the scapegoats for the failures of those in power. Thus the victims come to be blamed for the sins of the oppressors. This is what happened in London in the 1950s and 1960s, and it helped to shape and distort the climate in which issues of race have been discussed ever since.

4

Racism and Violence

In 1984 the *Guardian*, a newspaper which prides itself on its anti-racist posture (almost the only surviving British daily paper to do so), ran a front-page headline: 'Blackest day for pit violence'.[1] It was an unintentionally significant choice of words. I wrote to the Editor and asked whether it was a subtle way of making the point that the miners were now experiencing the kind of police violence which black people had been experiencing for some time, and which was to a great extent responsible for the uprisings of 1981. Somehow I doubted it, and needless to say my letter was not published. 'Black' was being used in its classical racist meaning of 'worst': black mark, blackmail, blacked.

However, the analogy with the miners' strike of 1984 brings out some important features which relate also to the question of race and racial violence. First, both commentators on racism and Arthur Scargill, the President of the National Union of Mine-workers, often use the concept of 'State violence', manifested through the police in a direct way but evident over a much wider field.[2] Second, in both the miners' strike and in the conflicts associated with black minorities, the question of class has been of crucial importance. People such as bishops and politicians who speak on these conflicts often reveal their class position and background to a far greater extent than they seem to realize. But in relation to black people, the interconnections between race and class are complex. It is all too easy, and fairly common in the white Left, to dissolve all racial matters into class ones. Nevertheless there is, in my experience, a growing chasm between the black bourgeoisie and the black underclass. The issues of race and class are inseparable, but they are not the same. Third, in both the miners' strike and in black protest, there is an acute sense that far more is at stake than particular policies and programmes. The future of whole communities, threatened with dereliction and despair, lies behind the immediate disputes. And there is a sense that one's own communities are no longer valued – in the case of black communities, perhaps never were valued by the white power structure – and are therefore dispensable. In the case of black people, of whom many were recruited in the post-war period by some of the very same people who now campaign for their removal, the sense of rejection is particularly bitter. And, finally, in both situations there is a serious breakdown of relationships with the police. It was this breakdown which erupted in violence in Brixton and Liverpool 8 in 1981. In the mining communities it may take many years to restore, if it is possible at all.[3]

It is a parallel which I am tempted to pursue, for the degree of support for the miners among many black people was evident at the 1984 Notting Hill Carnival, and was clearly displayed in posters and badges in many black neighbourhoods throughout the country. It took many miners and their families by surprise. Of course, parallels can be dangerous and misleading. But I want to stress the need to consider violence in relation to race and racism in a wider context than the specific experience of black people in Britain. And here there are three important general points to be made.

First, historically racism and violence are closely associated. In our own century the classic example is, of course, the Nazi experience. Here an anti-Semitic ideology generated vast destructive forces, leading to the extermination of millions of people, a world war, and the spiritual violation of a deeply Christian nation.[4] Whether Western Christianity can ever fully recover from the holocaust is not clear, but the roots of anti-Semitism in the Christian tradition are clear enough.[5] Racist doctrines can lead to genocide. But for black people, the essential background to the understanding of contemporary racism is the colonial experience, and for West Indian people the colonial and slave experience. It is impossible to understand the situation of the black minorities in Britain without taking account of the history of the colonial era and of slavery. The very presence of the 'new Commonwealth' immigrants is a post-colonial phenomenon. In simple terms, they are here because we were there. For black people, history is the record of the rape and dehumanizing of their identity and their communities, a record of exploitation, enslavement, poverty and systemic violence. No discussion of violence against or by black people in Britain can be meaningful which does not recognize this historic background.

Second, the colonial period has generated philosophies of liberation which include violence. This is as true of liberation struggles in the past as it is true today of the Irish and Latin American movements for freedom from domination. The theme that the powerful never voluntarily surrender their power is certainly not peculiar to black people. Different historical periods and structures produce their theorists of change. Thus Karl Marx was a product of nineteenth-century capitalism. But, however much the right-wing mass media would have it so, Marx is not all that popular among many black radicals. Frantz Fanon, the psychiatrist from Martinique and author of *The Wretched of the Earth*, is the product of white colonialism. And philosophically it is in the works of Fanon that the theme of liberating violence, the violence of the oppressed and dehumanized, is most powerfully expressed. If white revolutionaries look to Marx, Lenin and Trotsky for their understanding of the place of violence in social change, black revolutionaries are more likely to look to Fanon. In the literature of black liberation movements he holds a very special place. Again, there is no way of making sense of the black experience in Britain which fails to locate black thought and struggle in its international perspective.

Third, the day-by-day experience of black people in Britain is an experience of what is known as 'institutional racism'. Lord Scarman claimed that it did not exist in Britain. In fact, all racism is institutional. It is part of the definition of the word.[6] The discussion of racism at the individual level cannot be adequate unless it places individual attacks and individual experiences of violence against the background of the systemic attack on personal worth, dignity, liberty and security at the level of law, work, housing, and so on. Racism (as opposed to racial prejudice or racial discrimination) cannot exist apart from violence, for it presupposes the existence of a powerful group which is capable of enforcing its position. The experience of the racially disadvantaged is therefore essentially an experience of violence, of violation, of structural racism.

Violence, then, is built into the very nature of racism. It is not a series of freak, accidental or episodic occurrences. Racism is by its nature violent, although the forms that the violence will take will vary from time to time and from place to place. All this is part of the necessary background to this chapter, and it is hard to overemphasize it. I want now, against this background, to consider four phases of violence involving race and racism in post-war Britain.

The Notting Hill riots

First, I want to go back some thirty years, to the Notting Hill riots of 1958. I remember them well, for they took place as I arrived in London as a student. They are often remembered and referred to as the first race riots in Britain, although there had been serious incidents in 1919 in Liverpool and Cardiff, as well as earlier anti-Irish and anti-Jewish disturbances in nineteenth-century London, and indeed there were simultaneous disturbances in Nottingham. But it is Notting Hill, 1958, which is remembered as the first clear evidence of 'Britain's race problem'. The main events took place at the end of August and the beginning of September, although there had been earlier disturbances in July and mid-August.[7]

In fact, to call them 'Notting Hill riots' is not strictly accurate. For

> the disturbances fanned out from Shepherds Bush and adjacent Notting Dale to several pockets in Notting Hill, Kensal New Town, Paddington and Maida Vale. And while in Nottingham the troubles occurred in the centre of a district densely settled with coloured people, this was not so in London. On the contrary, the main explosions took place beyond the fringes of relatively concentrated coloured settlements or even further away; and the worst offenders came from housing estates and districts which were – and still are [1960] – almost wholly white. One of the most sordid zones of transition in North Kensington, which has a considerable cluster of coloured people, was comparatively quiet – though in a zone where 'marginal men', white and coloured, live side by side; which has generally a shady reputation; and where

trouble was, therefore, expected by local officials when it broke out elsewhere.[8]

Bramley Road, part of the parish of St Clement, Notting Dale, which figured prominently in the disturbances, had very few black people at the time.

As we look back at the 1958 disturbances, we can identify a number of features which recur in varying forms in later incidents. First, the disturbances occurred in an area, and at a time, which was marked by very low immigration from the 'new commonwealth'. Black people at this period formed 0.8 per cent of the population of Britain as a whole. The area where much of the rioting took place contained very few black people. At the 1961 census, there were only 5,806 people in Norland Ward who had been born outside the United Kingdom (34.4 per cent of the population), and only 384 of these were West Indians. Yet the myth has persisted that Notting Hill was a 'black ghetto' and that this was why the riots occurred.

Second, those involved in the rioting were white people, almost all young, and most of them came from districts which were wholly white. On 30 August some two hundred whites had gathered in Bramley Road, and this was followed by a gathering of between four hundred and seven hundred the next day. Two-thirds of those arrested on these two nights came from the Notting Hill area, in particular from Notting Dale.[9]

Third, racialist organizations, in particular the Union Movement (the successor of the British Union of Fascists), the National Labour Party and the White Defence League, were active in the area. The Union Movement was to contest the 1959 General Election with Sir Oswald Mosley as its candidate. The White Defence League had its headquarters in Princedale Road, close to the scene of the rioting.[10] Ruth Glass, in her study of the riots and their background, showed that the activity of these 'Keep Britain White' groups contributed to the hostile climate in which the rioting occurred.[11]

Fourth, the responses to the disturbances by those in authority included the assertion that the rioters were an insignificant section of the community (Lord Justice Salmon) and the demand for tighter controls of black immigration (George Rogers, the

Labour MP for North Kensington, and others). In other words, racialism – the word 'racism' was not in common use at this time – was seen as a freak phenomenon, alien to the English traditions and way of life; while the solution was seen in terms of racially discriminatory legislation to control entry of potential victims rather than in terms of any action to change public opinion, policy or practice.

Much of the support for immigration control came from the Labour Party. The local branch in North Kensington has been described as 'so right wing that Gaitskell [the party leader at this time] wouldn't attend its social functions'.[12] There were no black members. But Labour Party members elsewhere were also active in the campaign to control black entry. Although the official position of the party was one of opposition to controls – at least until the act was passed – there were Labour MPs in the forefront of the campaign for control from early days. Within days of the Notting Hill disturbances, the *Daily Mail* ran an article by Maurice Edelman, MP, entitled 'Should we keep them coming in?'[13] The following day, the same paper in its editorial urged control on the grounds that Britain was an 'overcrowded island'.[14]

I want now to take these four features out of the context of Notting Hill in 1958, and locate them within the general pattern of racial violence. We can, I suggest, recognize these features in the racially motivated outbreaks which have occurred since 1958 (though all four are not always present or of equal importance in each incident or cluster of incidents).

First, outbreaks of racial violence are not related to the size of the community under attack, but rather to the economic situation and to the prevailing climate of respectability of racialist activity. There is no necessary correlation between the numbers of black people, or other immigrants or minorities, within a nation or a neighbourhood, and the incidence of violence against them. Violent incidents have often occurred, as in 1919 and 1958, when black people have been few in number. The Jewish population in Germany was 1 per cent when Hitler decided that 0 per cent should be the optimum tolerable ratio. The 'number theory of prejudice' does not stand up to examination. Indeed, there is evidence to support the view that there is an inverse relationship between numbers and violence: that it is when the community is small in number that it is most likely to be the object of racial violence.

Secondly, white people are often recruited, or drawn in, as participants in violence from areas adjacent to the area of conflict itself, and sometimes from much further afield. Thus in the 1900s and in the 1930s the attacks on the Jews in Whitechapel were often organized in the entirely 'English' area of Bethnal Green a mile or so to the north.

Third, there is often (though not always) a causal relationship between the activity of racialist organizations and the incidence of violence in an area. This was true in the case of the anti-Jewish violence in East London in the 1930s, and in Notting Hill in 1958, and has been documented on many occasions since then. Sometimes the organizations deliberately incite and organize the violence, while at other times they simply create the climate of prejudice and hatred which makes it inevitable.

Fourth, a common reaction to racial violence is to punish the victims rather than the assailants, that is, to insist that it is their *presence* which is intrinsically problematic. Paul Gilroy has pointed to the central place of the view of black as problem in the construction of racist language and its close connection with that of black as victim.

> The idea that blacks comprise a problem, or, more accurately, a series of problems is today expressed at the core of racist reasoning. It is closely related to a second idea which is equally pernicious, just as popular, and again integral to racist meanings. This defines blacks as forever victims, objects rather than subjects, beings that feel yet lack the ability to think, and remain incapable of considered behaviour in an active mode. The oscillation between black as problem and black as victim has become today the principal mechanism through which 'race' is pushed outside of history and into the realm of natural, inevitable events.[15]

Racism is thus seen as a problem which only arises when there are black or other 'alien' groups to arouse it, rather than as something which is endemic within white society and which must therefore be tackled there. Racial conflict comes to be seen as an inevitable consequence of the presence of black people, who are seen as both problems and victims. But in terms of action in the aftermath of violence, it is the problem identity which comes to the fore.

Brick Lane 1978

I now turn to a second wave of racial violence, that which occurred in the Brick Lane area of Spitalfields and Bethnal Green in East London in 1978. I was parish priest of the northern part of Brick Lane at the time, and my church was a few minutes' walk from the scenes of the worst violence. Here the violence was directed principally against the Asian community, almost all of whom originated in Bangladesh. The assailants were mainly white 'skinhead' youths, inspired by the propaganda and the presence of the National Front, the British Movement, Column 88 and other fascist groups. The term 'Paki-bashing' had first been used in the Bethnal Green area in 1969–70, and there had been a history of attacks from then onwards. Racist slogans were common, and after 1976 the National Front, which was later to establish its national headquarters in Shoreditch half a mile away, became very active every Sunday at the corner of Brick Lane. Between May and September 1978 there were several murders, many incidents of violence against persons and property, and on 11 June 1978 a mob of several hundred skinheads rampaged through Brick Lane, attacking the homes of the Bengali community. The events and their significance are discussed in more detail in the following chapter.

Let me return to the four features which I identified in the context of Notting Hill 1958 and see how they apply to Brick Lane in 1978. First, unlike 1958, the 1978 disturbances involved a very large and concentrated black, in this case Bengali, community. Brick Lane was seen as a place of safety, and Bengalis were reluctant to move from it for fear of attack on isolated estates elsewhere. Although the incident on 11 June and several others involved direct entry of white gangs into the Bengali area, this was not the usual pattern of racial violence in the area. The worst and commonest attacks took place around side streets, and on estates further east where Bengalis were in the minority. The fewer the numbers of Bengalis on an estate, the more likely the incidence of racial violence; hence the demands by Bengalis that they be rehoused together on 'safe estates'.

Second, as in Notting Hill in 1958 and in the earlier East End disturbances involving the Jews, the assailants came mainly from white areas, particularly from Bethnal Green and Shoreditch (Mosley's strongholds from the 1930s, and the districts where fascist groups had been recruiting in the 1970s), but also from areas further north and east in Hertfordshire and Essex. One pub in Bethnal Green Road was identified as the main fascist gathering place, and a railway bridge in Brick Lane itself divided the Bengali, or more accurately the multiracial, area from the mainly white area where the NF and its satellites were active and gained support.

Third, the violence was directly related both to the presence and the propaganda of the fascist groups in the neighbourhood, and also, in my view, to the racial polemic of national politicians. It can be shown, for example, that each major speech of an anti-immigrant character in recent years has been followed by an increase in racial violence. Thus Enoch Powell's 'rivers of blood' speech of 1968, delivered ironically on Hitler's birthday, 20 April, was followed by the first outbreak of 'Paki-bashing' in East London in an area where Hitler's birthday was still being celebrated in my time in one local pub! Similarly, Margaret Thatcher's notorious interview on Granada TV in 1978 about the alleged 'swamping' of British culture was followed by an increase in racial attacks. Nobody would claim that it was the intention of these and other politicians to cause an increase in violence, but there seems little doubt that, knowingly or unknowingly, they helped to create the climate in which racial attacks were more likely to occur. So while, as in Notting Hill twenty years earlier, there was in 1978 a close connection between the activity of racist organizations and the increase in violence, the situation in 1978 was far more complex and more serious. The speeches and positions of major national figures and the media (in particular papers such as the *Daily Mail* and *The Daily Telegraph*) had created a climate in which racism was respectable.

Again, it was the victims who were blamed. Bengalis in 1978 were told to stay off the streets. It was their fault if they were attacked. If they were attacked and harassed on estates, they were advised to move. Even those who removed racist slogans from walls were arrested instead of those who had put them there. And while the National Front continued to sell its inflammatory literature for two years in Bethnal Green Road, when anti-racists nonviolently occupied the site, we were told that we were causing a breach of the peace! So it was the victims and opponents of racial incitement and violence rather than the perpetrators of it who were penalized. And, as in Notting Hill in 1958, the idea that racism was a minor aberration within a broadly decent and tolerant society still coloured the reaction of many people to the events of 1978. Individuals outside the East End, and even many in other parts of the East End, believed that the violence had been greatly exaggerated, and that, if only less were said about it, it would automatically subside.

Bradford 1981

I want now briefly to consider the events in Bradford, Yorkshire, in 1981, which led to the trial of the 'Bradford 12', a group of young Asians who were charged with making petrol bombs for self-defence and who were finally acquitted. I was a witness at the trial at Leeds Crown Court, as two of the defendants were known to me. The link with Brick Lane was clearly made at the trial. It was the fear that a similar state of seige might occur in Bradford which led to the decision of the young Asians to defend their community. As one of the accused said at the trial:

> My personal experience is that the police have never defended our community. There is an absence of the will to help . . . The police have always protected the fascists . . . Maybe you don't know what it is like to be black in a racist society. In such a situation, the only thing you can think of is the measures you might take to defend yourself.

Meanwhile, the unwillingness or extreme reluctance of the police to recognize the reality of racial violence was one of the central features of their position. A little while before the trial occurred, the Home Office study *Racial Attacks* had appeared.[16] It had surveyed thirteen police areas including West Yorkshire, of which Bradford was a part. Yet Detective Inspector Sidebottom, when questioned during the trial, admitted that he had never heard of the report, and that he was not aware of any high incidence of attacks in the Bradford area. The Home Office study had shown that Asians were fifty times more likely to be victims of racial attacks than were white people. Later studies showed that racial attacks were by no means restricted to the well-known areas such as Tower Hamlets and Newham, but were increasing in other parts of Britain also. In all the areas, Asian people were most at risk.[17]

The case of the Bradford 12 showed the extent to which the issue of self-defence, with its assumption that Asian people could not rely on the police to protect them, had grown in importance. Since then, self-defence has become a major issue in those areas where racial attacks are most common. And, in Bradford as in other areas, the features identified above were present: the prevalence of attacks in estates and streets where Asian families and individuals were isolated; the involvement of white youths from mainly white areas; the connection, at times very direct, with racist and para-military groups and with racist propaganda; and the tendency to blame and punish the victims rather than the attackers. Many Asians have reported that they no longer inform the police, because when they have done so, they themselves have been interrogated about their immigration and nationality status. Local authorities, when they have taken action, have tended to rehouse the victims of attack rather than remove the attackers.

The uprisings of 1981

Finally, I want to consider briefly the disturbances in Brixton and Liverpool in 1981, about which I shall say more in Chapter Six. Here it is important to make certain distinctions clear. These were not 'race riots' in the sense of conflicts *between* races. In both cases, as also in Bristol, Moss Side and elsewhere, black and white people were involved in the violence. At the heart of the disturbance, however, was not racial conflict but rather conflict with the police as symbols of white authority and white racism. The disturbances are better described as uprisings. They were certainly racial disturbances in the sense that racism, State racism, racism in policing and the criminalization of black communities were perceived to be the underlying issues.

Unlike Notting Hill in 1958, the 1981 uprisings were not related to immigration. The black community in Liverpool is not an immigrant community. It has been there for over a hundred years, and its historic roots are in Africa, not Asia or the Caribbean. Nor are most young blacks in Brixton immigrants. The uprisings were about black British communities, their status and their future. They were also about wider issues of poverty, unemployment and neglect in the inner-city neighbourhoods; evils suffered by black and white people together. Moreover, the most serious rioting took place in areas where well-informed people, black and white, had been predicting trouble for years, and had cited police tactics and behaviour as the most likely immediate cause.

Since 1981, Martin Luther King's statement that riots are 'the voice of the unheard' has often been quoted. What was most alarming and depressing about these occurrences was that they took place in some of the most over-researched districts in the world. They revealed the enormous comprehension gap between members of the government and the people of the inner city. Perhaps that was part of the revival of Victorian values. But by 1981 it seemed to be more than ignorance – rather a deliberate refusal to believe, an unwillingness to take the people of the inner areas seriously. Gabrielle Cox, who in 1981 was a Greater Manchester councillor for the Moss Side Ward and Chairperson of the Police Committee, drew attention to the feeling of powerlessness combined with the feeling of the government's carelessness.

> Inner cities are constantly being mercilessly battered, day after day after day. Almost any single governmental move for change at national or local level has a detrimental effect on the inner city . . . And here we see the sheer irrelevance of Orwell's view in *1984*. Winston Smith is surveyed constantly, but the supreme irony of our situation is that Big Sister doesn't care what the individual thinks or does. She has sufficient power, backed up by the complacent and the secure who don't mind what happens as long as it is fairly all right for them. She has the power to ignore what people in Moss Side think.[18]

It was this profound sense of inability to effect change, to make the powerful listen, which was the really fundamental cause of the 1981 uprisings. And in a sense they worked. Suddenly Michael Heseltine was rushed up to Merseyside, and money became available. A few days of rioting seemed to have achieved what years and years and many volumes of research had not. Lord Scarman produced a report on Brixton which said nothing in relation to the underlying issues which black people there had not known for years. But, it seemed, only when a respectable, elderly, white judge said it, did white society taken notice. And yet for how long? Would there have to be more uprisings before the lessons would be learned? Experience since 1981 suggests that the voice of the unheard has still to be heeded.

I have considered four types of racial violence associated with four different places and times. The response which is called for is different in each case, but there are some general comments which must be made. Certainly the law has an important, but limited, place in combating racism. Many of our laws are not used. For example, under Section 71 of the Race Relations Act of 1976, local authorities are obliged to 'eliminate unlawful racial discrimination and to promote equality of opportunity and good relations'. This surely involves an obligation to deal with racist attacks. Yet there are few cases of perpetrators of such attacks being removed from their tenancies on grounds of nuisance. Again, under Section 3 of the Criminal Law Act of 1967, the use of force in self-defence is allowed, and it is specifically stated that this applies also to the belief that an attack is imminent. Yet the experience of most Asian people is that it is they, not their attackers, who find themselves penalized. When Asian people contrast the lack of protection which they receive with, for example, the degree of protection afforded to non-striking miners in the NUM dispute, it is hardly surprising that they suspect partiality and political bias in the way in which the law is applied.

In all the areas where racial attacks have occurred, there are Christian churches. Is there evidence that these communities have responded in any positive and supportive way to the plight of the victim? There are some important examples, such as the work of Susan Davis, former Social Responsibility Officer for the Church in Tower Hamlets, who mobilized church workers to provide support and help for the victims of attacks. But for the most part it has been left to groups such as the Revolutionary Communist Party or local anti-racist committees to tackle these urgent questions. Churches have remained aloof, have not wanted to get their hands dirty with such issues – though they have also criticized those who have, accusing them of exploiting the situation for 'their own political ends'. Maybe the groups have. But the sad fact remains that the victims of attack have not, for the most part, seen the followers of Jesus to be on their side or concerned about their fate.

But at the end of the day, there will be no solution to the question of racial violence unless the underlying causes of the violence are tackled. And this means going beyond the immediate, and right, concern to reduce the level of violence, to the concern to change the social and economic conditions which make violence inevitable. If communities are battered, dehumanized, pushed further and further towards hopelessness, there should be no surprise if they explode. There comes a point when violence and vandalism become the last available forms of social action. And Christians who are committed to a gospel of love ought not to fail to recognize that, where the way of love and justice is not followed, the will of God may be achieved by violent means. Although Jesus preached a non-violent path, he recognized that the Kingdom of God would experience violence and that the violent would take it by force. We should not be afraid to recognize the hand of God in the events by which the mighty are put down and the poor are lifted up. When all has been said about the damage done by 'riots', do we not need to acknowledge that if, as a result, some powerless people have been empowered, have been given an identity, have made their voices to be heard, we should not deny that, in these events, the hand of God was at work?

5

Brick Lane and the Local Growth of Fascism

Brick Lane is a long street which runs from Whitechapel to Bethnal Green in the East End of London. It has experienced a good deal of publicity in recent years. But it has a long history. In 1576 Lolesworth Field, an early Roman cemetery, was broken up for brick manufacture, and it was as a result of this that the lane received its name. The sixteenth century saw the building there of the Red Lion Brewery, and this was followed in 1669 by the Black Eagle Brewery, which was taken over in 1694 by Joseph Truman. Today the brewery divides the Bangladeshi area to the south from the mainly white area of Bethnal Green to the north.

Brick Lane was one of the earliest parts of the East End to be built up. A writer in 1748 referred to the area as being 'close built and inhabited by an infinite number of people'. This writer described Brick Lane as a 'well-paved street', whereas in 1670 it had been 'a deep dirty road, frequented chiefly by carts fetching bricks that way into Whitechapel from brick kilns in those fields whence it had its name'.[1] By the nineteenth century, according to Mayhew, the lane and its offshoots consisted of lodging houses and brothels. It was in these streets that Jack the Ripper carried out his murders towards the end of the century, and so helped to focus more attention on the area. Brick Lane, claimed the Rector of Christ Church, Spitalfields in the 1880s, was 'a land of beer and blood'.[2] But during the following decade, the lane was transformed by the immigration of Jews from Eastern Europe, and it became the main street of the Jewish ghetto. Today a building at the corner of Brick Lane and Fournier Street stands as a symbol of the lane's religious history: once a Huguenot church, it later became a synagogue and is now a mosque. During the Jewish phase of Brick Lane's life, the divide at the brewery was even more marked than it is today. Beyond the brewery, and particularly beyond the railway bridge to the north, was Gentile territory. The immigrant population of Bethnal Green remained one of the smallest of any borough in London.

The Brick Lane area was at the centre of the anti-aliens agitation in the early years of the twentieth century. Thomas Benkin, Conservative candidate for South West Bethnal Green in 1892, told the electors: 'I consider the time has arrived when statesmen should consider measures which will directly benefit "John Bull" without due regard to outside and foreign interests. I am in favour of stringent measures to prohibit the wholesale immigration of pauper foreigners. I certainly support the principle of maintaining "Great Britain for the British."'[3] His statement could have come from almost any period in the modern history of the area. In 1901 the British Brothers' League was set up to build up anti-immigrant activity. Later, in 1937, the first of Sir Oswald Mosley's British Fascist candidates stood in the LCC elections for South West Bethnal Green and Shoreditch, the district which included the northern part of Brick Lane.

So the Asians who moved into Brick Lane after the Second World War entered an area with a long history both of immigration and of anti-immigrant polemic and organization.[4] The numbers were small until the prospect of controls in the early 1960s led to a 'beat the ban' influx. Thus the total number of people born in India in the Borough of Stepney was 371 at the 1951 census, growing to 905 in 1961. Pakistanis grew from 309 to 700. By the 1960s Brick Lane had become the centre for immigrants from East Pakistan, later to become Bangladesh. The overwhelming majority were single males. There were only 935 Pakistani women in the entire county of London in 1961, while the numbers of men were four times that figure. Although Brick Lane was being described as an Asian ghetto, there were in fact few heavy concentrations in 1961. The highest ratios of Asian-born people occurred around parts of Middlesex Street, Princeton Street and Old Montague Street. It was years later, after the creation of Bangladesh in 1974, that Brick Lane became the social centre of this new community on a much bigger scale.

The beginnings of racial violence

Although there were some minor outbreaks of violence in East London in 1958 after the Notting Hill incidents, it was not until the end of the 1960s that the deterioration in the situation became clear. In 1965 the Secretary of East Pakistan House had referred to 'a growing mass hysteria against the Pakistanis'.[5] This was one of the first public recognitions of the growth of specifically anti-Pakistani feeling, although the writer did not refer to physical violence. It was in 1969–70 that the East End witnessed attacks on the Pakistani community on a significant scale. A study by Louise London showed that the period from March to May 1970 was of particular importance.[6] The first actual reference to 'Paki-bashing' in the press appears to have been on 3 April 1970, when several papers mentioned attacks by skinheads (itself a word which had only recently come into use) on two Asian workers at the London Chest Hospital in Bethnal Green. But the term was in use in the East End in 1969 and probably originated on the Collingwood Estate in Bethnal Green.[7] On 5 April 1970 *The Observer* reported: 'The name of the game is Paki-bashing. In London's East End the skinheads might have learned the rules from the Hitler youth. Any Asian careless enough to be walking the streets alone at night is a fool.' Two days later Tosir Ali was murdered. During the period from March to May, some thirty-six racial attacks were documented in the East End. On 26 April about fifty young white people went on the rampage in Brick Lane, and five Pakistanis were injured. It was in this year that the issue of self-defence against racial attacks started to be seriously discussed. Mass meetings of the Asian community were held in various parts of Tower Hamlets, and there were discussions with MPs and the police.

It is important, therefore, to recognize that a pattern of racial attacks had been established in the East End by 1970, eleven years before the Home Office report and fifteen years before the police and the country as a whole came to recognize racial violence as a serious issue. Between 1970 and 1976 attacks continued on a sporadic basis. 'The situation is becoming both violent and unhealthy,' wrote Derek Cox, one of the most experienced youth workers in the Brick Lane area, 'and is evident in the schools as well as the streets.'[8] In 1976 the Anti-Racist Committee of Asians in East London (ARCAEL) was set up as a broad-based body to draw attention to the inadequacy of the protection offered to Asian people by the police and other authorities. There was a spin-off from the killing of Gurdip Singh Chaggar in Southall, and there was an increase in attacks in East London as a result. On the day that John Kingsley Read of the National Party (a shortlived split from the National Front) made his infamous 'One down – a million to go' comment in Newham on the Chaggar murder, ARCAEL organized a mass meeting at the Naz Cinema in Brick Lane. The meeting was addressed by Darcus Howe of the Race Today Collective, Trevor Huddleston, then Bishop of Stepney, and Dan Jones, Secretary of Bethnal Green and Stepney Trades Council. Huddleston continued to be held in considerable respect within the Asian community as did his successor, Jim Thompson, but the local churches on the whole did not seem to have seen the attacks on Asian people as any of their business. There was little, if any, evidence of Christians offering solidarity and support to the victims of violence.

In the weeks that followed, a number of victims of racial attacks were themselves arrested for threatening behaviour or for carrying offensive weapons. Meanwhile, the attacks continued. The press became interested in exaggerated stories of 'vigilante groups'. There was a germ of truth in all this, for the experience of the Asian community had led them away from passive acceptance of racism to a determined commitment to self-protection. Throughout 1976 there was a good deal of attention paid to Brick Lane in the national press. On 15 June 1976 the two Anglican priests whose parishes covered the Brick Lane district, Eddy Stride and myself, issued a statement. As this statement, issued at the height of the build-up of organized racism, was never printed in full in the press, it is perhaps worth reprinting it here.

> Considerable attention has been paid recently to this part of the East End, and it has been portrayed as a focus of hostility and violence against Asian, particularly Bengali, immigrants. Sections of the media, press and TV, have certainly helped to aggravate a tense situation. As the priests of the two parishes particularly affected, we wish to make the following points.
>
> (1) The Spitalfields district, including part of south-west

Bethnal Green, has for centuries been marked by severe social problems, particularly of housing. In each generation there has been a tendency, especially at times of crisis, to blame these problems on recent immigrants. The Irish suffered in this way in the 1840s, the Jews from Eastern Europe in the 1890s, and today the various black immigrant groups. We believe that this temptation to blame long-standing social evils onto the latest arrivals and victims, understandable as it is, needs to be resisted if the problems are to be solved.

(2) It is not helpful, in our view, to ignore the real social problems associated with immigration into already deprived and overcrowded districts, or to pretend that they do not exist. There is bound to be resentment when middle-class people who live comfortably away from the areas of conflict issue statements which sound to many working people like clichés. At the same time it is wrong to see immigrants as the *cause* of the problems which they help to highlight.

(3) It seems to us that much of the anger which is now rising to the surface among local people is basically righteous anger: anger at years of neglect and social injustice in this and other districts. But to direct this anger into a campaign of violence against immigrants is not only evil, but also is to identify the enemy wrongly. The anger needs to be directed into zeal for justice in society, for black and white people, and against all social systems which 'grind the faces of the poor' and ignore the demands of justice.

(4) As Christians we hold that both racialism and social injustice are manifestations of human sin, and that no amount of social reforms or attention to specific problems, important as these are, will get to the roots of these evils. Social change and spiritual renewal must go hand in hand if we are to create a world of justice and peace.

Eddy Stride and I disagreed on many issues, theological and political. The 15 June statement was an attempt to identify common ground. We were concerned to emphasize the need to resist scapegoating, to recognize the real problems of overcrowding and housing stress, to connect concern about race and racism with the wider struggle for social justice for all (without denying the specificity of racial oppression), and to unite the spiritual and social dimensions of our Christian discipleship. In all these emphases I am sure we were correct, and subsequent reflection and action by Christians of both evangelical and catholic traditions has focused to a large extent on these themes. Similarly, our stress on the spiritual significance of anger was a necessary and important corrective to much Christian talk which assumes that all anger is inherently and intrinsically sinful. Nevertheless, looking back on this period, I do not think our attempt at consensus was successful. The approach was wrong: we were trying to find a lowest common denominator. The kind of theological statement which would have been of value at this juncture was one which was drawn out of a common practice, a common struggle, and which sought to make sense of that struggle in the light of the gospel. But there was no such common struggle among Christians in the East End in the 1970s. There were Christians who took seriously the threat of organized racism and who threw themselves into the struggle against it. But for the most part Christians took the line of least resistance. They were, after all, a minority themselves, and their main concern was survival.

There was the additional factor that most of the Asians in the East End were Muslims, and contact with members of the Christian churches was minimal. 'Interfaith dialogue', if it existed at all, took place at a level which was removed from the pain and struggles of the back streets. The attitude taken by many Christians was that the claims about violence were greatly exaggerated. It was not within their range of experience. And yet in many cases their own children were involved. Moreover, by 1976 much of the violence was well documented. The magazine *Race Today* in June of that year devoted considerable space to the Brick Lane area, and spoke of the 'atmosphere of increasing racial and police intimidation'. The same issue listed 'the most serious assaults on Asians to have taken place between March and May this year'.[9] These amounted to some thirty cases, collected by the Spitalfields Bengali Action Group, almost all of them in the Brick Lane area.

On 20 November 1976 the East London Conference Against Racism took place at Queen Mary College. Organized by Bethnal

Green and Stepney Trades Council, and chaired by Brian Nicholson of the Transport and General Workers' Union, the conference brought together a wide range of people representing political, social, cultural and religious groups in the East End. Like most such gatherings, however, it was weak in representation from 'ordinary people', and many of those who attended were middle-class professionals, or professional attenders of meetings, who had moved into and were active within the East End. While it was useful in terms of mobilizing numbers of people, and in enabling a variety of views to be expressed, the conference did not help to hammer out strategy, nor did it lead to further gatherings. It did, however, pass a resolution relating to the growing NF presence in the Brick Lane area. 'Noting the attempts of the National Front to gain a base in East London, and especially their provocative newspaper sales in Brick Lane, conference decides to initiate a mass demonstration based on Labour and community organisations against the presence of the National Front, particularly in Brick Lane.' Again, it is worth noting that representation at the conference from the Christian churches in the area was very small indeed.

During the following year, 1977, the major ethnic minority organization continued to discuss the self-defence question in the light of the failure of the State, as represented by the police, to offer adequate protection to black people under attack. In May, *Race Today* called for patrols in the Brick Lane area in the face of 'a systematic campaign of deadly assaults against the Asian community'. They referred specifically to the case of an Asian youth whose ear was almost severed by a gang with knives, and to that of an Asian man who was critically ill after being beaten up.[10] A local newspaper pointed to the intimidating character of the NF presence in the area where attacks were increasing:

> Racial violence has recently centred around the Brick Lane area. The presence of National Front supporters at Sunday markets in the lane has prompted claims and counter claims of violent attacks. The National Front has been concentrating on utilising bands of white youths to give verbal support to Front members selling newspapers in the lane. An *Advertiser* reporter recently saw NF supporters swearing and spitting at

> Asians who walked past members selling papers near Bethnal Green.[11]

In the same month, June 1977, the Home Office, at the insistence of the Bangladesh High Commission, called for an urgent report from the Metropolitan Police on racial violence in the East End, and this was apparently prepared by the Community Relations Office at Scotland Yard. The Bengali Housing Action Group (BHAG) gave the Commissioner the dossier mentioned above listing thirty attacks. In June also the national press reported that Asian vigilante groups had been formed in the area.[12]

On 17 October 1977, more than 3,000 anti-racists marched through NF strongholds in Hoxton and Bethnal Green to a multicultural festival in Victoria Park. It was a foretaste of the much bigger rock festival which was to occur in the following year, and marked the beginnings in the East End of the association between the struggle against racism and rock music. Towards the end of the year, too, there was a good deal of activity in painting out racist slogans and graffiti. In December, five members of the Campaign Against Racist Slogans were found not guilty of defacing a railway bridge in Bethnal Green by painting over NF slogans.[13] On 4 December, anti-racists removed a large number of racist slogans from the wall of Cheshire Street baths, although they had earlier been prevented from doing so by the police. Even a British Movement symbol which had remained for several months on the wall of Bethnal Green Police Station was at last removed. Tower Hamlets Movement Against Racism and Fascism (THMARF), a group which had been formed in 1975, began to develop its activities towards the end of 1977. However, as the year ended *The Times* dismally reported: 'Police initiative fails to halt wave of violence against Asians'.[14]

The growth of the fascist groups

To understand the role of the NF and its satellites in the recent troubles in the East End, it is necessary to look back into earlier history. There had been a long tradition of anti-immigrant and racist polemic in the East End since the turn of the century, and particularly during the 1930s. The activities of Arnold White,

Major Evans Gordon and the British Brothers' League in the early years of the twentieth century have been well documented,[15] and the similarities have been shown between that campaign against the Jews and recent anti-Asian propaganda.[16] In the 1930s, Sir Oswald Mosley's British Union of Fascists concentrated its attack on the Jews in the East End.[17] A study by J. H. Robb showed the central place of Bethnal Green in the formation of anti-Semitic feeling and its mobilization into action.[18] Because Bethnal Green, adjacent to the Jewish ghetto of Whitechapel, was still largely a district of white, local-born residents, it was easy to exploit the sense of a threat from the alien presence to the south, and transform it into concrete anti-Jewish activity. The Hoxton district, also white and with a very low mobility rate, was similarly a major recruiting ground from the fascist movement.

Thus during the 1930s, fascist and racist groups were active in precisely the same districts where their successors based themselves in the late 1970s. In the mid-1930s the British Union of Fascists claimed 4,000 members in Bethnal Green, and in 1937 when the BUF contested Bethnal Green South West and Shoreditch, they polled more than 3,000 in Bethnal Green. The recent resurgence of organized fascism in the area must therefore be seen in the context of a long tradition.

In the period immediately after the Second World War, there was a revival of Mosleyite activity. Then in the 1950s a new wave of anti-immigrant polemic in the East End centred round the decayed district at the west end of Cable Street, which was discussed in Chapter Three. The racist groups focused their attention on prostitution and slum housing, both of which they attributed to immigrants. On 29 May 1958 an East London branch of the National Labour Party was formed at a pub in Cheshire Street, Bethnal Green, almost next door to St Matthew's Church. The NLP was led by John Bean, and later merged with Colin Jordan's White Defence League to form the British National Party. (This is not the same body as the present party of that name: there have been three groups calling themselves the British National Party since the early 1960s.) The BNP continued to hold regular meetings at the corner of Cheshire Street and Brick Lane, and their paper which was sold there, *Combat*, regularly featured East End issues. It was here, too, nearly twenty years later that Martin Webster, the NF parliamentary candidate, held his two Sunday meetings before the 1979 General Election. So in the 1960s Bethnal Green, with its mainly white population, was the base for an attack on Whitechapel with its immigrant communities. 'Stepney vice is a black problem,' announced *Combat* in March 1961. 'It has been left to the British National Party speakers at their regular Sunday meetings pitch in nearby Bethnal Green to denounce this blot on the face of East London.'

However, the main body which was involved in the events of 1978 was the National Front. The NF had been created in 1966–7 out of three earlier bodies: the League of Empire Loyalists, the British National Party and part of the Racial Preservation Society. In 1967 it was joined by John Tyndall's Greater Britain Movement, a more explicitly Nazi-type splinter group from the National Socialist Movement which Colin Jordan founded in 1962. The first chairman of the NF was A. K. Chesterton, a former Mosleyite who had edited the BUF magazine *Blackshirt*. From the outset, then, there were within the NF a range of political traditions: right-wing Tory imperialism, racial nationalism, crude religious fundamentalism with a British Israelite element, and National Socialism. The seeds of later divisions were present in the original formation.

At first the NF did not grow much in the East End, though they obtained 5.6 per cent of the poll in North Islington in the 1970 General Election. But after 1972 they began to show significant increases in a number of places. At the General Election of October 1974 the NF candidate in Hackney South and Shoreditch gained 9.4 per cent of the poll, the highest in Britain, while in Bethnal Green and Bow the candidate gained 7.6 per cent, one of the top six ratios. On 6 September 1975 the NF held an anti-mugging march through the East End, and from this point onwards their presence became more pronounced, although electorally they declined between the GLC elections of 1977 and the local elections of May 1978. Between 1976–8 there was a marked increase in racist graffiti, particularly NF symbols, all over Tower Hamlets, and in the presence both of NF 'heavies' and clusters of alienated young people at key fascist locations, especially in Bethnal Green. The NF aimed its propaganda particularly at the young, warning them of 'red teachers'. The Young National Front claimed to have distributed 250,000 copies of *How to spot a Red Teacher* during 1977. During the same period every school in the East End received a copy of the booklet *Did Six Million Really Die?*, which argued against the Holocaust.[19]

Of less importance in statistical or electoral terms, but at the local level more obnoxious and physically dangerous, was the British Movement, a more openly Nazi and anti-Semitic grouping. Formed in 1968, the BM was the successor to Jordan's National Socialist Movement. Its two main centres were Merseyside and the East End. BM members would attack the NF for being too liberal and insufficiently racist – 'Don't be fooled by the Kosher Front' was the title of one BM leaflet. Its bulletin openly advertised Nazi songs and literature as well as American racist publications such as *White Power* and *Thunderbolt*. Its paper, *British Patriot*, in January 1976 was advertising cassettes entitled 'Send Those Niggers Back' and William Joyce's 'Germany Calling', as well as the 'Battle Songs of the Third Reich' and copies of *Mein Kampf*. The Hoxton and Bethnal Green areas were littered with BM stickers and slogans, including the one on the wall of Bethnal Green Police Station mentioned earlier. There were a number of other groups which were active within the overall build-up of organized fascism in the area. One somewhat shadowy group was Column 88, a paramilitary network. Several anti-racists received death threats which purported to emanate from this group. More common was a letter from the 'Shoreditch Brigade' of the 'British Volunteer Force', which most people who wrote on race matters in the national or local press tended to receive.[20]

The atmosphere created by this concentration of Nazi-type groups was one of considerable tension, fear and violent hatred. In this situation the NF, as the most 'respectable' and publicly known of the groups, and the only one which put up candidates in elections in significant numbers, was able to exploit a situation of frustration, anger and disillusionment. It was able to attract to its ranks some of the most disturbed and problematic teenagers in the East End, for whom it provided an identity for the first time. Martin Webster was correct as far as this area was concerned when he claimed that 'the social base of the NF is made up of the desperate and the dispossessed among the white working class'.[21] For many of these young people, vandalism had become the last available form of social action. The coming of the NF into this situation can be seen at one level as the expansion of vandalism into a political movement.[22]

The events of 1978

On Saturday 29 April 1978 over 80,000 anti-racists from all over Britain processed, with rock bands and banners, through the streets of London from Trafalgar Square to Victoria Park for a 'Carnival Against the Nazis'. It was the biggest post-war demonstration of its kind in Britain, and it played a crucial role in stemming the tide of organized racism and fascism in the East End. The way in which Rock Against Racism, working in close liaison with the Anti-Nazi League (both of them initiated by members of the Socialist Workers' Party), was able to harness the cultural forces of rock music on the side of multiracialism was a major achievement.[23] The carnival was of crucial importance in making fascism culturally disreputable. But within days it was to be followed by tragedy. On 4 May 1978 Altab Ali, a young Bengali clothing worker, was murdered in Adler Street, Whitechapel. The murder sparked off a series of demonstrations, and the memory of Altab Ali remains a vital part of the tradition of struggle against racism in Britain. It was his murder which 'triggered a massive wave of protest throughout East London'.[24] On 14 May around 7,000 Bengalis held a protest march from the site of Altab Ali's death to Downing Street, behind his coffin. The Trades Council report, *Blood on the Streets*, described this march as 'one of the biggest demonstrations by Asians ever seen in Britain'.[25]

The murder struck fear into the heart of the local Asian community. Attendance at the English classes for Bengali women at Bethnal Green Institute fell by half.[26] The fear was not unjustified. On Sunday 11 June, a day which followed considerable press coverage of GLC plans for housing Bengalis in what were described as 'ghettoes', there was a major eruption of violence in Brick Lane. 'Mob of youths attack Bengali area in East End of London' was the headline in *The Times* on 12 June, and the incidents received major coverage in all the national press. About

150 youths rampaged through the Brick Lane district, smashing windows, throwing bottles and lumps of concrete, and damaging shops and cars. The day marked a new phase in the escalation of racial violence. I shall deal below with the connection between the violence and the alleged 'ghetto' proposals of the GLC. But it is important at this point to note the significance of this day as marking a shift in the character of racial attacks in the area. *The Times* noted: 'Attacks on Bengalis in the Brick Lane area of Spitalfields have usually been the work of relatively small groups. The destruction yesterday was carried out by the largest gang to assemble to threaten Asians in that area.' However, many people, including some of the police representatives, tended to play down the day's events, refusing to acknowledge that there was any organization or racial motivation in the incidents.

The following Sunday, 18 June, there was an anti-racist march organized by the Anti-Nazi League (ANL) and the Bengali Youth Movement Against Racist Attacks (a short-lived alliance between three of the major Bengali youth organizations). About 4,000 people, black and white, took part in this march. But the following Sunday there was further violence, many of the attacks taking place in side streets. During the whole period, many of the demonstrators against violence were themselves arrested: around fifty anti-racists, contrasted with only ten NF or BM supporters. A detailed study of police tactics in this period was prepared by the Brick Lane Defence Committee, the ANL and local lawyers, and was later published by the Trades Council. On 7 July David Lane, Chairperson of the Commission for Racial Equality, paid his first visit to the area, amid considerable publicity: he told 150 Bengalis at the Montefiore Centre that they should put their trust in the police, the CRE and the local Community Relations Council.

However on the previous Sunday, 2 July, a group of anti-racists, co-ordinated by THMARF, had occupied the site of the NF activity in Bethnal Green Road. This action began a period in which, Sunday by Sunday, the fascists were prevented from occupying their regular pitch in the area. The anti-racist numbers grew from around fifty to several thousands, though within a short time the police, who had allowed the NF access to the site for over two years, forbade access to anyone on the grounds that a breach of the peace would be caused. On 16–17 July the Bengali community became heavily involved, and organized mass sit-downs in the area. It was ironic that the unintentional initiator of the anti-racist activity was Chief Superintendent John Wallis, the officer in charge of community relations in the area, who had said at a public meeting that the anti-racists should arrive first if they objected to the NF presence.

During July and August the build-up of the police presence in the area was considerable, but it seemed to be related more to the organized anti-fascist activity than to the incidence of racist attacks. In August, Chief Superintendent Wallis declared that Brick Lane was 'the most heavily policed area in Britain'.[27] On Sunday 20 August there was a march, organized by the ANL, to celebrate the departure of the NF newspaper sellers from the area. This march involved some 5,000 people, mainly white. But the Asian community remained active, and one Asian journal in August in an editorial, drew attention to the symbolic importance of Brick Lane in the struggle of the Asian people:

> Brick Lane '78 is becoming the focus of attention as did Cable Street in the 30s and Notting Hill in the 50s, for the same forces are ranged in confrontation. However, there is a distinct danger that the more sensational aspects of the current situation are being given undue coverage by the media while the more positive, though less dramatic, developments go unnoticed. The bare facts of assaults and killing of Asians in the East End by the National Front's bully boys are known; what is not being sufficiently stressed is the strong multi-racial response that these acts have evoked, in particular among the Bengali youth, who have joined enthusiastically with their white friends in combating a menace which in its ultimate form will spell the death knell of a democratic Britain.[28]

These words carried particular weight in that they came from a man, Tassaduq Ahmed, who for many years had played a key role in educational and social provision within the Pakistani and Bengali communities in Britain. But they reflected accurately the feelings of the young Bangladeshis with whom he had remained in close contact.

The last major anti-racist demonstration of 1978 was a confused and painful one. On 24 September, while 100,000 people took part in a second Carnival Against the Nazis, organized by the ANL in Brockwell Park, Brixton, a large gathering took place in the East End to 'defend Brick Lane' against the possibility that a National Front march might come close to the Bengali district. Around 2,000 anti-racists blocked the entrance to Brick Lane, although in fact the NF had gone via side streets to a meeting in Hoxton. During the course of the day, the ANL came in for a good deal of criticism. The Hackney and Tower Hamlets Defence Committee, while it did not explicitly attack the ANL, insisted that the defence of Brick Lane was the 'top priority' for the struggle against fascism.[29] In their bulletin, issued before the demonstration, the Committee noted: 'Far fewer racist attacks have taken place in Brick Lane over the last few months, which the local people attribute not to the increased police presence but to the active defence which is being carried out by black people and anti-racists.'[30] However, an ANL leaflet of 1 October pointed out that a 'campaign of terror' was still taking place.[31] Both statements were correct. The mass invasions of Brick Lane itself did decline, but there were always occasional outbursts. The serious racial violence in side streets and on estates further east, extending into the neighbouring borough of Newham, continued and increased in frequency.

Other groups were less kind to the ANL. The Spartacist League, a small Marxist grouping, accused them of 'an organized betrayal of the fight against fascism', and claimed that the 24 September fiasco was simply the culmination of a process.

> The Anti-Nazi League has always been an organised betrayal of the fight against fascism. Today its treachery is clear for all to see. While the NF prepares to march to Brick Lane, the ANL is going ahead with its pacifist Carnival; telling anti-fascists to rally at Hyde Park for speeches by Tony Benn, that 'left' stalwart of the anti-working class, anti-immigrant Labour cabinet. Then it is parading off to Brockwell Park for fun, music and 'magic'. THIS CARNIVAL SHOULD BE CALLED OFF IMMEDIATELY! Everyone who seriously wants the fascists to be crushed should be in the East End today. Anyone who goes to Brixton with the Carnival is SCABBING on this struggle.

The ANL, the leaflet continued, was guilty of 'criminal, despicable, behaviour'.

> People are rallying in Brick Lane today for widely varying reasons. Supporters of small leftist organisations like the International Communist League (the left tail of the ANL), starting off with a sense of adventurist bravado and a desire to throw themselves onto the front lines against the fascists whatever the odds, now find themselves outflanked by larger forces. The local immigrant communities – organised in the Hackney and Tower Hamlets Defence Committee, an unstable coalition led by the opportunist Labour councillor Patrick Kodikara – are outraged at the Front terrorising their neighbourhoods yet again. Guilt-ridden members of the SWP (and its hanger-on the IMG) in the East End are reacting to pressure from the local immigrants to do something. And others are arriving from around the country for the simple reason that here, not the Carnival, is where the only meaningful protest against the NF will take place.[32]

The day represented more than a lost opportunity for the ANL. Created as a national and broadly based single-issue movement, the League lacked the roots in local communities which would have enabled it to respond to the very concrete, localized threats presented by organized fascism. So, faced with the threat to Brick Lane in September, the ANL was celebrating a Carnival Against the Nazis miles away. The ANL spokesman who claimed that 'the NF's feeble attempt to disrupt the carnival and invade Brick Lane was completely defeated' missed the point entirely. The NF march was a crucial part of their build-up in the Shoreditch area. It was on that day that they announced the establishment of their new national headquarters in Great Eastern Street, only half a mile from the Bengali area. And the ANL failed to notice it. By focusing on opposing the fascists in public celebration, they neglected the more sinister growth of the fascist movement in the back streets. More seriously, by isolating organized fascism from the racism of State and of street, they confused and obscured the nature of the struggle.

The 'ghetto' controversy

As far as the East End was concerned, organized fascism, racial violence and the racism of the local State apparatus were closely connected. The violence of 11 June occurred at the end of a week which had seen tremendous media coverage of a GLC plan to set aside blocks of flats for the exclusive use of Bengalis. The background to the story began on 22 May, when the GLC's Director of Housing, Leonard Bennett, produced a report, *Housing of Bengalis in the London Borough of Tower Hamlets*. The report began by stressing the need for additional dwellings, and the concern of the Bangladeshi community that they should be rehoused in safe areas. It then suggested

> that we might continue to meet the wishes of the Bengali community by earmarking blocks of flats, or indeed a whole estate if necessary, for their community, *provided* the existing tenants wish to move away and could be given the necessary transfers.

The suggestion was linked in the report to the fact that the Bengali Housing Action Group (BHAG) had given to the GLC a list of estates in Tower Hamlets which it considered safe. Bennett ended his report with a formal request that he should be authorized

> to set aside a few blocks of flats in or near Spitalfields specifically for the occupation of people from Bangladesh . . . Such a step to be in the nature of an experiment to see whether a specific estate or area set aside for a particular community group achieves a desirable solution to a difficult social problem.

There was no reference to 'ghettoes' – the word was not used at all. A report in the *Guardian* several weeks later commented: 'The GLC supporters of the scheme were anxious to deny that they were creating all-Asian ghettoes, although this is clearly the recommendation of the report on which the decision was based.'[33]

It was on Sunday 4 June that the storm broke, with an article in *The Observer*. 'GLC Plans Ghetto for Bengalis', it proclaimed. The following day the *Evening Standard* had a headline 'Labour split over GLC ghettoes plan'. *The Daily Telegraph*, in a characteristically unpleasant editorial on 6 June, said that ghettoes were 'not an obviously bad thing' and that their creation should not be discouraged, for 'there will be fewer cases of friction if races live separately. Admittedly there will be forays into these areas by hooligans of other races. But, alas, the harmonious, multiracial Utopia cannot exist outside the minds of those who are striving so disastrously to bring it about.' It was only a few days before just such a foray of hooligans did occur in Brick Lane. It occurred after a week of intensive press coverage of the 'ghetto' plan.

The 'ghetto' controversy was important for another reason. It brought together groups of white residents in Tower Hamlets with representatives of the Bengali community, and forged a new unity between various groups. The reactions of most of the Bengali groups to the plan was hostile. A meeting of two mainly white tenants' organizations with three Bengali groups on 6 June strongly opposed the proposals, and on 13 June these groups held a meeting with Jean Tatham, Chair of the GLC Housing Committee. Although one paper claimed that she had 'refused to withdraw the plan',[34] Lindsey Mackie reported in the *Guardian*: 'The proposed scheme to house Bengalis in the East End of London on segregated housing estates was finally buried last night when the Greater London Council committee chairman who approved the proposal said that she had been misunderstood and that Bengalis would be housed in mixed estates.'[35] The five organizations who had arranged the meeting with Jean Tatham claimed that the plan would play into the hands of those who preach and use violence. The group which had been named in the original report as having called for such a plan, the Bengali Housing Action Group (BHAG), denied that this was what they had in mind.

> We have been told that the GLC plan to segregate us on slum estates because 'it is a demand that comes from within the Bengali community'. It has been claimed that we in the Bengali Housing Action Group (BHAG) support this move. We do not . . . At no stage did we ask for a 'ghetto'. Nor did we ask for segregated slum blocks to be set aside for our members. If this is what the GLC propose, we intend to fight them in the same

way that we have fought them before. We will not settle for segregated slums.[36]

What BHAG had asked for was that Bengali families should be rehoused on safe estates, and they had produced a list of thirteen estates with empty flats. Only three of these were in Spitalfields.

On 20 June the GLC debated the scheme and passed a motion reaffirming that GLC housing stock would be allocated solely on the basis of housing need and not on a racially segregated basis. The Bennett plan had been shortlived, but it had led to two unexpected results: on the one hand, the escalation of organized racial violence and, on the other, a new commitment by white and Bengali tenants to multiracial housing and multiracial living. In the meantime, the fascist presence remained as a constant reminder that violence was not far away.

The responses to the troubles

The ANL and its offshoot, Rock Against Racism, played a very important role in making the fascist presence in Brick Lane into a national issue. The ANL was deliberately created as a single-issue movement, and soon after the Tory victory of 1979 it virtually ceased to exist. Within its own terms, the ANL had been highly successful: it had isolated the NF, undermined its electoral potential, helped to erode its cultural base and pushed it into the back streets. Yet it was precisely here that another danger lay. On the one hand, the physical danger of the fascist movements to black people did not disappear after 1979. Indeed Sivanandan has claimed that the achievement of the ANL was that fascism was 'driven from the (white) high street into the (black) alley ways of the inner city, there to continue their depredations and their recruitments'.[37] On the other hand, there was, after 1979, an increased acceptance, or at least tolerance, of crude racist polemic of a type previously associated with groups such as the NF, within the Conservative Party. In her interview on Granada TV's *World in Action* on 30 January 1978, Mrs Thatcher was asked, 'So, some of the support that the National Front has been attracting in recent by-elections you would hope to bring back behind the Tory Party ?' She replied, 'Oh, very much back, certainly . . .'[38] And in fact in 1979 the NF vote collapsed. Layton-Henry, in a study of the politics of race, comments:

> It seems clear that the major reason for the electoral reverse was Mrs Thatcher's pubic identification of the Conservative Party with a tough line on immigration. The massive swings to the Conservatives in the ten constituencies stretching from Islington Central through the East End to Dagenham, which averaged 14.2 per cent, were areas where the National Front had achieved some of its highest support and it appears to have lost much of it to the Conservatives.[39]

Since then, as far as Tower Hamlets is concerned, there has been the curious and worrying phenomenon of the Liberal success, originally rooted in the former NF strongholds, and deriving much of its support from local grass-roots racism.

At the same time, it would be churlish and incorrect to deny the major positive contribution of the ANL, in alliance (albeit often an uneasy alliance) with local anti-fascist groups, in undermining the hold of the NF in areas such as the East End. The same cannot be said of other bodies. The Commission for Racial Equality remained aloof from the troubles, until in April 1979 they published a seriously inaccurate and unhelpful report, *Brick Lane and Beyond*.[40] The local Community Relations Council, known at this time as the Council of Citizens of Tower Hamlets, was so out of touch and absorbed with its own internal conflicts that it could be of no help. It was not trusted by the Bangladeshi community, many of whom were unaware of its existence. Even the CRE report described it as 'the main organisation which was seen to have failed to respond to the needs of the Bengali community'.[41] But the CRE continued to fund this ineffective body, thus making the creation of a new and stronger group more difficult. Such a group – the Tower Hamlets Association for Racial Justice[42] – was established and quickly gained support from within the Bangladeshi community. But the fact that for years, and particularly during the troubled years of 1970–8, the East End had no effective community relations structure which could bring together and act for all the ethnic minority groupings in the area, was a serious disadvantage in the struggle against organized racism.

The Churches were weak and timid in their response to the growth of fascism. Most of the clergy disliked the NF presence, though there were suggestions that some clergy, particularly in

Hackney, had made sympathetic noises. The lay membership, as represented at synod and conference level, was hesitant and tended to see the troubles as none of their business. The fear of becoming contaminated and compromised by involvement at street or political level goes very deep in the Churches. So they prayed and occasionally talked, and the clergy sometimes (though not often in my experience) preached anti-racist sermons. But for the most part the Churches were on the sidelines, watching the NF grow and gain support among the disaffected youth in a way which they themselves had rarely done. It was some years before the threat posed by the fascist groups began to be taken seriously by the churches in the East End. In 1983 the Bishop of Stepney wrote:

> Our experience in East London confirms that for too many people it [the danger of fascism] is more than a temptation. There are organisations at work publishing material to disprove the Holocaust. There are many youngsters who, while not being members, are infected by their neo-Nazi teaching. The undercurrents of racism, the violent harassment of ethnic minorities and the weak, the fear in which many people live (afraid to go out at night), the debates about citizenship, the scapegoating of easily identifiable people for our economic ills, the profound effects of discrimination and the 'send them home' slogans are the springs of a very dangerous river.[43]

Yet how far his sentiments reflected the consciousness of the Church as a whole is open to doubt.

The really important shift in consciousness which the experience of 1978 brought about was among the Bangladeshis. The commonly held white myth of the oppressed Asian victim, passive and fearful, helpless in the face of vicious racist attacks, certainly did for some time correspond with reality as far as some Asian people in the East End were concerned. There was a sense of isolation combined with a sense of terror. 'The whole community is now stricken with fear,' was one newspaper's response to the events of 1978.[44] But it would be a serious mistake to see fear and despair as the dominant emotions motivating the Bangladeshi community today. For out of the events of 1978 a new Bengali radicalism has emerged, and it is this which is the most important feature of the period.

However, the radicalization of Bangladeshi youth in Spitalfields goes back some years. Prior to 1974, local councillors and bureaucrats had tended to ignore the existence of the Bangladeshi community, and most Bangladeshis ignored local affairs, preferring to focus on the politics of Bangladesh. But during 1974, as new groups were forming to tackle slum clearance, lack of playspaces and so on, the Spitalfields Bengali Action Group was formed, and established close links with the mainly white Spitalfields Community Action Group (SCAG). The following year the Bangladesh Youth Movement was created which, under the leadership of Jalal Uddin, became one of the major influences on the thinking and awareness of young Asians in the area. In 1976 the creation of the Anti-Racist Committee of Asians in East London (ARCAEL), in response to the racial violence, marked a major stage in the politicization of the new leadership. Caroline Adams, who has written the history of the early Bengali settlers in the East End, claims that ARCAEL was of crucial significance.

> ARCAEL and the activity around it transformed the consciousness of many young people and laid the foundations for crucial changes in the community's relationship with the world around as the police, the council, local whites, the Left, learned to regard Bengalis in a new light. The Bengali community had come of age and could no longer be patronised or ignored, at least not without a comeback.[45]

Later in 1976 the Bengali Housing Action Group (BHAG), mentioned earlier, came into existence, and two years later the Spitalfields-based Bangladesh Youth Front appeared on the scene. The community had become increasingly organized and articulate, and was to become a significant force within the local political context.

I have told this part of East End history in some detail because it illustrates the way in which a community under attack can become mobilized, and how political awareness emerges through pain and struggle. The Christian community, to its shame, played little part in supporting the community under attack and in its struggle to hold its head high with dignity. Yet there was an earlier period of East End history, the struggle against fascism in the 1930s, when Church leaders played a crucial role. One of these was Father John Groser of Christ Church, Watney Street, and his words, addressed to the local community and the police during the Mosley period, are still relevant in the context of today's struggles:

> Chief Inspector, we wanted our meeting at that corner, you made us come here instead. If we had called it here, you would have made us go there. It does not matter to us whether we are here or there, but it does matter to you that where we speak shall be a matter for your decision, not ours. Comrades, I am saying this in your hearing, because I want you to realise what is happening. If you know what is happening and why it is happening, you won't let it break your spirit and that is what matters most. They don't want you to feel that you are persons with the right to make decisions for yourselves. They want you to feel that you have no will of your own, for they are afraid of what will happen if you begin to act as persons. Don't let any of these things destroy your self-respect and the knowledge that each one of you matters because you are a child of God. If you lose that, you lose everything. If you retain that, one day you will win through, and people will again treat you as men and women who matter.[46]

6

After Scarman: The Events of 1981 in Retrospect

In this final chapter of Part One, I shall consider the events which occurred in Brixton, south London, and elsewhere in 1981, events which led to the Scarman Report of that year, and shall consider some of the wider issues and lessons of that year. In doing this I shall draw together much of the material presented in the preceding chapters. I shall attempt to place the disturbances of 1981, as well as those which preceded and followed them, in the wider context of the state of the inner city and of the racial minorities within it.

The first disturbances in Brixton occurred over the weekend of 10–12 April 1981, and they were followed in July by a series of similar disturbances elsewhere, particularly in the Liverpool 8 district. During July, in fact, there were disturbances in twelve cities and towns. In London, in addition to Brixton, Dalston, Stoke Newington, Hounslow, Clapham and Acton were affected. The Scarman Report, published in November, dealt only with the events in Brixton in April. Apparently Lord Scarman was told by the Home Secretary that he must deal only with policing issues, not with social conditions. Scarman refused to be so restricted, and the result was a compromise: a document with a heavy stress on the policing aspects, with some comments on social conditions accompanied by suggestions. On the policing questions, Scarman made a number of recommendations, including making racially prejudiced behaviour within the police force an offence, and establishing obligatory police community liaison groups. He emphasized consultation, but said nothing about the composition or power of police authorities. The police, Scarman claimed, must carry some of the responsibility for the disturbances. He spoke of police prejudice and of the failure to adjust policies in the light of changes in society. But the manifestation of such prejudice in the form of police racism was said to be 'occasional'. No attention was paid to the long-term condition and context of the events, although there was a recognition that social conditions could create a predisposition to violent protest.[1]

While Scarman dealt only with the events in Brixton over one weekend, the general approach, and the responses it provoked among police, politicians, the media and others, can be taken as applicable to other disturbances elsewhere, not only in 1981 but in later years. I shall therefore take Scarman as a point of reference and a point of departure in considering some of the wider implications of the events of 1981.

In fact, some of the responses to the disturbances were more disturbing than the events themselves, for they revealed the enormous and growing comprehension gap between the 'establishment' and the residents of the inner city. We heard expressions of horror and surprise that these events could have occurred at all in Britain, even though those closest to the situation in the districts affected had been issuing warnings for years. Indeed some of them had been shouting warnings until they were blue in the face. And what their warnings had proclaimed, research over many years had supported and documented. For the areas where violence erupted in 1981 were among the most 'researched' areas in the world. It has been said, for example, that Liverpool 8 (Toxteth) had been 'subjected to more sociological studies and surveys than the people of Samoa'.[2] The Bishop of Liverpool described it as 'the most surveyed district in Britain'.[3] 'What has become known as Toxteth', wrote Margaret Simey, councillor for the Granby Ward and at that time Chairperson of the Merseyside Police Authority, 'had been the subject of reports galore in the past, so there was really no need for further inquiries so far as social and economic conditions were concerned.'[4] Six volumes of a government survey were devoted to conditions in Liverpool 8, along with Small Heath (Birmingham) and Lambeth (which includes Brixton). But in the week of the riots in July, the six volumes were said to be 'so deeply buried in the Department of the Environment that it took three days to find them'.[5]

It is essential, therefore, to grasp the fact that the areas of disturbance were well studied and the conditions there were well documented. This was particularly true of Liverpool, but it was true also of Brixton and Moss Side, Manchester. What the responses to the events revealed, however, was a frightening gulf between reality and the awareness of those in power. Thus after Mrs Thatcher's visit to Liverpool, the black leader Wally Brown made the sad comment that, although she did listen to what was being said, it was so far beyond her experience that she simply could not understand. Other well-educated men and women expressed horror and surprise at the conditions. The Chief General Manager of the Abbey National Building Society said that he was 'shocked' by Liverpool, and Patrick Jenkin, then Secretary of State for the Environment, was also disturbed (see p. 35).[6]

We were witnessing different perceptions of reality. If government ministers were relying on the reports of senior police officers, it is not surprising that they were unprepared for the events. After all, the Chief Constable of Merseyside had said, only a few months earlier in his Annual Report: 'I am confident that these relationships with all sections of the community are in a very healthy position, and I do not see any serious difficulties developing in the future.' The black inhabitants of Liverpool were not surprised, nor was the Brixton Council of Churches, nor was anyone with close knowledge of the districts affected. But as the population of the inner cities continues to decline, and that of the more affluent suburbs to increase, the comprehension gap will continue to grow.

Within a short time of the events, we were being treated to quick explanations by police, political figures and the media. We were told, first, that the disturbances had nothing to do with unemployment or deprivation, and were simply the work of criminals and hooligans – black criminals, according to the Chief Constable of Merseyside. Liverpool blacks, he had said earlier, were 'the product of liaisons between white prostitutes and African sailors',[7] while the former Chief Constable of Bootle, in a letter to the police journal *Merseybeat*, said that Liverpool blacks had a history of crime and had created inner-city ghettoes.[8] Such statements were hardly conducive to the creation of a climate of mutual respect or understanding. Yet the response to the disturbances which laid the stress purely on criminality was not peculiar to some policemen. The Prime Minister, in a speech in the House of Commons on 9 July 1981, cited as her source of reference the *Daily Mirror*: 'I agree with the leader in the *Daily Mirror* that the violence in Liverpool had nothing to do with the city's problems of pay, housing and unemployment, but said it was a "spree of naked greed"'. This statement must have been something of an embarrassment to William Whitelaw and James Prior, both of whom, within twenty-four hours, were stating the contrary view that unemployment could not be so quickly dismissed.[9] Lord Scarman would have nothing to do with this kind of nonsense, and recognized the obvious fact that social conditions created a predisposition to violent protest. He stressed this again in an impressive, though not entirely applicable, quotation from President Johnson towards the end of his report.[10]

Nevertheless, since 1981 the tradition of ignoring the deeper roots of urban conflict and focusing exclusively and simplistically on criminal 'explanations' has been sustained. Among the police, the tendency to focus on 'keeping people off the streets' has often led to a disregard of what actually happens to those people in terms of their life expectations, job prospects, and so on. As long as they are 'off the streets' that is the sum total of police responsibility. 'If you keep off the streets of London and behave yourself, you won't have the SPG [Special Patrol Group] to worry about,' said Commissioner McNee in 1979.[11] NcNee believed that 'policing a multi-racial society is putting the fabric of our policing philosophy under greater stress than at any time since the years immediately after the Metropolitan Police was established in 1829'.[12] His successor, Sir Kenneth Newman, implicitly linked the growth of multiracial communities with the growth of terrorism, as presenting similar problems for policing. 'There are two particular problems in the western societies which have the potential to affect the balance between order and freedom. The first is concerned with the growth of multi-ethnic communities. The second is related to indigenous terrorism to promote separatism or an extreme ideology.'[13] On other occasions, Newman described the riots as the work of criminals.[14]

The tabloid media have, of course, preferred the criminal or 'wickedness' explanation to any attempt to dig deeper into underlying causes (which no doubt would include a good deal of wickedness in various people and places!). Thus the *Daily Mail*, in its treatment of Winston Silcott, sentenced as a result of the Broadwater Farm disturbances of 1985, described him as 'full of malice and hate' and as having 'evil in his heart', and denied that deprivation was relevant.[15] At a slightly more sophisticated level, we have seen among police and sections of the media an increased tendency to use the language of 'law and order' to disguise a fundamentally racist position. Often there is no reference to race or colour, but there is a 'sanitary coding' in the language.[16] Decoded, what it means is that black people are intrinsically problematic, a black area is by definition a criminal area, and any gathering of black people is a potential riot.

The practice of playing down the effect of social conditions and laying the emphasis on crime is still common among government ministers. The Prime Minister put the view strongly and crudely in her comments after Handsworth in October 1985. The disturbances, she claimed, had 'no excuse, no justification whatsoever'.

> We utterly condemn anyone and everyone who takes part in riots in Britain. Whoever these people are who riot, burn and murder – whoever they are organised by – there is no excuse, no justification whatsoever for such crime and vandalism. Those who take to the streets on the first available pretext, to fire, loot and plunder, will be subject to the full rigours of the criminal law.[17]

Similarly, Douglas Hurd, as Home Secretary, described the events as 'senseless occasions, completely without reason'. They were 'not a case history for sociologists to pore over, but a case for the police'. They were not a 'social phenomenon' but simply crime, 'not a cry for help but a cry for loot'.[18] Replying to a letter from some inner-city clergy, Hurd criticized those who would gloss over murder and rape by 'pleading social deprivation'. What the clergy had actually said was that they 'repudiate utterly the suggestion that the causes behind the recent unrest are purely criminal; or that the solution to the present situation lies merely in strengthening the forces of law and order'.[19] The same point was made in a statement by the Executive Committee of the British Council of Churches on 2 October 1985. But the view of the disturbances as purely criminal has prevailed.

In fact the social conditions provided the raw material, but there were other more immediate factors which made upheaval more likely in some places than in others. The essential point to grasp is that there was no simple and constant pattern, no slick analysis that could apply to all the events, and certainly no 'conspiratorial' model that will serve. The issues are too serious and too complex for cliché responses, and it is particularly depressing that, for much of the time, this is what we have had. Certainly there were some common features in most of the disturbances. Most of them took place in cities, and in the deprived, run-down districts of cities; but there were exceptions. Most involved young people from working-class backgrounds; though again there were significant exceptions. Almost all, of necessity, involved conflict with the police. But there were some key differences. Southall, for example, was a unique situation, in which it is known that organized fascist and racist groups from the East End moved into an Asian area for a rock concert by the Four Skins. In contrast to the situation some years earlier (discussed in Chapters Four and Five), this was virtually the only case where organized racist groups played any significant role in creating, or contributing to, the violence.

It is now beyond dispute that, in the words used by the Brixton Council of Churches and confirmed by Scarman, the disturbances were an 'outburst of anger directed at the police'. The Council of Churches, in a careful statement, pointed out that the final report of Lambeth Council's working party had warned in January 1981 of serious consequences of the policing in Brixton, and that the police had declined to respond to this. The churches and community groups in Brixton were frustrated at the failure of their efforts to liaise with the police. 'It seems as though the police force can never allow itself to be seen to be taking any advice, let alone the faintest hint of criticism.'[20] In this the Brixton Churches and groups were not alone. The London Churches Group claimed in 1981 that they had been 'persistently snubbed' by Scotland Yard for three years. The experience of other groups was similar.

In no way can such comments be dismissed as emanating from irresponsible, wild, leftist agitators, or what James Jardine of the Police Federation called 'the bleeding hearts, the so-called liberals and Marxist agitators who can do nothing but complain about police brutality'.[21] Jardine attacked the bishops in Liverpool for showing too much sympathy for the rioters. Language of this defensive and more or less hysterical type was, and remains, all too common, and has been a major factor in the deterioration of police community relations. Church and community groups have become accustomed to having their serious, responsible, often very moderately worded criticisms of the police dismissed by language which is lacking in seriousness, irresponsible and immoderate in tone. Police officers and their public defenders often speak as if all criticism of them were 'virulent', 'perverse responses' or emanated solely from 'certain groups on the far left'.[22] Yet clearly this is not the case. The Hytner Committee which reported on the Manchester disturbances felt it necessary to remind the Chief Constable, James Anderton, that 'not everybody who makes suggestions for the improvement of the police force is a subversive'.[23] Yet it is not clear that the point has been taken, and such claims continue to be made. One former Chief Constable, writing in August 1981, claimed that criticism of the police was 'mostly unfair, by members of left wing organisations out to discredit authority as a whole and the police in particular'.[24] A Police Federation spokesman in 1985 described two political activists in Tottenham as inflaming the criminal minority and causing 'open incitement to riot'.[25] And the tabloid media has supported this view. Thus after the sentencing of the young man charged with killing a policeman in the uprising in Tottenham in 1985, two daily papers attacked 'left wing politicians' and 'doctrinaires' for stirring up anti-police sentiments,[26] while clergy in the St Paul's area of Bristol who criticized police tactics during the notorious 'Operation Delivery' in September 1986 were accused, by 'respectable' newspapers, of 'making rioting respectable' and of being 'apologists for anarchy'.[27]

It was good, therefore, that Lord Scarman, who presumably did not fit these descriptions, stressed that the police must carry some responsibility for the outbreak of disorder, that they were partly to blame for the breakdown in community relations, that there were instances of harassment and of racial prejudice among junior officers, and that there was a failure to adjust policies and methods to meet the needs of policing a multiracial society. None of that was new. It had all been known for a long time and often said. But, it seemed, it was only when a respectable, elderly, white judge said it that many people were prepared to hear. And that, in fact, may be the main significance of the report.

Finally, and predictably, we were told of outside agitators, Marxists, anarchists, and so on. The 'conspiracy theory' was as popular in the coverage of the 1981 events as it had been in the United States in the 1960s, in Britain in the eighteenth and nineteenth centuries, and even as far back as 1381 when 'Lollards' and 'heretics' were seen as the instigators of the Peasants' Revolt. In Chicago in the 1950s, the famous community organizer Saul Alinsky observed that 'outside agitators' were always the first to be blamed when long-standing injustices and frustrations led to civil disorder. Indeed some even blamed Alinsky (who had been dead for years) for the riots in Liverpool, seeing them as part of an internationally organized radical strategy![28]

One leading exponent of conspiracy theory is James Anderton, Chief Constable of Manchester. Anderton holds that the greatest danger facing the police is the 'creation in this country of a society based on Marxist/Communist principles' and of a 'totalitarian one party state'.[29] So in 1981 he described 'a kind of military strategy' behind the Manchester events. 'This was carefully planned guerrilla warfare . . . and London accents were heard in Moss Side.' He spoke of individuals who were 'intent on causing disruption and anarchy within the inner city areas of Manchester and elsewhere'.[30] Similar noises came from Liverpool. 'Someone is instructing them,' said Fred Jones, Chairperson of the Police Federation in Liverpool. 'The hard left have now jumped on the bandwagon.'[31] William Whitelaw, the Home Secretary, also spoke of 'agitators' in a speech at Warrington on 10 July, while the press had headlines such as 'Search for the masked men', 'Riots: four men hunted', 'Four behind the riots' and 'Extremists' master plan for chaos'.[32] Scarman used the less emotive word 'strangers', to whom he ascribed some slight role in what he termed a 'shadowy area', and he referred to extreme groups who exploited the situation for their own ends.[33]

The belief that urban unrest is fermented by small groups of political activists is a well-established one among the police, almost part of the deposit of faith, even among those with a 'liberal' reputation. Thus John Alderson in 1973, when he was Chief Constable of Devon and Cornwall: 'The reality of the malevolent activities of a society of extremist groups . . . Marxists of every brand, anarchists, nihilists, and at least some elements of the various nationalist movements, all these have a determined interest in subverting existing British society.'[34] Thus Sir David McNee, then Commissioner, speaking of the activity around the Deptford fire (see below), commented: 'I think if we look at what is happening in Deptford and what has been happening, you would find there the same individuals that we get in Notting Hill, or wherever there is difficulty. They are also in Deptford, motivating and urging the black community to confront the police.'[35] In his comments on the events in Handsworth in 1985, the Chief Constable of the West Midlands, Geoffrey Dear, also referred to 'outside agitators'.[36]

Of course there is some organization in all disturbances. But to blame the Militant Tendency, the Workers' Revolutionary Party, the National Front, anarchists or Saul Alinsky – or even, as in some articles, the Institute of Race Relations and the British Council of Churches – for the disturbances is not only to attribute to these groups a power which they do not possess, it is profoundly insulting to the deprived districts and to the anger of neglected and harassed communities to suggest that they *need* to be organized from outside. Certainly, once the rioting had changed to looting different people were involved, and there was both organization and direction. But, like Commissioner Kerner in 1968, Lord Scarman rejected the conspiracy model. Indeed, what was most striking in both Brixton and Liverpool was how little a role the white Left played in the uprisings. In Brixton the headquarters of the WRP was burnt, while black militants from elsewhere who tried to get in on the action were told, as were their white counterparts – not too politely in some cases – that their services were not required.

A slightly milder version of the agitators theory is the view that black people who rebelled were 'imitating' the behaviour of blacks elsewhere, whether in Soweto or in the USA. As long ago as 1973, a White Paper on *Police/Immigrant Relations* argued that problems for the police were caused by 'a small minority of young coloured people . . . apparently anxious to imitate behaviour amongst the black community in the United States'.[37] In 1976 the Metropolitan Police, in their evidence to the Select Committee on Race Relations, claimed that there was an increased tendency for West Indians to interfere with the police in their work, and that each small incident 'carries the potential for large scale disorder'. They argued that such disorder was likely to occur in the summer months.[38]

There was one mistake which even the least responsible of the popular dailies did not make: these were not race riots. Certainly the racial element was crucial, but they were not conflicts *between* races. In Brixton there was a fair cross-section of black and white people. In Moss Side the majority of those arrested were white.[39] 'Racism has never entered into it' said David Webb, the former Handsworth Chief Superintendant, after the events of 1985.[40] Only Enoch Powell and sections of the American press seem to have got this wrong. The former spoke of a 'battle map' which corresponded with immigration, and linked the events with his previous predictions of civil war.[41] American local papers such as the *Chicago Tribune* assumed that Brixton was a slum black ghetto like 47th Street, a comparison which might have been reinforced by Chief Superintendent Plowman's claim, in his evidence to Scarman, that Brixton might become like Harlem.

In fact, the comparison with the United States is confusing at two points. There is much to be learned from the 1967–8 disturbances in American cities and from the subsequent responses. There are striking parallels both in the aetiology of events and in the types of reaction (and non-reaction). But there are two fundamental differences. First, the districts in Britain where conflicts occurred were not racial ghettoes such as Harlem or the South Side of Chicago; there are no such districts in British cities, and it is difficult to see how they could develop. That is not, of course, to deny that 'there are alarming signs that Britain is well on the way to creating a new black underclass', or that this is 'a phenomenon which has no parallel in British working-class history'.[42] But the areas of deprivation are in no sense comparable to the American districts. Second, no one has ever disputed that black Americans are US citizens. They are not immigrants, there is no talk of controls, deportation, repatriation or loss of citizenship. The British events were multiracial in character, and the 'ghettoes' are ghettoes of the poor of all races. The specific oppression and harassment of young blacks focused and exposed in an extreme form the long-standing oppression of whole communities.

The events in context

I want now to place the events of 1981 in a wider context, and this will involve moving both behind and beyond Scarman: behind, because there is no real attempt in the report to examine the long-term background to the events; beyond, because, as Scarman himself admitted, the future of the inner city as such was outside his terms of reference.[43] First, it is essential to grasp the fact that the Brixton disturbances did not occur in a vacuum, and that policing was not the only factor involved. There had been a buildup of anger among the black communities in South London since the terrible fire in New Cross on 18 January 1981 when thirteen young blacks died. The fact that it was not until 24 February that any message of sympathy came from the Prime Minister (and even then it was not sent to the parents but to a local community worker), and the way in which the inquiry and the inquest were handled, had created a climate of bitterness, anger, and a feeling that the nation did not care and had averted its eyes. The fire led directly to the Black People's March on 2 March, a mainly peaceful act of protest which almost all the daily papers, with the striking exception of the *Guardian*, described in terms of mob violence and of an 'orgy of destruction'.[44]

Among the black community nationally there was also the growing anxiety about the Nationality Bill and the fears that many might lose their status as British citizens, fears which were intensified by the experience of many blacks of being treated, by police and other officials, as if they were illegal entrants. In Brixton itself there had been a long history of incidents of conflict between the police and black people, culminating in the police operation 'Swamp 81', in the week preceding 10–12 April.

Elsewhere in London there had been conflicts involving racist organizations, and these had contributed to the oppressive atmosphere. There had been the well-documented cases of racist attacks which were discussed in earlier chapters. And, of course, there had been 'sus', the 'suspicion' clause which was used predominantly against young blacks.[45] What is often not realized is that there had been two sus laws, not one, in operation against black people. The first was the use of Section 4 of the Vagrancy Act 1824. Around half of those arrested under this section were black people. While the 'sus' offence as such has now been abolished, there is no evidence that the new Police and Criminal Evidence Act has improved the situation. The operation of sus, however, extended also to the area of passport raids and checks as a result of the 1971 Immigration Act, and as this was used mainly against the Asian community, it contributed to the increasing sense that to be black was to be alien.

The disturbances of 1981, then, did not occur in a vacuum, but in the context of a build-up of hostility to black people; an experience, as one report expressed it, of 'police against black people',[46] and of racially discriminatory legislation with the prospect of more of the same. The experience of the police as a hostile and racist force was expressed well by the former chairperson of a police authority, a white woman and former youth worker:

> Young people from ethnic minorities fear the police. They do not respect them. Their fear springs from experience: they are often stopped in the streets to be questioned or searched; many are racially abused; some are beaten in police custody; and others are criminalised on the perjured evidence of policemen. Parents of these young people have gradually come to realise that a Christian upbringing and the instilling of standards of honesty and integrity do not safeguard their children from such practices since racism discriminates in terms of colour not behaviour. This is not the judgment of blinkered political extremism: it is a sad and bitter witness of church members from multi-racial inner city communities throughout the country.[47]

Against this background, Scarman's claim that '"institutional racism'' does not exist in Britain' must have a hollow and unconvincing ring. The police are one of the main institutions through which race relations are mediated. The experience of police racism is well known and well documented. But, it seems, this knowledge and experience is not recognized as valid by those in power. Thus the refusal to recognize the validity of the experience of racism contributes to its persistence and growth.

Again, the disturbances occurred at a time of economic recession and under an administration with a distinctive approach to social welfare and to the poor. Scarman argued that 'it would be unfair to criticise the government for lack of effort',[48] though his own report, taken as a whole, is a pretty damning indictment. For clearly the Thatcher government, with its explicit commitment to inequality, its onslaught on the poor, its apparent contempt for working people, and its own fundamental remoteness from the issues must take a very large share of the blame for the events of 1981. Even *The Times* felt it necessary to point out:

> It can hardly be said to have shown much concern for young blacks – or whites. In addition, it has put through parliament a Nationality Bill which is regarded by the minority groups as being racist; it has failed to make its disapproval as sharp as it might of the neo-Nazi groups; and it has shown little interest in the perplexing problem of racial discrimination.[49]

Undoubtedly we have witnessed in recent years an increased belief among the marginalized sections of society, black and white, that the government not only does not care but is actually against them. Not only the unemployed but also those dependent on supplementary benefits, one parent families, immigrants, and a large number of poor people who are struggling to keep their heads above water, can have little to reassure them that the present administration is on the side of the poor and disadvantaged.

Scarman's report consisted of 124 pages, of which 91 were about the police compared with 22 about social conditions. While the neglect of the wider aspects of the urban scene was bound to produce a report of restricted value, the emphasis on the role of policing was correct. The depressing aspect, however, is that even the policing side of the story was not new. In Brixton there had been a long history of conflict between the police and the black community. In Liverpool 8 the documentation of the effects of (to put it in its mildest form) insensitive or (as Liverpool blacks would put it) racist policing methods in Upper Parliament Street goes back not months but years and decades. It is almost legendary. Margaret Simey, that very courageous and much-maligned lady, was warning of civil disorder as a result of police activity in Liverpool 8 in 1971, not 1981, and indeed there were disturbances there in 1972.[50] At that time one reporter wrote of an atmosphere 'close to despair' among the people of the area. 'The reports in which some of them have described what they see as a reality have been suppressed, censored or ignored: they don't feel that politicians, local or national, will hear what is happening and act this side of visible breakdown.'[51] This was not an isolated report. Two years later the local Young Conservatives warned of the dangers of the concentrated police presence, pointing out that 'the scope for antagonism' was very great. They referred also to the existence of racism and prejudice among the local police.[52]

Nor has the central point been missed among some more thoughtful figures within the police force. Thus while Scarman rejected the claim that the police in Brixton had over-reacted, John Alderson, then Chief Constable of Devon and Cornwall, was not so restrained in his comments on possible future developments and their implications for policing practice. 'One hundred and fifty years of British police heritage down the drain,' he complained in his evidence to Scarman. He went on to speak of 'dehumanising equipment' and of the police 'tooling up to declare war on the public'.[53] It was not Alderson's first word on the matter. It was he who had first warned of the danger, dismissed by Mrs Thatcher as 'absolute nonsense' in her immediate reactions to Brixton,[54] that the police might develop into an 'army of occupation'.[55] The full implications of his warning were to be manifested some years later in the course of the miners' strike of 1984.

There seems little evidence that the attempts by men such as John Alderson and David Webb, former Chief Superintendent in Handsworth, to introduce some self-examination and self-criticism into the force has met with much serious response outside the senior ranks and the staff colleges. One would have thought that the fact that both these men felt that they had to leave the force would have produced some serious reflection among police officers. Yet one of the saddest aspects of the post-Scarman scene has been the apparent inability of the police to admit that they had made any mistakes. Although one senior officer, in evidence to Scarman, did concede that 'Swamp 81' had been a serious mistake,[56] others speaking in the immediate aftermath of Brixton were not prepared to admit this.[57] While Sir Kenneth Newman publicly committed himself to 'the Scarman line', he seemed not to be prepared to accept the police's share of blame for the events.[58]

And this inability to admit mistakes has continued. The West Midlands Police, in their report on the events in Handsworth in 1985, claimed: 'If it can be said that anything good has emerged from the riots, then perhaps it has been the fact that unemployed disenchanted youth and the police have been drawn together in positive and constructive consultation.'[59] Now if this has occurred it is all to the good. But positive and constructive consultation can only take place in an atmosphere of mutual trust, and mutual trust involves the acceptance of mutual blame. All too often, as in St Paul's, Bristol, relations with the community have been undermined, and communication made impossible, by the refusal of the police to admit the disastrous effect of their policies.

Those who argued that 'community policing' methods are only appropriate to the 'safe' regions of Devon and Cornwall would have had more credibility had their own alternative methods shown even the slightest indication of success. On the contrary, experience in Handsworth showed that the former methods were more, not less, relevant to the urban context. This is not to deny that community policing raises serious problems, including the relationship between the police and other agencies, such as youth workers and community projects. Some of these problems are unlikely to be resolved, since they are rooted in conflicting ideologies. But at least an atmosphere could be created in which discussion could occur, and this has happened in some places.

On the other hand, the trend within the police force towards a concern with technology and surveillance has continued, as has the shift to a paramilitary or 'fire brigade' style of policing. These trends reached their climax during the miners' strike of 1984, and specifically in the events of Orgreave on 18 June 1984. Orgreave represented the culmination of a process which had begun some years before and within which the events of 1981 were crucial. Again, it was Alderson who pointed out that Orgreave marked the appearance on the British scene of a paramilitary type of policing which had previously been associated with continental European States.[60] The effect of what was in fact a 'state of seige'[61] on the mining communities was appalling. In Barnsley, a town in which there had been no particular hostility to the police before 1984, the experience of the policing of the strike led to a feeling of deep hatred.[62] And, as black people experienced the police as a racist presence in their neighbourhoods, so the miners came to see and describe the police as 'Thatcher's private army'.

But it was not necessary to go to Europe to see the origins of the new repressive type of policing. Across the sea to the west, developments in Northern Ireland had provided a laboratory for the use of riot-control technology and methods of control of civil populations, which were now being transferred to the mainland. 'If we lose in Belfast,' said the Tory MP John Biggs-Davison in 1973, 'we may have to fight in Brixton and Birmingham.'[63] For years methods of policing, of investigation and of trial, as well as an entire technology of repression, had been accepted in Northern Ireland in a way which would never have been tolerated in mainland Britain. We are now seeing calls for a more repressive posture in relation to the black community here. Not surprisingly, some have described the black neighbourhoods in terms drawn from colonial experience. One writer has referred to the 'jungle conditions' in the inner cities, and has argued that such areas call for precisely those qualities which were needed in policing the colonies.[64] Yet research has shown what common sense might have suggested, that the application of so-called 'less lethal equipment' serves to escalate, rather than to defuse, confrontation, and exacerbates conflict.[65] The Northern Ireland experience has not exactly been a successful one, even from the policing perspective. The prospect of techniques and approaches developed there spreading to British cities is not a happy one.

Beyond Scarman

In recent years the Scarman Report has been widely accepted as authoritative, and is often quoted almost as if it were holy Scripture. Thus the Silverman Report on the Handsworth disturbances of 1985 looks back to its distinguished predecessor.

> The Scarman Report is now almost the definitive classic in relation to British inner city riots. It is completely full of information, wisdom and experience. When I turn to many of its passages I find that they would apply word for word to the events in Handsworth/Lozells and I certainly could not express it better.[66]

But if it is so definitive, it seems odd that other reports saying basically the same things need to go on appearing. Either inner-city riots are purely automatic, periodic occurrences like hurricanes or lightning, to which Scarman is a valuable handbook; or they arise out of specific causes which have not been dealt with, and are therefore likely to occur again. In fact, the uncritical devotion to Scarman is mistaken and is in fact part of the problem. And, since we are likely to see more Scarmanite documents, whether expressed in better language or not, we ought to conclude this chapter with some observations on the weaknesses and inadequacies of its approach.

First, Scarman ignores the long-term context of the disturbances. The decline and decay of the inner-city districts, as previous chapters have shown, did not happen by accident. Nor is it adequate to point, as Lord Scarman does, to 'the lack of an effective co-ordinated approach to tackling inner city problems'.[67] The fact is that it *was* an 'effective co-ordinated approach' which led to inner-city decline. It was the result of a conscious policy of dispersal and decentralization, of letting the inner city run down. The problem, therefore, is not simply one of 'more resources' or of improving police methods, important as these are; but of reversing the policies which have led to, and reinforced, urban decay and the oppression and paralysis of the urban poor. And here there has been little progress, as a study of government responses to urban poverty makes clear. 'The conditions that gave rise to violence and protest in Notting Hill in the 1950s, in Watts, Chicago and Detroit in the 1960s, in the whole series of incidents in the 1970s and 1980s culminating in riots in St Paul's, Brixton, Toxteth and Moss Side remain virtually unchanged.'[68] Yet all that Scarman tells us of all this is that it is 'a field which is for others, not me, to cultivate'.[69] Maybe it is. But the neglect of the wider context should be a warning to future writers to cease relying on Scarman as if it were definitive.

Second, racism tends to be seen in terms of 'feelings of rejection' or 'alienation' rather than in terms of concrete reality. In this Scarman is followed by Silverman, who writes: 'Racial discrimination and the feeling of being discriminated against is an important part of the social and psychological background of Handsworth. It is part of the alienation felt by ethnic communities and in my view it is an essential element in the cause of the riots.[70] Now of course, how people feel is very important, and both Scarman and Silverman are very sensitive to the feelings of discrimination which they identify. But racism is not essentially to do with how people *feel* about reality, but about whether their feelings correspond to reality. What matters is not just that people *feel* discriminated against, but that they *are* discriminated against. Yet Scarman believes that institutional racism does not exist in Britain.

Third, the racism within the police force is minimized. Scarman speaks of 'occasional' manifestations by a 'few officers'.[71] The research by Chief Inspector Paul Gorman, which is mentioned briefly in Scarman, presents a more disturbing picture. According to Gorman, the police force attracts authoritarian personalities, and the liberalizing tendencies in training do not survive entry into the police subculture.[72] The evidence of police racism is considerable. The report by the Policy Studies Insitute, for example, presents a picture which one writer has described as 'a shared anti-black rhetoric' and as being 'little short of scandalous'.[73] Yet there seems little recognition by the police of the seriousness of the problem. One advert for recruits to the Metropolitan Police, for example, conceded that there was prejudice in the force, but in a way which effectively dismissed it as specifically a police problem. 'We could say there are no prejudiced people in the Met. But you'd quite rightly call us liars. There's no doubt that there are prejudiced people in the Met just as there are in the population at large.'[74] But this is totally to dodge the issue of whether there is *more* racism in the police than in the population at large, and whether it has a specific character and manifestation. Some police publications suggest something close to self-inflicted blindness on the issue. Thus a booklet issued by the police in the Bristol area and circulated at the time of the disturbances in 1986, says this about the police in St Paul's: 'St Paul's 1986. Officers policing multi-racial areas become involved in their communities and have become familiar and accepted figures. Despite occasional setbacks the goodwill and increasing understanding of men and women policing multi-racial communities has led to a gradual reduction in tension.'[75] This is either naive to a frightening degree or it is simple, straightforward dishonesty. Now of course, Scarman cannot be blamed for this, and he does recognize that the police must take their share of blame. But the seriousness of racism within the force, which is well known to everyone living and working in multiracial areas, is not brought out in his report.

Fourth, the crucial issue of accountability is not dealt with. At the end of the day, this is what matters most in the inner cities. Are the police to be subject to any form of democratic control, or are we to continue to act on the basis of what one writer has called the infallibility of chief constables?[76] The question of accountability is at the root of most of the problems of policing in the urban areas. Consultation may take place, but if the police then do as they please, nothing will change. And on this central issue Scarman fails us.

Finally, in Scarman there is a sense of *déjà vu*. We have been here before. The Kerner Commission, set up by President Johnson after the disturbances in the United States in 1967, reached much the same conclusions.[77] The disorders were not inter-racial, not directed against white people but against the police and against 'symbols of the white American society' – authority and property. Kerner's description of police practice sounds only too familiar:

> These practices, sometimes known as 'aggressive preventive patrol', take a number of forms but invariably they involve a large number of police–citizen contacts, initiated by police rather than in response to a call for help or service. One such

> practice involves a roving task force which moves into high crime districts without prior notice and conducts intensive, often indiscriminate, street stops and searches.[78]

Again, despite 'extremist rhetoric', the attacks there were not seen as an attempt to overthrow the existing order, but rather to share in its advantages. (The research on black youth in Brixton by Gaskell and Smith, quoted approvingly in Scarman, made precisely the same point.[79]) There was 'a clear pattern of social disadvantage'. There was no evidence of conspiracy or outside organization. There was, however, 'an increasingly disturbed atmosphere' and 'severely disadvantaged social and economic conditions'.[80] The only aspect that seems really new about Scarman is the date!

However, at the end of the Kerner Report the authors expressed a worry that their recommendations might simply be shelved, not carried out, or that the responses might be totally inadequate. Lord Hunt, who had chaired a government committee on young immigrants and the youth service in Britain in 1970, made the same point in a letter to *The Times* in 1980. Reports such as these, he complained, were simply 'a costly waste of time', for there was no action.[81] The Kerner Report concluded with a quotation from the distinguished black activist Dr Kenneth Clarke, who referred to the reports of earlier riot commissions.

> I read that report . . . of the 1919 riot in Chicago, and it is as if I were reading the report of the investigating committee on the Harlem riot of '35, the report of the investigating committee on the Harlem riot of '43, the report of the McCone Commission on the Watts riot. I must again in candour say to you members of this Commission – it is a kind of Alice in Wonderland – with the same moving picture shown over and over again, the same analysis, the same recommendations, and the same inaction.[82]

Will Scarman meet the same fate?

PART TWO

THE CHURCH IN A RACIST SOCIETY

7

The Church in a Plural Society

'The creed of the English is that there is no God and that it is wise to pray to him from time to time.'[1] In saying this in 1963, in the aftermath of the controversy over John Robinson's *Honest to God*, the philosopher Alasdair MacIntyre was summing up the substance of an important lecture which he had given on the BBC Third Programme in 1956 entitled 'A Society Without a Metaphysics'. MacIntyre has over the years been one of the most perceptive critics both of contemporary society and of Christian thinking. Having read his lecture in 1956 at the age of seventeen, and returned to it several years ago, I want to take it as the starting-point for a discussion of the nature of our society and of the Church's response.

MacIntyre took as his starting-point a comment made by the Soviet leader Bukharin just before he was executed in the Stalinist purges of the 1930s. Bukharin said that it was no longer possible in Russia to find a 'Dostoyevskian existence'. Dostoyevsky's characters, torn by hate and doubt and love, saw their experiences against the background not simply of Russia but of the universe. That kind of universe, MacIntyre claimed, had been destroyed by a revolution offering metaphysical certainty. But, he argued, our society also had made a Dostoyevskian existence impossible. However,

> whereas the Russians have exchanged one metaphysics for another, we have become a society without a metaphysics . . . This lack of beliefs is fundamental to our situation, characteristic of our way of life, and until this is appreciated, most argument about metaphysical beliefs – about religion, for instance – must proceed in an unreal way.

The lack of any framework of fundamental beliefs holding our society together was not accidental – as if we might somehow, tomorrow or next year, acquire a new set of beliefs. Rather, this lack of belief was fundamental to our condition and to the nature of our society. MacIntyre argued that one consequence of this was that British society was marked by the 'loss of any overall sense of significance'. He concluded: 'The curious flavour that a combination of liberal morality and metaphysical meaningless gives to life is the characteristic flavour of our time.'[2]

MacIntyre's assessment seems to me to be more true now than it was when he made it in 1956. He was asserting more than the fact that Britain could no longer be described in any convincing sense as a Christian society. But he was at least asserting that. I want to reassert it as the essential basis for our discussion. My assumption is that, even if it were once the case that some kind of Christian culture existed throughout Britain, this has not been so for some time. The urban cores of the post-industrial Revolution era have never been 'Christianized' except in the most superficial sense. And today it is in the inner-city districts that we see the reality which is obscured by conventional factors in countryside and in suburb: the reality that organized Christianity, represented most clearly by the visible structures of the Church of England, is one of a number of minority groups within a post-Christian society.

I want to emphasize that I am claiming that our society is post-Christian, not post-religious. T. S. Eliot rejected the use of the term 'post-Christian' on the grounds that a Christian culture had not been positively replaced by something else.[3] Others would argue that the concept of 'secularization' has been over-used. However, the point which I wish to stress here is that, however important the Christian faith has been in moulding our society in the past, anything resembling a Christian worldview is now of marginal significance in modern urban society. And the spread of this reality from the inner city to the suburbs, in which church-going is still an accepted part of the mainstream culture, is only a matter of time. Of course, a kind of residual religiousness survives (sometimes called folk religion or, after Bellah, civic religion – though the notions differ not only from the phenomenon which I am describing but also from one another), and is in some places and at some points very resistant to decay. And the ways of presenting the data on this phenomenon will vary.

Thus, when one survey showed that half of the teenagers interviewed claimed to be Christian in some sense, the *Guardian* announced 'Teenagers reveal belief in God', while *The Times* proclaimed 'School-age faith in rapid decline'.[4] But the point is that what survives is a decayed form of a Christian, or pre-Christian, culture which is long past. To pretend otherwise is to risk building one's houses on sand.

And yet, while all the data indicate a continuing decline in mainstream Christianity, there is considerable evidence of a resurgence of religions and faiths of various kinds. The oft-repeated myth of the 1960s that religion was in a state of decline was heavily criticized by the Chicago sociologist Andrew Greeley in his polemical study *The Persistence of Religion* (1973). The religious needs of humanity, Greeley argued, had not essentially changed since the late Ice Age. 'Secular man', 'technological man', 'man come of age' – if these beings existed at all, they existed only on university campuses in the West, and increasingly among the white, middle-aged, senior faculty members, while the students indulged in astrology, the occult and other cultic practices.[5] Like much of Greeley's writing, it was an overstated reaction to an overstated case. But it seemed to bear out Tawney's observation many years earlier that 'the alternative to religion is rarely irreligion: it is a counter-religion'.[6]

What we are seeing in Britain is partly the transmission of ancient faiths from elsewhere, partly the emergence of new forms of religious expression, and to a great extent the desperate search for spiritual nourishment from any source, a charisma hunger of the kind that often follows the 'twilight of the gods'. So, as conventional white religion declines, other forms of religious life flourish. I want to point to five clear examples: there are many others which are not so clear.

First, we are seeing the appearance on a significant scale of what I would term 'Third World Christianity'. Christianity is far more powerful and creative in the Third World, in Latin America, Asia, Africa and the Caribbean, as well as in the USSR and China, than it is in Europe. The Third World is, in theological terms, the developed and developing world. So it is not surprising that the forms of Christian presence which show the highest growth rates in Britain are the black Churches, those which involve people of

Third World origin. A study in the 1970s suggested that the black-led Churches showed a growth rate of 4.2 per cent per annum.[7]

The black Churches in Britain are a fusion of various traditions ranging from Catholic, Orthodox, Holiness, Pentecostal and independent African and Asian streams, to black versions of nineteenth-century white revivalist Churches originating in the USA. While many of the latter exhibit the otherworldly and conservative traditions of the white Churches from which they grew, others have drawn on the liberation tradition in black Christianity. This tradition goes back to the slave rebellions, and was expressed in the movements of black protest which reached their climax in Martin Luther King and the Civil Rights Movement in the USA. It is represented today by black theologians such as Cornel West, James Cone and Gayraud Wilmore in the USA, and by such African leaders as Allan Boesak and Desmond Tutu. The influence of these trends in transnational black Christian thought and action are being felt among black Christians in Britain. In addition, the movement of liberation theology is manifesting itself among the black Churches, as it is also influencing those on the edges of the mainstream white Churches.

W. J. Hollenweger, who has devoted much of his life to an intensive study of the growth of Pentecostalism all over the world, has claimed that the numerical, and perhaps also spiritual, centre of world Christianity is shifting from the white Western type to this new Third World type. The Christianity of the future will not be predominantly a white person's religion.[8] It is very likely that the future of Christianity in Britain will lie to a great extent with the black Christians.

In considering the Third World religious traditions of black people in Britain, it is important not to ignore the significance of Ras Tafari, which, in spite of a Home Office circular which classified it along with teddy boys, skinheads and the Beatles, is an authentic religious movement. Large numbers of black youth have looked to Rasta as a spiritual alternative to white-dominated Christianity.

Second, we see the transmission of Eastern religions other than Christianity – Christianity is, of course, an Eastern religion – to the British urban environment. Hinduism, Buddhism and Islam in particular have grown and flourished in recent years, the last two having gained sizeable numbers of adherents from the indigenous population. To a large extent, of course, the growth of Eastern religions is a result of immigration. In London there are now more Patels than Robinsons in the telephone directory. In one East London school with six hundred pupils, eleven world religions are represented; most of the Christians are Greek Orthodox. The Hindu community in Leicester is the second largest outside India. Buddhism in Britain saw a 28 per cent increase in the first half of the 1970s.[9] Even if one allowed for no developments and shifts among the indigenous white population, the presence of these communities of Third World origin has undermined earlier ideas of secularization and of the 'death of God'. As Kenneth Cracknell and Christopher Lamb have written:

> The *anima naturaliter spiritualis* is alive and well in the Muslims of Bradford, the Sikhs of Handsworth, and the Hindus and Jains of Leicester. It may be that they will in time succumb to the western disease, but currently some young people of purely Anglo-Saxon or Celtic origins are being drawn to Islam and other faiths from the desolation of contemporary British life and the emptiness, spiritual and literal, of many of the churches.[10]

In fact, there is evidence that many young people from Hindu and Muslim backgrounds have lapsed after some years of exposure to the British context, but the spiritual vitality of these great religious traditions is not significantly eroded.

Third, we see the continued popularity of the 'private religions', meditation schools, syncretistic cults of theosophical type, the occult, forms of magic, as well as the revival of pagan cults of the kind which have always appealed to fascists and racial purists. A study in 1978 suggested that more young people believed in UFOs and life on other planets than believed in God.[11] I documented much of the spiritual enthusiasm among the young in the 1960s and early 1970s in my study *Youthquake: The Growth of a Counter-Culture Through Two Decades* (1973).[12] While it is fashionable now to dismiss the counter-culture and the movements of the 1960s in general as having led nowhere, this is, in my view, a serious error. The 1960s marked the beginning of a movement which is still continuing. One of the religious aspects of that period was the quest for a spirituality of an entirely private and inward kind. The popularity of this kind of spirituality has increased, not least in the suburban areas.

Fourth, we see the popularity of various forms of Christian fundamentalism and adventism. Most of these movements originated in North America in the nineteenth century, though there have been many developments and changes since those days. Jehovah's Witnesses, which grew out of the apocalyptic speculations of William Miller in the 1840s, still attracts disciples, not least among the black community in Britain. Newer groups such as the Family of Love, formerly the Children of God,[13] and the Unification Church, have also gained large followings, while fundamentalism is on the upsurge within the mainstream Churches, including the Church of England.

Finally, I would include Marxism as a religious movement, where it is held as a total world-view rather than as an analytic method. It is impossible to discount the deeply religious elements in modern Marxism; and the devotion of some of its adherents to the writings of the founding fathers is closely akin to religious fundamentalism.

Pluralism and anti-pluralism

If my argument is correct, we need to reject the view that a Christian society has now received into its midst a number of minority faiths, and equally the view that our society is wholly secularized apart from a few pockets of insignificant freaks. It is more correct to say that our society is *plural*, a society containing a variety of ethnic and religious groupings. But it is not yet *pluralist*, that is, it is not yet a society which has accepted its new character. And so policies are often shaped, campaigns are launched, appeals are made, which assume the essentially Christian – and white – character of the nation. And this applies not only to the State but also to the Church within it. Bishops, for example, still address the nation as if they were the spokesmen of a national Church (as they are in law), rather than as the leaders of a minority among minorities (as they are in fact). Often churchpeople seem to be living in a world which is carefully insulated and protected from these recent developments and changes in society.

Thus it is only in recent years that religious education syllabuses have begun to take account of the multi-faith dimension not only in British society but anywhere else! In the years immediately after the Second World War, the attention given to other faiths was minimal. The London Syllabus of Religious Education (1947) contained ten lines on Judaism and very little on Islam. The very influential Cambridgeshire syllabus, *Religious Training for Schools* (1949), which within four years was used by 113 local authorities, contained only one reference to a non-Christian religion. And there was no significant change until the 1960s.[14] Within theological education, studies have shown the paucity of multiracial and multi-faith materials in many colleges.[15] A study of Roman Catholic seminaries in England and Wales concluded that there was less multicultural education material in the seminaries than in many primary and secondary schools. What attention was given to issues of race and other faiths tended to be 'dealt with' under the heading of pastoralia.[16]

However, we are not simply confronted with a situation of confusion and lack of awareness of the nature of our society. There is clear evidence of a mounting campaign, both in the United States and Britain, to recall the nation to its 'Christian foundations', as a kind of war cry against what is seen as moral decline, left-wing infiltration, permissiveness, racial suicide, and so on. Christianity is, in this approach, virtually identified with the national character and way of life. The rise of the Moral Majority and other forms of the 'Christian Right', which helped to sweep Reagan to power, is one part of an international growth which is extremely dangerous. The histories of Nazi Germany, Franco's Spain and South Africa show how successful a call to mobilize the Christian nation against the threats from Marxism, liberalism and the 'alien invasion' can be. And yet to respond to such a call is to clothe insecurity and confusion with the mantle of moral conviction and the crusading spirit. The insecure person, armed with religious zeal, easily becomes fanatical. But today we are confronted by a whole society which is insecure, and there is a natural attraction in movements offering apparent certainties, certainties which merely hide the bewilderment which is too painful to face.

So in our plural society we see MacIntyre's combination of liberal morality and metaphysical meaninglessness. But MacIntyre had warned in 1956 that such a society was in a highly dangerous state.

> To have got rid of our metaphysical beliefs is to have swept the house and garnished it with science and morality: that there are evil spirits that may come and dwell in the house we learned in the fate of Nazi Germany. Those for whom life is emotionally empty may be at first content with limited perspectives; but later they may become cynical and disillusioned; and later still they may become the prey of any passing evangelist of unreason who will promise a coherent view of the world and a coherent programme for changing it.[17]

This is in fact what has happened, although its manifestations are immensely varied. In the United States the phenomenon has the characteristic features of a national epidemic, though the potential for indefinite spread has probably been exaggerated. In Britain, where fundamentalism is less a part of the dominant culture, the position is more complex. But, as in the United States, divisions among Christians along traditional denominational lines have become more and more unreal. The crucial divisions now are rather between the city Church and the suburban Church, between progressive and conservative forces in all the Churches, between those who see the Church as a community committed to the struggle for justice and change in the world and those who see it as a preservative force, a ritual enactment of the stable order of the past.

The alternatives before the Church

The Christian community in this situation is faced with a number of alternative directions in which it might move. Indeed it is already clear that Christians are moving in opposite directions, and that positions are becoming increasingly polarized. What are these alternative directions?

First, the Church could accept its role as a stabilizer, even a tranquillizer, a force for tranquillity and calm in the midst of conflict. It is a role with a long pedigree. The movement of the Churches into the poor districts of cities in the eighteenth and nineteenth centuries was seen largely in terms of social control. As a nineteenth-century Bishop of Rochester commented, the clergy were the cheapest policemen available.

However, recently many Christians in the inner city have, in the aftermath of the uprisings since 1981, been seen to reject this role of pouring oil on justly troubled waters. The resulting position is well illustrated by the controversy in 1981 over the British Council of Churches' grant to the Liverpool 8 Defence Committee.[18] The purposes to which the very small grant of £500 was put were, on the surface, beyond controversy: paying the cost of fares to hospitals where victims of the events were; paying the costs of the funeral of a young man killed by a police vehicle; and paying the cost of travel to courts and police stations. But critics of the grant saw beneath this the sinister manifestation of a Church supporting, and therefore condoning, the perpetrators of riot and upheaval. The Church, the critics argued, should not be supporting riot but maintaining peace.

Clearly the tranquillizer/sedative role of religion is one which attracts much support, particularly in the suburbs. I have used the terms 'tranquillizer' and 'sedative' rather than Marx's stronger word 'opiate'. An opiate is an extremely powerful, and addictive, painkiller. What I am suggesting is that the role of religion and the Church is more often analogous to a drug such as Librium: a mild tranquillizer which keeps the lid on the explosive powers within, bringing a temporary calm. But it does not, and cannot, reach to the roots of the trouble. (We should perhaps also remember that Librium is easily resisted, often prescribed as a placebo, and was shown some years ago to be extremely expensive! Maybe the parallel with conventional Anglicanism is even closer.)

Second, the Church could opt for a form of 'spiritualized' religion in which its attention is focused on the next world rather than the Third World. This phrase was quoted, apparently with approval, by Dr Edward Norman in his Reith Lectures of 1978, published as *Christianity and the World Order*. For Norman, true Christianity should be concerned not with social transformation but with 'the condition of the inner soul of man' and 'the ethereal qualities of immortality'.[19] The comparison of religion to ether rather than opium is at least an original way of dissociating oneself from Marxist categories. But ether is also a drug of addiction, and its use spread in nineteenth-century Ulster as a reaction to a temperance campaign led by one Father Matthew.[20] It seems likely that the current revival of 'otherworldly' Christianity, stressing inner experience and personal spirituality more than justice and freedom in the world, is a similar reaction against the often shallow liberalism of the 1960s. But to respond to the present crisis by offering a religion of inner experience and otherworldly hope is to fall into the same trap which made many Christians in Nazi Germany incapable of offering any effective resistance to Hitler. It is an error against which all the great spiritual theologians have consistently warned us.

The third possible direction for the Church is that it accepts, joyfully, honestly and humbly, its essentially minority role within a plural society. Within this society it has to learn to be salt and leaven. Salt is not a meal in itself, nor is the purpose of leaven to produce more leaven. The symbolism of salt and leaven points to the fact that the Church is meant to be not a vague religious club spread throughout the nation, but a dynamic minority, disturbing and exploding like leaven in a lump of dough.

In a period in which conventional religion is in decline, the Church is in a position from which it could seriously examine its new role. It is in fact an old role, for it was the position of the primitive Church in the Roman Empire. For centuries, after the unfortunate conversion of Constantine, it was obscured by the fatal alliance in many countries between the Church and civil power. Today, as the Constantine era grinds to its close, in some places more slowly than in others, the essential minority character of the Church is again exposed to view. The danger is that church leaders and church members may run away from what they mistakenly see as their nakedness, and seek the emperor's clothes.

But it is only by the recovery of the notion of the Church as a community which stands as a sign of contradiction to every established order, that we can develop a genuinely liberating theology. As the Church is pushed to the margins of society, it will begin to discover that it is not there alone: that there are other marginal people there, too. Some of them have been there for rather a long time. The rediscovery of our weakness and apparent powerlessness will be a painful but healing experience for a Church such as the Church of England, which sees itself as belonging more in the corridors of power than in the back streets. But I suspect that the role of the Church in the corridors of power is passing. More and more the Church is becoming, in spite of itself, a counter-culture, a deviant minority within a society without a metaphysics. The question is whether it will accept this role joyfully, or whether it will choose the long-trodden path of compromise with Mammon, clinging to its formerly privileged position of alliance with the State.

Perhaps it is only as the Church is pushed to the margins of society that it will be forced to take up the agenda of the marginalized communities in society. For, as Cain Felder has written:

> Of all the mandates which confront the church in the world today, the mandate of world community predicated on a renewed commitment to pluralism and the attendant acknowledgment of the integrity of all racial groups constitutes an urgent agenda for Bible scholars and the laity alike. It is an agenda for too long neglected in the vast array of Eurocentric theological and ecclesial traditions which continue to marginalise people of colour throughout the world.[21]

8

The Archbishop's Commission and Beyond

It was at the beginning of December 1985 that the report *Faith in the City: A Call for Action by Church and Nation* appeared. It was the report of the Archbishop of Canterbury's Commission on Urban Priority Areas, and it had been preceded by two-and-a-half years of evidence from a wide range of people and groups inside and outside the Church of England. The Commission had been set up in July 1983 'to examine the strengths, insights, problems and needs of the Church's life in Urban Priority Areas', these areas being described as including 'inner city districts and many large Corporation estates and other areas of social deprivation'.[1] In fact, the report devoted more space to the social and economic aspects of the Urban Priority Areas (UPAs) than it did to the specific role of the Church of England, although the majority of the recommendations were addressed to the Church rather than to government and nation (38 compared with 23).[2]

The report defined UPAs in this way: 'What are now called urban priority areas are districts of specially disadvantaged character. They are places which suffer from economic decline, physical decay and social disintegration.'[3] In the UPAs are to be found disproportionate numbers of vulnerable people – the unemployed, the unskilled, the uneducated, the sick, the old, those disadvantaged through their ethnic origins and colour, those on low incomes or State benefits, and so on. 'The sombre statistics of all these conditions', say the authors, 'provide the details of the map of inequality.'[4]

In earlier pages of this book I have shown that reports and commissions of inquiry on the state of the inner urban areas are not new. The nineteenth century abounded with such reports, running into many volumes. During the last twenty years we have had Educational Priority Areas (1966), the Urban Programme (1968), the Community Development Projects (1969) which produced over two hundred reports, the Inner Area Studies (1972), the Urban Deprivation Unit at the Home Office (1973) and the Comprehensive Community Programme (1974). In launching the Inner Area Studies, Peter Walker had spoken of the need for a 'total approach', while his Labour successor Peter Shore, in his promotion of the White Paper *Policy for the Inner Cities* (1977), spoke of the 'first comprehensive policy' for the inner areas.[5] Yet in 1981 Lord Scarman was still complaining of the 'lack of an effective co-ordinated approach to tackling inner city problems'.[6]

Moreover, there is a long tradition of Church-initiated reports going back to the late Victorian period. One of these, the Archbishop's Commission on Industrial Problems of 1919, made some quite radical statements, not unlike those of the present report. George Lansbury was one of those who was not impressed, pointing out that 'though the Church of England, when driven to it, was bound in the light of the gospel to come to some such conclusions, she had no intention of doing anything about it, and was, in fact, becoming more and more reactionary as the crisis developed'.[7] Against that kind of background, it was hardly surprising that one reaction to the setting up of an Archbishop's Commission on Urban Priority Areas (ACUPA) was to ask: is this to be yet another contribution to the list of failed urban initiatives? And is the Church of England yet again to limit itself to impressive words with no accompanying action?

The report in fact begins with the 1977 White Paper, and notes that since then the situation of the inner areas has deteriorated. In an impressive passage of personal testimony, the commission members describe the impact which their travels and studies have made on them.

> We have to report that we have been deeply disturbed by what we have seen and heard. We have been confronted with the human consequences of unemployment, which in some urban areas may be over 50 per cent of the labour force, and which occasionally reaches a level as high as 80 per cent – consequences which may be compounded by the effects of racial

> discrimination. We have seen physical decay, whether of Victorian terraced housing or of inferior system-built blocks of flats, which has in places created an environment so degrading that some people have set fire to their own homes rather than be condemned to living in them indefinitely. Social disintegration has reached a point in some areas that shop windows are boarded up, cars cannot be left on the street, residents are afraid either to go out themselves or to ask others in, and there is a pervading sense of powerlessness and despair.
>
> Our own observations and the official statistics tell the same story. Clearly these are symptoms of something seriously wrong in our cities. Physical appearances, and the responses of those affected, may vary greatly from place to place; but the underlying factors are the same: unemployment, decayed housing, sub-standard educational and medical provision, and social disintegration.[8]

The report goes on to present a thorough and well-researched analysis of the position of the UPAs and of the Church within them. It is a scholarly piece of work of abiding significance. Sadly, it will not soon date.

Even before the report was published it was attacked, and the word 'Marxist' was being used, apparently by a senior member of the government. 'Tory anger at C of E Marxists' announced *The Daily Telegraph* on 2 December.[9] The references to 'Marxist theology' must have perplexed Canon Anthony Harvey, the theologian on the Commission, a man whom no one had hitherto suspected of Marxist tendencies. He need not have worried, for the use of the word was instinctive and unintelligent. It was taken up, equally if not more unintelligently, by Auberon Waugh in *The Spectator*. The conclusions of the report, he claimed, were rather similar to those of the Beveridge Report but were 'more overtly Marxist and anti-religious in tone'. Among the 'overtly Marxist' passages, he cited that which cautiously welcomed liberation theology, and went on to speak of 'the Archbishop's explicit adoption of Marx'.[10] Digby Anderson, a right-wing sociologist, now an Anglican priest, who had sprung to fame as a result of a poorly researched volume entitled *The Kindness that Kills*,[11] in his regular column in *The Times* criticized the report for using the concept of powerlessness which, he said cryptically, was 'ideologically flawed' – presumably another reference to Marxism, although powerlessness is not a term or concept which is associated particularly with the Marxist tradition.[12] Paul Johnson, however, writing in the *Daily Mail*, a paper which is keen to spot Marxists under most beds, preferred to see the report merely as 'an entirely secular treatise'.[13]

Anderson's fellow columnist Ronald Butt had once written, apparently with some regret, that 'unlike Fascist, Marxist can be accepted simply as a description . . . rather than as a term of abuse'.[14] But it is as a term of abuse, an accusation, that it has been, and is, mainly used. This becomes apparent when one asks the simple question: in what sense is the report Marxist? Which elements in Marxist thought are being referred to? Surplus value? The falling rate of profit? Alienation? Dialectical method? Which Marxist theorists do they draw on? Gramsci? Rosa Luxemburg? Trotsky? The Frankfurt School? Marx himself? Even to ask such elementary questions as these is to realize the absurdity of the situation. For the attacks on this report, as on other Church statements on social justice issues, as 'Marxist' have nothing to do with Marx and Marxist thinkers. They are utterly devoid of thoughtful reflection and are merely insults, thrown out randomly and haphazardly. As descriptions of anything, they have no content or meaning.

In fact, there are many influences on the report, some of which are easy to detect, but Marx is not one of them. The origins of ACUPA lie in the mainstream (and predominantly Anglican) tradition of Christian social action and reflection, with its long history of concern with the inner urban areas. Specifically, they are linked with the work of Canon Eric James. For years, during his ministry in Southwark in the 1960s and later as Director of Christian Action, James was pointing to the desperate situation of the Church in the inner areas, and expressing alarm that the hierarchy seemed incapable of any real response. In 1968 he wrote sadly:

> In all honesty I have to say that I hardly know one archbishop or diocesan bishop in the Church of England who seems really

> to understand the realities of our urban industrial situation, or is willing with anything like the urgency that is required to lead his diocese toward the radical action the situation demands.[15]

On 27 May 1981 a letter from Eric James was published in *The Times*. He wrote: 'I should myself like to see the immediate appointment of an Archbishop's Commission – to report within a year – called the 'Staying There' Commission . . . It would report on the Church's strategy for the inner city . . .' On 23 April 1982 the Bishop of Stepney wrote to James, inviting him to attend a meeting of the urban bishops on 22 June to discuss the idea of 'some sort of Commission about the inner cities'. The Bishop of Stepney, Jim Thompson, was known to be concerned about the future of the Church in the inner areas and had in fact been suggested by James, in his *Times* letter, as the chairperson of the proposed Commission. While he was not in the end directly involved with ACUPA, its origins seem to lie in this exchange of correspondence and the meetings which followed.

The Commission consisted of eighteen members, fifteen of them men and three women, plus six advisors and a secretary (all men). Although the blurb on the back cover described them as coming from a 'wide range of backgrounds', two were bishops, seven were clergymen, six were academics, and all were professionals of one kind or another.

The strengths of the report

In the light of the hostility which the report received, much of it from people who had apparently not read it, it is important for socially conscious Christians in the present unfavourable climate to stand by its positive aspects. And it should be said at the outset that, descriptively and analytically, it is very good indeed. Clearly the Commissioners had listened carefully to people throughout the country. The report is marked by a sensitivity and an ability to listen which is refreshing in a church document and almost unknown in many reports from secular and particularly government sources.

Again, the report recognizes the reality of the Church of England and its precarious position in the inner city. There is nothing new in this, and all that the report is doing is recognizing what social historians have been saying for years. The influence of Hugh McLeod is particularly evident in Chapter Two on 'Church and City'. The middle-class character of the Church of England is emphasized: it has always lacked that 'pervasive influence transcending the boundaries of class' which, the authors claim, was true of both the Roman Church and of sections of Nonconformity. They do not mention the fact that the Roman Church has declined as a working-class religion as the sense of Irish identity has declined, or the fact that many Nonconformist churches have abandoned the inner city or have stayed purely as eclectic churches drawing on the suburbs.

The report reinforces what the anti-poverty lobby has been saying for years: that there has been a significant persistence and growth of urban poverty and deprivation. There is, the report claims, 'severe and increasing deprivation'.[16] It points to the clear correlation between population change and the social index: that is, the lower the population, the higher the degree of deprivation. So there has grown up 'a different Britain whose people are prevented from entering fully into the mainstream of the normal life of the nation'.[17] It lays particular emphasis on the notion of polarization between rich and poor, 'the increasing divide between rich and poor'.[18] They see the process of polarization as 'a general one in Britain today'[19] and one which manifests 'a grave and fundamental injustice' within British society.[20]

The authors suggest, and they are certainly correct, that many politicians do not understand the level of despair within the UPAs. The gulf between the present government and the run-down communities in the north in particular has grown wider and more unbridgeable. Yet the position is more serious: for the policies of the government have actually added to the sufferings of the poor and of deprived areas as they have improved the conditions of the already affluent and comfortable. The authors warn that

> if the policies of any government can be shown to be making the plight of some classes of citizens actually worse, and if moreover the resources available to those who seek to alleviate this plight are being reduced, it is a clear duty for the Church to

> sound a warning that our society may be losing the 'compassionate' character which is still desired by the majority of its members.[21]

Finally, the report does give attention to the position of black people within British society and within the churches. It devotes five pages to 'The Church and Minority Ethnic Groups',[22] and calls for 'a clear lead from the centre . . . We believe that the Church must make a clear response not only to racial discrimination and disadvantage but also to the alienation, hurt and rejection experienced by many black people in relation to the Church of England.'[23] In this, of course, it represents an advance on earlier church reports which had tended to ignore the existence of the black community altogether. The 'Tiller Report', for example, which offered guidelines for the Church's ministry from 1963 to 2023, made one passing reference to 'black and coloured people' among a list of 'losers in the urban race', and ignored the existence of black Anglicans altogether.[24] In the UPAs where West Indians constitute 15 per cent of the population, the report claims, they form 19 per cent of congregations (but only 13 per cent of membership of Parochial Church Councils.[25] In fact in many urban areas, churchgoing increases in direct relation to the presence of an Afro-Caribbean community. As one researcher has observed, 'the Anglican Church is surprisingly important for the Afro-Caribbean population'.[26] In addition to the mainstream Churches, there are the newer black-led Churches which, as the Evangelical Race Relations Group noted in its evidence to ACUPA, 'have largely replaced the older denominations as the authentic Christian presence in the UPAs' in many places.[27]

However, although this is true, it is also the case that black people are leaving the Churches, including the black-led Churches, in droves. Clearly race and cultural issues are not the only factors involved. But, as far as the Church of England is concerned, the question must be asked: does its very Englishness, combined with its degree of entanglement with the white power structure and with the established order, make it exceptionally difficult for *this* Church to adjust to the major cultural shifts in our society? In fact, this close involvement of the

Church of England with the mainstream English culture was used as a major argument for the establishment of the Church in all four Church and State reports of 1917, 1935, 1952 and 1970. Only in the 1970 report was it suggested, by Valerie Pitt in her dissenting memorandum, that the result of this essentially tribal attitude to religion might be to associate the Church disastrously with a dying order.[28] And while Pitt did not raise the question of the Church in a multiracial society, this must now be on the agenda. The Commission for Racial Equality, in its evidence to ACUPA, had urged upon the Church 'its need to have a total commitment to racial justice and to adopt a race relations programme which extends to every part of its structure and influences every aspect of its work.' The report is in fact the first semi-official response to the issue of structural racism within the Church of England.

It recommends that the work on education for racial justice, begun within the Church of England's Board for Social Responsibility in 1981, should be continued, preferably under black leadership; that a senior black person should be appointed to the staff of the Advisory Council for the Church's Ministry; and that a Standing Commission on Black Anglican Concerns should be established within the central structures of the Church. However, the subsequent history of these proposals is depressing. On 6 February 1986 the General Synod debated the proposed Black Commission and rejected it by 207 votes to 197 with 17 abstentions. The arguments used were familiar ones to those who have followed the Black Sections debate in the Labour Party, and of course, almost all the speakers were white. However, as a result of some discussion between the black members of the Synod and the Standing Committee, in September 1986 the Standing Committee issued a document urging a reconsideration of the matter, and presenting a modified proposal for a Black Advisory Group. This was passed at the Synod in November. However, only one full-time person was to be appointed, to be responsible both for the new group and for the enormous body of work which had been built up within the BSR.[29] So, at a very early stage, the ACUPA proposal for three senior black officers, presumably with full secretarial support, has been reduced to one person doing two major jobs. This retreat so early on is not a good omen for the future of the Church's response to the very positive proposals of the report.

The weaknesses of the report

Having stressed the positive aspects of the report, it is important to draw attention to some weaknesses. In doing so, it is necessary to avoid giving ammunition to right-wing critics who will seize on any scraps they can find to attack the Church's social witness. At the same time, nothing could be more dangerous than to regard ACUPA as a final statement which was beyond criticism, rather than as a stage in an ongoing search for a Church committed to justice.

One weakness in the report is a tendency to raise problems and then run away from them. An obvious example is its statement that the Church of England, in its ministry in the UPAs, should avoid reflecting an inherited middle-class culture.[30] But the report has already stressed that this *is* the culture and ethos of the Church. How can it avoid reflecting what is in fact the case? It goes on to deplore the continuation of a predominantly white, male, middle-class leadership of the church.[31] But it offers no advice as to how this can be avoided.

Again, there is an interesting passage in which the report recommends the development of Local Non-Stipendiary Ministry (LNSM) within the UPAs. This may well be a valuable move, and the report certainly sees it as an 'important prophetic action'.[32] However, there is an obvious danger that LNSMs will come to be viewed as a second-class, inferior form of ministry. This is what happened, in fact, in the original experiment in Bethnal Green, and the report recognizes that it is a real danger. But having recognized it, no more is heard of it.

Again, the report suggests that theological training may not adequately prepare people for urban ministry. It even cites the evidence of the Urban Ministry Project that their training 'positively unfitted' them for their ministry.[33] Yet this also is left in mid-air. And the class issue in theological education is not tackled. Theological colleges have always expressed a middle-class, white, male culture, and have sought to reinforce it upon those under their influence. Some colleges have expressed, and continue to express and maintain, the rarified ethos of the world of Oxbridge and the public schools. The urgent question must therefore be raised: are these institutions reformable? Do they contribute to the gulf between Church and city of which the report complains, and indirectly reinforce the polarization which it deplores? It is no answer to say that the Church of England has, in recent years, introduced new, non-residential styles of training. It has indeed done so, following the model set by the Southwark Ordination Course in 1960. But it is clear from the unpublished papers of the late Canon Stanley Evans (who established the course), that he saw this development as a way to undermine the class bias in ministerial training. Is there any evidence that this has worked? I do not think so, and ACUPA would seem to agree. But in any case, the non-residential courses have not *replaced* the fashionable Oxbridge colleges from which the bulk of the bishops and other church leaders are drawn.

And, not surprisingly, the report dodges the issue of the public schools. In Chapter One I pointed to the central place of the public schools in the education of the bishops of the Church of England. Moyser's study of the composition of the General Synod showed that around 46 per cent of the members had attended public schools.[34] And it is well known that most senior members of government are products of the public school system. The authors of the report recognize that there is a real problem. They were told that

> the Church's involvement in education might reveal a bias towards the 6 per cent of young people who attend private schools . . . it has been put to us in evidence that many of them [i.e. clergy and laity], especially bishops, spend a disproportionate amount of time at the schools attended by 6 per cent of the population of the country and rarely visit the schools which educate the other 94 per cent.[35]

But having received the point, they ignore it. Yet if any institutions contribute to polarization, surely the public schools do. Is this yet another example of the Church of England witnessing to a 'bias to the poor' with its left hand, while its right hand is stuck firmly in the eye of the needle?

A further weakness of the report is its inability to call a spade a spade. Thus it speaks of the 'modern consumer economy' when presumably what it means is capitalism.[36] It is modern capitalism that we are talking about in the whole discussion on inequality, wealth and poverty, and polarization. Yet the authors seem afraid of using the word. At times one suspects that they want to say more. Thus they tell us that UPAs are 'the geographical dimension of an unequal society'.[37] Moreover, this inequality is neither new nor accidental, but is built into the nature of our society. 'Our own time has witnessed a more or less crude exaltation of the alleged benign social consequences of individual self-interest and competition. The inner city may justly be seen as the disfigured battleground of this modern phase of an age-old conflict.[38] The present government are clearly firmly located on one side of this conflict, committed to the maintenance and extension of inequality.

The authors seem at times to recognize this, and yet at others they write as if inequality and individualism – not to mention racism – could somehow be removed without disturbing the basic framework of the social order. Thus they write of individualism:

> *We believe that at present too much emphasis is being given to individualism, and not enough to collective obligation.* In the absence of a spirit of collective obligation, or the political will to foster it, there is no guarantee that the pursuit of innumerable self-interests will add up to an improvement in the common good.[39]

In an earlier passage they stress that there is a 'strong Christian tradition' which encourages individuals to serve others. But they then continue:

> Many people are outstandingly generous today: but it must be said that a society which requires for its prosperity the encouragement of personal acquisition and the maximum consumption of material goods may be one which gives insufficient encouragement to restraint and self-denial. Not that there is less instinctive altruism than there was: there is an amazing response, for example, to disaster appeals and to calls for voluntary blood donors. But in a highly competitive and consumer-oriented society, the chance to elicit and encourage such motivation is rarely seen, and a concern for social justice,

> and a human and compassionate response to the plight of the disadvantaged has become harder to elicit. This is as true within the Church as in the country at large. Christians have a responsibility to give a lead in this respect; but when they do so they run counter to the prevailing ethos of society. Ultimately it is only an absolute commitment to our solidarity one with another, a recognition of the importance of all forms of collective action for the common good, and a passionate concern for the rights and well-being of those least able to help themselves, which can redress the balance of the excessive individualism which has crept into both public and private life today.[40]

The authors complain that individualism has somehow 'crept into both public and private life' as if, having crept in, it could equally easily creep out. Yet individualism is central to a system in which profit, property and the market, the key institutions within capitalist society, are the prime determinants of inequality. Religious individualism also has a long history of giving ideological support for market forces. When it fails to do so, as in the United States at present, more corporate types of Christian political actions will arise to defend capitalism in a more aggressive way. But it is individualism which they defend, albeit by corporate means.

The report is weak in its treatment of racism. While it devotes a number of pages to the role of black people in the Church of England, and contains various references to racial discrimination, it has nothing to say about racism as a structural reality in Church and nation. Of course, discrimination and disadvantage are very serious matters on which the documentation is enormous and thorough. It is regrettable, therefore, that the report, having 'heard numerous complaints from black people of alleged discrimination against them' by police and magistrates, and admitting that some of these are well substantiated, then says that it 'would not wish to use such evidence . . . to level criticism specifically at the police or the magistracy'. Indeed, it concludes this paragraph with the statement: 'Such treatment is stoically endured by the great majority of black people.'[41] Surely the authors are not commending such endurance as an appropriate response to a perceived injustice. Nobody would claim that police and magistrates were the only groups guilty of racial discrimination; but if they are so guilty, and the evidence is surely more than hearsay, then should it not be said? Racism manifests itself in minute particulars, and cannot be combated purely at the level of generalized critique.

On the other hand, racism is more than the sum total of acts of discrimination, more than the under-representation of blacks within the power structure. It is a pervasive atmosphere, an integral part of the cultural climate of our society. Of course, discrimination and disadvantage are its public manifestations, and the report rightly draws attention to the need to tackle these evils. But there is a failure to recognize the degree to which racism is an integral part of our culture – of the sense of 'Britishness' – and the role of the Church of England in reinforcing this cultural nationalism. As with the treatment of individualism, it is as if, with some efforts here and there, racism could be removed without too much disturbance of the body politic. But what if racism is endemic within that body, so that to threaten racism is to threaten the stability of the unjust order of which it is a central part? The report does not consider such a possibility.

In the same way, little attention is paid to class and class conflict beyond the recommendation that the Church of England should shed something of its middle-class ethos. One would have thought that a report which had been dubbed as 'Marxist' might have shown some interest in an area which was so central to Marx's thought. Or that a report on urban issues would have devoted some space to the class struggle over housing which has been described as 'the central process of the city as a social unit'.[42] To bring Marx back into the discussion is to raise the question of what a Marxist critique both of the urban scene and of the Church of England would have to contribute. British theologians and Christian social thinkers have in the main ignored the Marxist tradition. In this they are not unique, for the widespread obsession with Marxism as a bogey goes hand in hand with an effective ignorance of Marxism as a system of thought.

A closer attention to Marx would have helped the authors of the report to understand class, race and migration within the context of modern capitalism, and to see the connections between them. It would have enabled them to recognize that no discussion of poverty can be of value which does not first examine the structure of wealth and property of which poverty is the reverse side: in Tawney's memorable words, what thoughtful rich people call the problem of poverty, thoughtful poor people call the problem of riches.[43] Tawney was no Marxist, but he saw that the problems of poverty and disadvantage cannot be solved unless one begins the critique further up the scale. Again, some insights from Marx would have led the authors to devote far more attention to the concentration of wealth and of economic and political power in city and suburb, including city and suburban churches, than they do. None of this is, of course, to suggest that Marxism is an adequate conceptual tool for approaching the issues of the 1980s, nor is it to ignore the weaknesses and datedness of much traditional Marxist analysis. But there are important insights about the urban scene and about the role of large institutions within capitalism (such as the Church of England) which are not available from any other source.

And in fact the report does not examine the class and cultural role of the Church of England itself as a major institution within State and nation. At the heart of the Church's role is the Church/State alliance, the establishment. The report ignores this central aspect altogether. Indeed, Professor Halsey, in an article on the report in *The Times*, claimed that 'in practice the Church of England is established only in theory'[44] – which seems to mean that the matter is of no practical relevance. Yet apart from the obvious aspects of establishment in terms of wealth and power, it plays a crucial role as myth in helping to perpetuate the confusion between Church and nation, a confusion which the authors themselves also imply in their address 'to Church and nation'. As long ago as 1913, J. N. Figgis in *Churches in the Modern State* criticized what he called 'a wholly unreal identification of the Church with the nation, an identification which had ceased to represent all the facts even in the time of Hooker and has been becoming less true ever since.'[45]

Today the myth of a national Church, the religious arm of the nation, is blatant nonsense. Yet the Church of England clings to it as a way of 'influencing' the national scene. The authors of the report are very concerned that the Church's influence should be felt. But have we not perhaps moved beyond this stage? And is not the Church's entanglement with the structures and value system of the ruling class a major obstacle to its influence being taken seriously? Is the idea of 'influencing society', which seems to dominate the thinking of the report as it does many church statements, an adequate model for the Church's social witness?

Marx did not write much about the Church of England, but one thing he did say was that it would sooner abandon thirty-eight of its thirty-nine articles than one thirty-ninth of its income.[46] What matters most is not what the Church *says* but what it *does* and whose interests it serves. This also is an insight which the authors might have gained from Marx, although the New Testament itself is fairly explicit: individuals and groups are known by their fruits. Where an institution's treasure is, there will its heart be also. Or, in Marxist terms, it is the material world which determines consciousness.

Now the public face of the Church of England within the material world, the world of finance and property, is presented by the Church Commissioners. And the report is gently critical of the Church Commissioners, referring to 'the potential conflict between financial return and social responsibility'.[47] But it does not convey the seriousness of the position. All over the country, ordinary people judge the commitments and priorities of the Church of England not by what reports say, but by the behaviour of the Church Commissioners in the handling of property and wealth. And clergy in urban areas often defend and justify the Commissioners' commitment to the principle of the highest return, on the grounds that it enables their own pastoral work to continue. But what if the credibility of their work is being undermined by the very processes which are meant to maintain it? While *Faith in the City* was being written, the Committee for Social Responsibility in Tower Hamlets, one of the most deprived areas in Britain, was attempting to stop the sale of a disused vicarage in Grove Road, Bow, to the highest bidder, and to obtain its use for a local black project. It did in fact succeed, after a long battle, though mainly, it seems, because the financial difference was not very great. Other properties continue to be sold without any apparent concern for the issues in social justice to which the report witnesses. I say 'apparent', because if there is such concern it is virtually impossible to locate it, since in the Church of England decision-making, like episcopal appointments, seems deeply mysterious. As the chairperson wrote to the Bishop, 'It does seem almost impossible to discover where these decisions are made.' Words that could be repeated of every diocese. Accountability has never been one of the Anglican virtues.

Moreover in recent years, since the abolition of exchange controls, the Church Commissioners have been increasingly investing overseas. So, while ACUPA calls for a Christian response to inner-city problems, the Commissioners (who in terms of power *are* the Church as far as the general public is concerned) can be viewed as contributing to the very problems which the report documents.

The theology of ACUPA

The theological chapter of the report is Chapter Three (although one critic, Frank Field, claimed that 'the theological analysis is tacked on at the end' – presumably because that is where he expected it to be[48]). However, at the very beginning of the report the authors tell us of the 'basic Christian principles of justice and compassion which we believe we share with the great majority of the people of Britain'.[49] This is a revealing and significant statement, for it excludes from the start the view that Christian principles and values might be in conflict with those of the dominant society. The authors are very committed to the view that the mass of the people, if not the government, share certain assumptions, for example that compassion should be a governing feature of our society. Thus they speak of 'Jesus' call to show compassion on those in need', a call which 'finds an immediate response in the hearts of Christians (and not only Christians)'; and of the '"compassionate" character' of society which 'is still desired by the majority of its members'.[50] However, whether this is the case or not, it is confusing to blur the distinction between shared compassion and shared Christian commitment. There is more to Christian faith, ethics and discipleship than compassion. And it is not self-evident that the values of the gospel *are* common to society as a whole. Indeed the evidence to the contrary is considerable.

It is the implicit assumption that the majority of the population, perhaps including the government, are basically 'closet Christians' needing gentle persuasion, rather than basically secular people needing conversion, which underlies the theology of the report and determines its style. For if the authors and their constituency are fundamentally on the same side, then it is appropriate to tread gently, to explain carefully, even to adopt a defensive posture. And the theological sections do have an unfortunately defensive, even apologetic, tone. 'Social comment of this kind is a legitimate option for the Church', we are assured, 'and proceeds from a long tradition of Christian social concern.'[51] This is hardly the language of the Church militant, the community of those who hunger and thirst for justice. Not only is the Christian social tradition reduced to 'comment' and 'concern', but these are no more than a 'legitimate option'. And no doubt, faced with this option, some Christians will legitimately opt in while others will opt out.

Perhaps it is because the authors do not feel the need to proclaim the gospel or to convert anyone, that the theological chapter makes no reference to any of the central Christian doctrines. The chapter begins with the New Testament maxim to 'remember the poor', a phrase which is repeated several times, and with a brief reference to the parable of the Good Samaritan. (This is perhaps an unfortunate choice in a chapter which uses so little of the Bible, since it is one of the few parts of the New Testament which both Margaret Thatcher and Norman Tebbit have used in order to defend their policies: the Samaritan is only remembered because he had money in his pocket.[52]) And we are then told: 'There is a sense in which no further "theology" is required.'[53] Indeed Canon Harvey has subsequently said that 'there was a sense in which we did not want too much theology'.[54]

And indeed there is not too much theology. There is a passing reference to Jesus' proclamation of the Kingdom of God which, we are told, 'had from the start profound social and political implications',[55] while in the one further reference to the Kingdom we are told of its 'realization . . . in a form of human society'.[56] But beyond these brief allusions there is no gospel in the report. We are told nothing of incarnation, redemption, transformation or sanctification. There is no Kingdom theology beyond the two brief references. Instead there is a stress on what is called 'concern' within a framework which is broadly accepted. No alternative vision is offered or even suggested. Indeed, such a vision is positively excluded as being beyond the scope of Christian people. 'Christians can hardly be expected to propose a realistic alternative to the entire economic system: but there is ample precedent in the Christian tradition for exposing the system we have to moral judgment.'[57] But this is highly questionable. The authors may well be able to argue a case for a reformist approach rather than any other, but it cannot simply be assumed that reformism is the only Christian option. The American theologian Stanley Hauerwas has written: 'The church's great failure in social ethics has not merely been her willingness to support the status quo but her inability to stand as an alternative to the current forms of the political.'[58] What ACUPA sees as the only Christian option, Hauerwas sees as a sign of failure. *Faith in the City* is in fact the theological equivalent of the Scarman report. But it begs the question of whether the role of the Church is to witness to a different set of values and therefore to a different ordering of society which will embody those values more adequately.

Some wider issues

What is the value of reports such as this? In all honesty, their value is limited. They can be quoted. One can use them to remind people of what they have said and the positions to which they have committed themselves. But today we are in a society in which the powers that be are beyond the range of rational and moral criticism, beyond shame. We are in a post-Fabian society. And this calls for a prophetic rather than a reformist response. Yet the authors of the report seem to be trapped within the reformist conventions and assumptions.

But this raises a further question. What is the nature of Christian social criticism? Within a short time of the publication of the report, we were told in a newspaper headline: 'Church and State agree on inner cities'. The account was of a meeting between Archbishop Runcie and government minister Kenneth Baker. They were, said Runcie, 'talking along common lines'.[59] So soon after what must be seen, in spite of all the criticisms, as a formidable and devastating attack on the ethos and ideology of the government, we find that a little chat can make all the difference. Church and government are not so far apart after all. Here lies the fundamental error behind the Commission's approach. It assumes that, with a little give and take, Church and government can find common ground. It assumes the existence of common values, common concerns, common priorities, common lines of thought. It fails to take sufficiently seriously the reality of evil within the structures of the fallen world. And it misses the Church's essential role, which is not to influence or reform society but to challenge the very foundations of its life. In Jim Wallis's words: 'Our churches need to be disoriented from the patterns of the present order and transformed biblically. The church must again become pilgrim and prophet – a community in the process of continual disentanglement from the values that dominate the age.'[60] It is because, at the end of the day, the Commission did not see the need for such disentanglement that, for all its positive features, it fails to be a witness to the transforming power of the Kingdom of God.

9

The Urban Church in Retreat: Some Lessons from Chicago

'I would not want to live there for anything in the world [but] I think that whoever ignores it is not entirely acquainted with our century and of what it is the ultimate expression.' Thus wrote Guiseppe Giacosa in 1933 of the city of Chicago.[1] Some thirty years earlier, an American liberal clergyman had reflected on the ambivalence to be found in the great cities of the United States.

> On the one hand the city stands for all that is evil – a city that is full of devils, foul and corrupting; and on the other hand the city stands for all that is noble, full of the glory of God, and shining with a clear and brilliant light . . . The greatest corruption, the greatest vice, the greatest crime are to be found in the great city. The greatest philanthropy, the greatest purity, the most aggressive and noble courage are to be found in the great city. San Francisco, St Louis, Chicago, Cincinnati, Philadelphia, Boston, and Brooklyn are full of devils – and also of the glory of God.[2]

Of the great cities he mentions, it is Chicago which has aroused the greatest interest both from urban sociologists and from churchpeople concerned with ministry in the urban cores. It was the sociologists at the University of Chicago ('the Chicago School') who dominated urban sociology for many years. Later, in the 1960s, much attention was given to the various urban training programmes and courses which were established there.[3] A whole issue of *The City Church* in 1963 was devoted to Chicago.[4] But the immense activity of the 1960s has been followed by retreat, decline and some degree of disillusionment in the 1970s and 1980s.

Since 1978 I have spent about six weeks each year in Chicago as

Visiting Theologian at St Stephen's House, an ecumenical retreat and study centre on the South Side. St Stephen's House has been an interesting vantage point from which to view the position of the Church in the city. In the first place, it has a unique status in that it is not technically part of any church establishment, and is described by its Director, Richard Young, as an ecumenical centre in communion with the (Anglican) Diocese of Chicago. It has very close links with the Catholic Theological Union, one of the largest Roman Catholic seminaries in the United States, with the Chicago cluster of Theological Schools which includes Lutherans, Presbyterians, Disciples and others, with the Orthodox communities, and with the Episcopal churches in city and suburb. It is also important in so far as it works with large numbers of people outside all Churches, with many who have left the Churches, and it has particular concerns for work with medical and law students in the university. Close to the University of Chicago in Hyde Park (ten to fifteen minutes walk away), it is also close (three minutes walk away) to 47th Street where the large poor black ghetto begins.

My role in Chicago has been mixed: conducting retreats, quiet days and seminars for local students, parishes, clergy and others; being available for personal meetings and consultations; preaching and teaching in Anglican parishes in the affluent suburbs as well as in the inner city; and doing a certain amount of study of the issues facing Church and community. The following reflections are based on my experience over the past decade. They are open to criticism, and there is much which I may have simply misinterpreted or presented unfairly. I would be grateful for such criticisms and corrections. However, there are some important contrasts with the position of the urban churches in Britain, and some important lessons to be learnt from the Chicago experience.

Early history of Chicago

Early American life was rural. In 1790 only 5.1 per cent of the population was urban. But from the 1830s the urban centres began to grow. According to tradition, Chicago was founded by Jean Baptiste Point du Sable, a French-speaking black man from Santa Domingo. (Ironically, in 1853 blacks were banned from entering the State of Illinois.) In 1830 Chicago was merely a swamp on the south-west shore of Lake Michigan. It contained fifty people in twelve log huts. By 1890 it had become the second-largest city of the western hemisphere, and one of the five great cities of the world.

In 1837 the city census gave the population as 4,170, including 3,989 white people, 77 'Negroes'[5] and 105 sailors. By 1850 half of the population were immigrants. One of the largest immigrant groups was the Poles. In 1890 there were five large Polish areas in the city. In 1898 eleven precincts in what was called 'Polish downtown', forming an area three-quarters of a mile long and half a mile wide, were together 86.3 per cent Polish. One precinct was 99.9 per cent Polish, that is, one non-Pole out of 2,500 people. Here were two of the largest Roman Catholic parishes in the world, St Stanislaus Kostka and Holy Trinity.[6]

By 1890, too, a community of very poor people had grown up in Chicago, and it was the poverty of the working people which caused the English Christian Socialist writer W. T. Stead to publish his book *If Christ Came to Chicago* in 1893. Many of the urban poor were immigrants. At the census of 1890, 77.9 per cent of the city's population were foreign-born or of foreign parentage. The main groups were German, Irish and Scandinavian, but there were also large groups from Poland, Lithuania and elsewhere.

The slum and the ghetto

However, it was not the immigrants from overseas who were the principal victims of urban poverty but the blacks from elsewhere in the USA. The movement from the south to Chicago grew rapidly in the 1890s. In the early years most of the blacks who came lived in mixed neighbourhoods. But the years from 1890 to 1915 saw the growth of the black ghetto. By 1900 16 wards in the city were 99.6 to 100 per cent black. However, in this period the black community in Chicago was not large. In 1890 blacks formed only 1.3 per cent of the population, and this had grown to 1.8 per cent in 1900. Between 1900 and 1910 both the black community and the ghetto grew. In 1910 over 30 per cent of blacks lived in neighbourhoods which were mainly or wholly black. In this year two wards, Second and Third Wards, were 25 per cent black.

There were not many neighbourhoods which were wholly black at this period. But the ghetto was spreading. It had taken shape before the First World War, and the war and the post-war years saw it strengthened to become a permanent part of the structure of Chicago.

The Chicago ghetto was a product of white hostility. It was not like Harlem in New York City where a black community took over a previously white area. The ghetto in Chicago was black from the start. In 1919 the first serious race riots occurred, and the Governor of Illinois called for a permanent local commission on race relations.[7] But since that time, the ghetto has become a permanent enclosure, unlike the concentrations of other ethnic minorities who lived together for a time and then moved on. The black ghetto is 'a uniquely urban phenomenon',[8] essentially different from those temporary enclaves. Most of the neighbourhoods in which the foreign-born lived were in fact mixed neighbourhoods. The only homogeneous neighbourhoods were the black neighbourhoods. They comprised 'a kind of residential confinement which was unique'.[9] The ghetto characterizes the social geography of Chicago to this day. The lines of demarcation are very clear. It is the most segregated city in the Western world.

In 1945 the major work *Black Metropolis* was produced by Drake and Cayton.[10] A study of black Chicago, it portrayed the city as the second-largest black city in the world. In his preface to the book, the black writer Richard Wright issued a warning that the ghetto might contain the seeds of later conflicts and upheavals.

> Do not hold a light attitude towards the slums of Chicago's South Side. Remember that Hitler came out of such a slum. Remember that Chicago could be the Vienna of American Fascism! Out of these mucky slums can come ideas quickening life or hastening death, giving us peace or carrying us into another war.[11]

His words were probably not taken seriously for many years. The ghetto was seen by many as a place of despair rather than revolt. Indeed, as late as 1963 Mayor Daley was insisting that there were no ghettoes in Chicago![12] Two years later Martin Luther King came to Chicago, and was shaken by the experience, commenting that he had never seen such hostility and hatred in all his years in the south. 1966 saw riots in the white suburb of Cicero, while openly Nazi groups grew up in other white areas.

At the end of the 1960s the black population had grown considerably. Between 1950 and 1960 the black community in Chicago as a whole increased by 65.1 per cent. But in some neighbourhoods the increase was far higher: in North Lawndale it was 765.9, in Hyde Park (the university area) 876.8 and in Kenwood (where St Stephen's House is located) 908.9 per cent. By 1960 North Lawndale was 91.1. per cent black and Kenwood 83.9 per cent. The biggest black concentrations were in Grand Boulevard (99.4 per cent) and Washington Park (99.1 per cent). Hyde Park, which had a long earlier history of preventing black entry, had a black community which formed 37.7 per cent of its population.[13]

By the 1970s Chicago was home for 64 per cent of the metropolitan area's unemployed, 75 per cent of its families below the poverty level, 76 per cent of its Spanish-speaking people, 85 per cent of its welfare recipients and 90 per cent of its black population. Between 1940 and 1970 the city had lost half a million whites and gained a third of a million blacks. These were the years when the suburbanization of housing and jobs grew apace among the white population. So there grew up in the Chicago area an extreme example of a uniquely American phenomenon: the city in which the poor live at the centre and the rich in the suburbs.[14] The contrasts with Britain hardly need stating. The most clearly observable one is the absence of the black ghetto. Instead, in British cities one sees the social class 'ghettoes' of the poor and disadvantaged of all colours.

Today Chicago is more racially segregated than ever before. 90 per cent of blacks live in neighbourhoods which are over 90 per cent black. The 1960–70 period saw an *increase* in segregation –the very years in which attention was focused on the Civil Rights Movement and on the growth of Black Power. A recent report comments:

> Chicago became blacker and poorer in the 1970s, and the fact that these two trends occurred in the same period is no coincidence. The city's black population grew from 32 per cent to 40 per cent between 1970 and 1980, while the proportion of

> residents with incomes below the poverty line rose from 14.5 per cent to 19.9 per cent. While most areas of the city saw some increase in poverty, it was in the black and Latino communities that poverty worsened the most.[15]

The study goes on to point out that this strong link between race and poverty is found at the neighbourhood level, especially in those areas which had undergone little change in the 1970s (that is, areas which had remained either mainly white or mainly black). More than half of the black areas (56 per cent) had suffered significant increases in poverty in the inter-censal period, compared with 14 per cent in white areas. Poverty also follows blacks as they move within the city. In areas which changed from white to racially mixed, 42 per cent saw increases in poverty.

It was the entrenched correlation between race and poverty which was the central feature of a book which appeared from Chicago in 1978 and which caused a national debate, the ripples of which have still not subsided. The book was unfortunately entitled *The Declining Significance of Race*, and its author, William Julius Wilson, is Professor of Urban Sociology at the University of Chicago.[16] In spite of much confusion and misrepresentation, not helped by the title, Wilson's central thesis continues to be examined. Basically Wilson was seeking to shift attention away from racial identity as such to the essentially economic and class issues facing the black underclass in the cities. For, he argued, there was a growing class division within the black community, most marked in Chicago itself. 35 per cent of blacks were in the underclass, the black poor. It was impossible to make sense of the inner city by focusing on race alone. Nor could affirmative action affect the status of the non-privileged groups. Subsequent work has confirmed Wilson's pessimism about the fate of the black poor. In Chicago, the division at 47th Street symbolizes his point. South of the 47th Street divide one enters a middle-class, multiracial area, the area where Jesse Jackson has his stronghold and where Wilson himself lives. Yet the crowds of blacks who arrive at Operation Push on Saturday mornings for Jackson's meetings, and the smaller numbers who gain entry into the University of Chicago and attend Wilson's classes, seem more and more out of touch with the black poor north of 47th Street.

Again, the contrasts and connections with Britain stand out: the impossibility, within the British context, of a simple identification of race with poverty; and the impossibility, in both countries, of seeing race as separable from class.

The Church in the city

> In 1915 the cry was heard 'The Negroes are coming.' The church reported . . . in 1918 'Our church has been greatly handicapped during the past year by the great influx of coloured people and the removal of many whites.'

So a Chicago Baptist church reflected. The author continued:

> The church was face to face with catastrophe. No eloquent preaching, no social service, could save a church in a community that was nearly 100 per cent Negro . . . Meanwhile the Negroes are steadily pushing down the alleys southward with their carts of furniture, but 47th Street running east and west still stands as a breakwater against the oncoming tide. If it crumbles, there will be some new history for the First Church.[17]

The subsequent history of the Church in Chicago has been marked by the phenomenon of 'white flight' and by what later became known as the 'suburban captivity of the churches'.[18] As the blacks have moved into the inner-city areas, so whites, and the churches catering for them, have moved out. It has been suggested that there are theological roots to the suburban movement in the understanding of the congregation or parish as a community of like-minded people.[19] This view has been reinforced by, and restated in, the contemporary 'church growth' movement.

The flight from the cities was well under way between 1920–30. By the 1930s, the notion of a 'parish' in the sense in which that term is used in England had disappeared from American Protestantism. (The Roman Church has maintained it to this day.) The term 'parish' had come to mean not a neighbourhood but a collection of like-minded people who gathered together into a church. It was a non-spatial concept to which the neighbourhood context was irrelevant: if a church did not 'succeed' or 'grow' in one place, let it move and flourish elsewhere. A writer on urban church strategy in 1932 noted that 'the old geographical parish in the exclusive sense has practically disappeared from American life'.[20] This disappearance is of crucial importance in understanding the Church's suburban flight, and the relative lack of guilt it has felt about it. By the 1930s it was estimated that over half of Protestant Christians in the United States left their home neighbourhood regularly to attend church.[21] But in the same period, writing of 47th Street, another author observed that the 'race churches' were dominant.[22] So by the 1930s one already had the pattern of white Christians travelling to a church which suited their liking; and of black Christians, residentially segregated in ghetto neighbourhoods, forming their own local black churches.

After the Second World War there was a revival of concern with inner-city ministry, and initiatives in Pittsburgh, Detroit and elsewhere attracted attention. Among Anglicans the work of Paul Moore and Kilmer Myers (both later to become bishops) in Jersey City became well known. But these inner-city parishes were very exceptional. While Moore entitled his book of the mid-1960s *The Church Reclaims the City*,[23] there was no way in which this could or did happen. In the main, Anglicanism remained affluent, white and suburban.[24]

The 1960s produced a mass of material on urban issues, much of it emanating from Chicago.[25] Elsewhere in the USA, these were the years of the East Harlem Protestant Parish in New York City (while nearby its less publicized Anglican neighbour St Edward the Martyr in East 109th Street flourished under Frank Voelcker's leadership).[26] Writers such as Harvey Cox and Gibson Winter extolled the virtues and possibilities of urban life.[27] But in the same period two-thirds of American population growth was in the suburbs. Today, in the minds of church spokespersons, not much is left of the 1960s vision except nostalgia. It is widely viewed as a 'temporary respite from the traditional anti-urban mentality in the United States'.[28] As far as Anglicans were concerned, the suburban Church grew in the 1960s, leaving the inner city largely unaffected.[29] Yet in 1978 the Urban Bishops' Coalition could claim, with some exaggeration: 'The life of the Episcopal Church is inextricably interwoven with the life of our cities. In the great cities of our land the church finds its greatest numerical strength.'[30] In a sense this is true. Some fashionable churches in the inner city are well filled by Anglicans who travel in from miles away. One church in downtown Chicago is full every Sunday with Anglo-Catholic people from miles around, but nobody living close to the church itself attends. In many of the poor parts of the city the Anglican presence is pitifully small and may be non-existent.

The 1960s in the South Side of Chicago were marked by the work of Saul Alinsky, the Woodlawn Organization, street gangs and riots. Alinsky's work had begun many years earlier in the poor white neighbourhoods known as 'Back of the Yards', known now to millions through the story of Studs Lonergan.[31] Alinsky was an urban populist whose methods caused much controversy and anger, not least within the Churches. The Chicago-based *Christian Century* was strongly opposed to him, as was Walter Kloetzli who developed his critique into a study of the urban challenge facing the Churches.[32] Yet Alinsky's work would not have made the progress it did without the collaboration of sections of the church community. One of his strongest supporters was Father Leonard Dubi of the parish of St Daniel the Prophet in the very poor Garfield Ridge area of South West Chicago.

In the Woodlawn area, where Alinsky's Woodlawn Organization had grown up, the large youth gang known as the Blackstone Rangers, and later as the Black P Stone Nation, flourished in the late 1960s, and there was some attempt to work with this gang by a group of Christians based at First Presbyterian Church in Woodlawn.[33] But work with street youth or with neighbourhood issues was the exception rather than the norm of Chicago churches. A report from the Community Renewal Society in 1971 noted dismally:

> Generally as the white residents vacate a neighbourhood, the churches have become increasingly disengaged from the immediate neighbourhood around their building, and eventually have disbanded or moved to new locations . . . The major white denominations are retreating to the suburban and satellite areas while Negro sectarian Protestantism is beginning to dominate central city areas.[34]

The exception to this pattern was, and is, the Roman Catholic Church, which has retained a presence in the ghetto and inner-city districts, but whose leadership is almost entirely white.[35]

It is important to stress this dominant pattern of disengagement from neighbourhood ministry, for a myth has growth up in Britain that Chicago churches have led the way in 'urban ministry'. It is certainly true that much of the community work on the South Side in the 1960s could not have happened without the support of the churches; the Organization for a South West Community is a good example.[36] And there was the well-publicized work of the Urban Training Centre (which inspired various projects in Britain such as Donald Reeves' Urban Ministry Project) and the controversial Ecumenical Institute.[37] But, as George Younger wrote in 1974, 'many of the projects and efforts which were considered to be most significant or promising have disappeared today or are greatly diminished in both range and hope'.[38]

The Ecumenical Institute had moved from its old quarters in a black area on the West Side to larger premises in a white area on the North Side. Gibson Winter, one of the founders of the Urban Training Centre, has written that 'it is astonishing that we hoped for so much and accomplished so little'. Winter has called the 1960s 'a miserable exercise in futility'.[39] Yet the work which he and Dick Luecke pioneered does continue, and Luecke is still based in Chicago, running the Community Renewal Society from premises in Michigan Avenue opposite the Art Institute. Here, too, are the offices of the *Chicago Reporter* which monitors race issues in the city. Founded by John McDermott, a Roman Catholic layman from St Thomas's Parish in Hyde Park, it is now edited by Roy Larson, an Anglican layman and long-time Chicago journalist. At the time of writing, the offices of the Institute for the Church in Urban Industrial Society (ICUIS) in Woodlawn stand empty and locked. Here are archival materials covering a whole range of urban issues, a major and unique source for people involved in urban ministry. But it stands deserted and unused, a glaring case of a centre which has lost its purpose. And around the area are many individuals who were active in the urban social movements of the 1960s; they now seem tired, confused: history has passed them by.

Yet most of Chicago's Anglican community were never involved in any of this work or thinking. Anglicanism is, with a few startling and impressive exceptions, a conservative and establishment force, liturgically backward, socially uninvolved, politically conservative, the Church of the well-to-do, and almost wholly white. The two main black parishes on the South Side attract the middle-class elements of the black community. The strength of Anglicanism lies in the affluent suburbs such as Kenilworth, Lake Forest and Flossmoor. John Atherton, after a short visit, summed up the situation accurately in comments inspired by the pastoral work of the Cathedral shelter.

> From this base the church offered what was essentially a counselling and food parcel service of a very organised kind and very dependent on government finance. For the rest, the church was noticeable for its almost total absence from the inner city and from the commercial, financial and industrial life of the city. This absence reflected a deliberate strategy of withdrawing from the deprived inner city into the more affluent suburbs and into the personal and pastoral side of a very bourgeois Christianity. It provided one of the starkest examples of the ecclesiastical bias to the rich.[40]

Lessons for Britain

I am conscious of the danger of simplistic contrasts and comparisons, as also that of generalizations based on an inadequate evidence. The following reflections should therefore be read as my tentative thoughts on the basis of some acquaintance with churches in Chicago over a decade and in Britain over three decades. I would point to eight areas where the Chicago experience can throw some light on our situation in Britain and can confront us with important but uncomfortable areas for debate.

First, the danger that the Church becomes a self-perpetuating institution. 'Danger' is too mild a word, for it has become a reality not only in Chicago but in parts of Britain. It is twenty-five years since Chicago's best-known theologian Martin Marty observed that 'since the institutional self-interest preoccupies the churches, and does not serve the community, it seems to incarnate irrelevance'.[41] Younger, in similar vein, claims that most churches in Chicago are 'still rooted in the post-Constantinian assumption that the spread of the church is the principal aim of the mission of Christ'.[42] My impression is that the churches in Chicago, and in the United States generally, see themselves as clubs or corporations which should be maintained for their own sakes. So churches often compete with one another and local co-operation is rare even within the same communion, let alone across denominational divides. The churches reflect, and ritually re-enact, the capitalist values of competition and free enterprise. Hence the relative lack of interest in doctrine (except, of course, the hard core of individualism and national pride which lies at the heart of 'civic religion' as practised in all the churches). Hence, too, the priority of church maintenance and preservation over the proclamation of the Kingdom of God. The church which is an end in itself is in very grave danger.

Second, the Church as a class institution. As in the USA as a whole, churches in Chicago reinforce class divisions. Nor is there any widespread recognition that there is anything wrong with such a situation. The church growth movement, which has been gaining in Britain for some years, bases its work on the belief that churches are communities of similar and like-minded people. Churches are institutions within class society: on this view they also reinforce and sanctify, but in no way transcend, class divisions. The spread of church growth ideas in the British suburban churches is likely to bring similar dangers in its train.

Third, the middle-class Church which cares *for* the poor. There is at present much talk, in the USA as in Britain, of 'bias to the poor' and of solidarity with the poor. But there seems to be little awareness of the class dimensions of the Church's position. Hence it is possible to help to 'organise the poor against the working class',[43] to minister to, and even become an advocate for, the very deprived in a paternalistic way, while bypassing the industrial proletariat, the group from which the Church has always been alienated. Much ministry to the poor is rooted in middle-class assumptions about the survival of the Church as a class phenomenon. From its position of great wealth and influence, it pleads the cause of the poor. It is likely that it will seek to maintain the position in order that its voice will continue to be heard. But can such a Church which speaks *for* the poor ever be a Church *of* the poor?

Fourth, the Church as a racially segregated institution. Church life in the USA, it has been claimed, is as segregated now as before the Civil Rights Movement.[44] On the South Side there are white parishes and black parishes, to some extent reflecting the neighbourhoods. Again, there seems little consciousness of racism as a threat to the identity of the Church. When I preached at the main Roman Catholic church in Hyde Park several years ago on the theme of race, I was told by an old member of the parish that it was the first time that he could recall the subject being raised in a sermon in fifteen years. Racial segregation and inequality seem to be accepted as part of the way things always have been and will be.

Fifth, the suburban church as an irrelevance to the city. Clearly the wealth and power of the suburban churches is tremendous. And yet there seems to be a tendency to ignore the responsibility of suburban Christians and to leave them to organize themselves in self-sufficient and self-authenticating communities. It is vital to get across to the suburbs their responsibility for, and potential influence on, what happens in the inner city. That task does not seem to be a priority here any more than it is in the USA.

Sixth, the mystique of reconciliation (on which I will have more to say in Chapter Twelve). Essentially, the critique of Saul Alinsky focused on the issues of reconciliation and conflict. It is widely assumed that the Church exists to reconcile, and that this excludes the adoption of positions which may lead to conflict and controversy. This view needs to be questioned and rejected; it lies at the root of much of the Church's ineffectiveness on issues of racial justice.

Seventh, the question of the black underclass. I think Wilson's pessimism is justified. Undoubtedly there has been significant progress in the black middle class. Chicago has had a black mayor – Harold Washington – and many blacks are in key positions. Affirmative action has been valuable, and it remains necessary. But the situation of the black poor has deteriorated, and the gulf between the black bourgeoisie and the black poor has grown wider. Again, there are clear parallels in Britain.

Finally, the indivisibility of race and class. While the urban geography is different, the Chicago experience underlines the impossibility of treating race in isolation from the issues of social justice and the conflicts of a class society. At the same time, it is mistaken and dangerous to dissolve race issues into class ones. Race and class are interlocked: they are not the same, but they cannot be separated.

In all these areas there are clear pointers and warnings for the Churches in Britain. We need to make the connections.

10

Religion and the Rise of Racism

'Racism dies in order that capital might survive.'[1] So wrote the black activist A. Sivanandan at the conclusion of a review of the development of race legislation and attitudes in Britain in the 1960s and 1970s. As immigration control reduced non-white immigrants to a trickle, so race relations legislation sought to curb the incidence of racism within Britain in the interests of social stability. The theory was that, while in terms of immigration policy black people were to be considered merely as labour units, those who managed to beat the controls and settle here were to be seen as equal citizens. Racism at the doors of Britain was seen as necessary in order to achieve inter-racial harmony within Britain. However, since then, the fatal flaws in the theory have come to seem increasingly irrelevant as Thatcherism has ushered in an era more obviously hostile both to racial and social justice. Today Sivanandan's words seem excessively optimistic. In the aftermath of the Nationality Act, the conflicts in Brixton, Liverpool and elsewhere, and the government's response to them, the breaking up of family life through the immigration rules, and the general lack of interest in government circles in any sustained attack on racial disadvantage, reports of the death of racism can only be seen as exaggerated rumours. The evidence, both internally and internationally, points to the persistence of racism as an integral dimension within capitalism.

In view of this, it is surprising that while Christian social thinkers continue to develop the debate initiated by Max Weber[2] and developed by Tawney,[3] on the relationship between religion and capitalism, the study by Ronald Preston being the latest contribution,[4] little attention has been paid to one aspect of the relationship which is of crucial importance for the future of both: the role of the Christian religion in aiding and abetting the rise of racism. I want therefore in this chapter to discuss the growth, persistence and spread of racism in our society, its connections with, and implications for, organized Christianity, and the relevance of Tawney's thinking for this discussion.

However, if the neglect of discussion of racism within the English Christian social tradition is striking, its almost total absence from Tawney's work is even more so. As far as I can see, Tawney nowhere wrote about race or racism, except indirectly in his two studies of China.[5] From one perspective, there is perhaps nothing very surprising about this. The concern within the labour movement with race, colonialism and the issue of racial justice is, for the most part, a post-war phenomenon. The word 'racism' did not enter common vocabulary until the end of the 1960s. The Fabians in particular gave scant attention to colonial issues. Some of their early material, such as Bernard Shaw's *Fabianism and the Empire*, was appalling. As late as 1949 it is interesting to see the topics which the Fabian Society conference did not get round to discussing: they were international trade, colonial development, foreign policy and Commonwealth relations.[6]

In other respects, however, Tawney's silence on race is odd. For he was 'not a typical Fabian' and was highly critical of them at times.[7] His early experience at Toynbee Hall in Whitechapel took place at the height of the anti-aliens agitation, a highly racist and anti-Semitic campaign. His friendship with William Temple might, one would think, have led him to consider the issue of race. For there were isolated figures among Christian social thinkers, notably J. H. Oldham, who were relating Christian theology to race as early as 1924. Reviewing Oldham's book *Christianity and the Race Problem*, published in 1924, Temple observed that race was the greatest of all practical problems facing humanity.[8] However, this early concern does not seem to have affected Tawney's studies, published over the same period. And so *Religion and the Rise of Capitalism* (1926) does not consider the relationship between Calvinism and racial superiority, nor does *Equality* (1931) discuss racial equality. Tawney was a giant among Christian social thinkers, and his neglect of race issues is typical of the Christian social tradition as a whole in this period. Nevertheless, a study of Tawney's thinking is relevant to our current debates on racism and the Church, and it is relevant at two levels. First, his insight into religion, socialism, equality and social change have important consequences for the anti-racist struggle today. Second, the limitations of his approach help to highlight some weaknesses in our own.

Tawney's insights

First, Tawney saw that Protestant Christianity, and particularly Calvinism, had both aided the growth of capitalist society and capitalist values, and in return had itself been shaped and distorted in the process. Of the growth of the capitalist spirit, he wrote: 'The force which produced it was the creed associated with the name of Calvin. Capitalism was the social counterpart of Calvinist theology.'[9] In *Religion and the Rise of Capitalism* he also analysed the 'growth of individualism', the process by which Christian social action was reduced to the realm of individual rescue work, a process from which it is only now recovering. 'It was therefore in the sphere of providing succour for the non-combatants and for the wounded, not in inspiring the main army, that the social work of the church was conceived to lie.' So the Church 'abandoned the fundamental brainwork of criticism and construction'.[10]

It is, of course, impossible to make sense of the contemporary racial scene unless we relate it to the international spread of capitalism, the colonial, and in the case of the Caribbean the colonial and slave, background to migration, and the ideology of racial superiority for which Christianity provided a theological basis. It is equally impossible to understand the inadequacy of Christian resistance to racial oppression without some grasp of the false dualism to which Tawney drew attention. Today when some radical Christians in the Reformation traditions are speaking of the need for a second Reformation,[11] we need to learn from Tawney how grievously the tradition of the first Reformation has damaged our witness.

Second, Tawney held that the fundamental socialist dogma was that of the dignity of the human person,[12] and that this involved the struggle for equality. His Christianity and his socialism were egalitarian, and it is worth noting how essential theology was to his approach to this issue, to such an extent that he held that only a believer in God could be consistently and faithfully egalitarian. 'In order to believe in human equality', he wrote in 1912, 'it is necessary to believe in God.'[13] He went on: 'The essence of all morality is this: to believe that every human being is of infinite importance and therefore that no consideration of expediency can justify the oppression of one by another. But to believe this it is necessary to believe in God.'[14] It was the recognition of the inequality between God and humanity, he argued, which made any claim for inequality between human persons so absurd.

Today, however, the Christian roots of the labour movement are diminishing. No longer is religion a major influence on the Labour Party.[15] The question of the survival of a commitment to equality once the spiritual basis of that commitment has been removed is both important and difficult. However, what is even more apparent is the persistence, and in recent years the resurgence, of a 'Christian' defence of inequality. I refer, of course, to the claim of Thatcherism not only to promote inequality as the condition of social progress but also to link this promotion with a commitment to Christian doctrine. Indeed, some Conservatives, including probably the Prime Minister herself, would see Christianity as the basis of this ideology and practice. What we have in the philosophy of the Conservative Party, as expressed in the present government, is a passionate belief in human inequality.

Thus Sir Keith Joseph has written of 'tyranny hidden in the pursuit of equality'. The very pursuit of equality is 'an instrument . . . of impoverishment and tyranny'.[16] It was close to the fiftieth anniversary of the publication of Tawney's *Equality* when a book of the same name appeared from the pen of Sir Keith Joseph, and was commended by an East London clergyman as 'a profoundly Christian book' which 'takes the doctrine of original sin seriously'. Equality, he claimed, was not possible because 'men are different to an *infinite* degree'.[17] Similarly, Dr Rhodes Boyson has told us that equality restricts the human spirit, while progress comes from inequality.[18] Even the dangerously 'wet' Peter Walker, whose concern for racial justice puts him streets ahead of most Conservatives, prefers inequality to an egalitarian philosophy.[19] But it was George Gale, the right-wing journalist, who in a contribution to the influential volume *Conservative Essays* (1978) summed up the Conservative belief most succinctly. 'The

Conservative Party is not egalitarian and never can be. It is a waste of time pretending that equality is what it is about. It is about inequality.'[20]

Christians should not therefore be under illusions, imagining that by some process of moistening, or by the continued use of the Prayer of St Francis (even in its accurate version), there might be progress towards social and racial equality in the Conservative Party. They cannot and will not promote equality because they do not believe in it. They are not hypocrites but passionate believers in everything that Tawney opposed. This is not to deny that there may well be individuals within the Conservative ranks who can be allies in the struggle for racial justice, and it is an urgent task to identify such people and build alliances with them, for they are becoming increasingly difficult to find and their path is a lonely one.

If there were any doubt about the *belief*, the actual *practice* presents overwhelming evidence for the commitment to inequality. The research by Townsend, Atkinson, Goldthorpe, Field and others has shown how little inequalities of wealth and income have changed over a century, and how, under the present regime, there has been a positive policy in favour of the wealthy and against the underprivileged and the deprived.[21] The Judaeo-Christian tradition holds that the test of belief is practical: it is those who do justice who know the Lord (Jer. 22.16). By the prophetic criteria of the pursuit of justice, the correcting of oppression and the defence of the poor, the present regime in Britain must be seen as utterly irreligious and apostate. Tawney's critique is of abiding significance. There is, he claimed, 'no touchstone, except the treatment of childhood, which reveals the true character of a social philosophy more clearly than the spirit in which it regards the misfortunes of those who fall by the way'.[22] There could be no more damning indictment of Thatcherism than that.

Equally, Tawney saw, as long ago as 1912, the injustice in Sir Geoffrey Howe's belief that the creation of wealth is more important than its distribution,[23] a belief expressed regularly in Conservative budget provisions. The social problem, Tawney insisted, was not about quantities but about proportions, not about the amount of wealth but about moral justice.[24]

And this brings me to a third aspect of Tawney's thought: the relationship between facts and justice. The Fabian tradition was concerned to a great degree with the collection of data. Sidney Webb believed that statistics should be gathered in order that the informed élite could run society. The underlying assumption was that if good men and women were given the facts, social change would follow. We should now recognize that this assumption is naive and false (though it still seems to govern much of the thinking of the institutional Church). Indeed, in many areas of social policy there is an inverse relationship between data and action. On matters of race and migration, Ruth Glass noted in 1964, 'when facts contradict fiction, it is the facts which are regarded as dubious'.[25] Tawney was critical of the Fabian obsession with fact-gathering and their neglect of principle and vision. 'They tidy the room but they open no windows in the soul.'[26]

Finally, Tawney's view of the role of the Church. Like Temple and Gore, he held that individualism, the 'privatization' of religion, far from being integral to the Christian tradition was a modern aberration. From Gore he had adopted the concept of a Christian society in which the principles of the Sermon on the Mount would be applied in social life.[27] So in *The Acquisitive Society* (1921) he could argue for 'a new kind, and a Christian kind, of civilisation'.[28] Hence his attachment to medieval society with its sense of a common order and a common purpose. The section in *Religion and the Rise of Capitalism* on the medieval background[29] contains a good deal which represents Tawney's own idea of Christian society. Like the Christendom Group, Tawney had an element of nostalgia for a Christian order of the past. In our plural society his view must appear archaic and romantic, and he never really pursued it to its logical conclusion. Nevertheless, he did recognize and maintain the inseparable link between Christian theology and a just social order. Like Temple, he was a Christian humanist and a Christian materialist.

The rise of racism

I want to consider some aspects of the rise of racism, drawing on the insights from Tawney. It is necessary to extend Tawney's analysis of religion and capitalism to the issues of race and colonialism. In the development of colonialism into a cohesive system, racist ideology was of central importance. Not that racism was a product of capitalist expansion. But racism was liberated by the growth of capitalism, and the colonial church, as the church of the expanding white capitalist world, was an essential part of this process. Nowhere was Tawney's analysis more relevant than in South Africa, where the developing racist ideology was justified theologically by Dutch Calvinism. Its doctrine of the elect, its insistence that spirituality was as earthly and as bound to creation as dust and blood, and its belief that the black person was the descendant of the accursed Ham were vital elements in the ideology of apartheid. As Trevor Huddleston wrote in 1956, 'Calvinism, with its great insistence on "election", is the ideally suitable religious doctrine for South Africa.'[30] Thus the Christian religion, in its Dutch Calvinist form, aided the rise of institutional racism and became an integral part of that racism's ideological apparatus.[31]

However, it would be a mark of appalling insularity to see in South Africa a unique and deviant example of the Christian contribution to the rise of racism. The historic association of Christianity with whiteness all over the world has had devastating effects and led to dehumanizing and negative images of black people.[32] I want, however, to refer to two areas in which Christian churches have supported or connived at racist movements in North America and Europe.

The first example is the growth, and during the last few years the revival, of the Ku Klux Klan and related movements in the United States. Studies in the late 1960s showed that Protestant clergy were disproportionately represented in the membership and leadership of the Klan, and a detailed analysis of Klan membership in Knoxville, Tennessee, showed that 71 per cent belonged to Baptist churches and 24 per cent to Methodist ones. In other words, in statistical terms the KKK is a deeply Christian organization, rooted and grounded in the Christian churches. Nor is the organization dead. In recent years there has been a revival of the Klan, and it has been estimated that its membership doubled between 1975 and 1980. The Anti-Defamation League has estimated its membership at around 10,000 with some 100,000 sympathizers.[33]

However, what is much more significant is the more widespread phenomenon of the resurgence, in Britain and the USA, of a species of crude biblical fundamentalism combined with an authoritarian right-wing posture of a kind which has for over a century provided support for racism and anti-Semitism. The powerful fundamentalist lobby around Reagan is too significant an element in American life for it to be written off as marginal derangement. Fundamentalist Christianity plays a much more central role in American society than is the case in Britain. Nevertheless, the atmosphere created by both Reagan and Thatcher, an atmosphere marked by paranoia, fears of subversion, a façade of moral rectitude and the use of elements from the Christian vocabulary, provides the ideological air in which such groups can breathe and breed. So in Britain we see the growth of movements of religious intolerance and fanaticism of a type similar to the Moral Majority and Christian Voice in the USA. At present most such groups focus their attention on issues such as homosexuality and AIDS, pornography and child abuse, drugs and the defence of the family. However, the record of fundamentalists on race is a very bad one, and they are simply one part of a larger whole. The fact is that, historically, Christian believers have often been in the forefront of organized racial hatred, Jewish conspiracy theories and fanatical anti-communism with all its accompanying evils.[34] In an increasingly authoritarian and repressive climate there is no guarantee that those days are over.[35]

My second example is the contribution of Christianity to the growth of Nazi anti-Semitism, and the inability of most Christians in Germany in the 1930s to offer any resistance to Nazism. Again, my purpose is not to throw stones, but to urge us to self-scrutiny lest we succumb to similar seductions. And here Tawney's critique of Christian dualism is highly relevant. The Lutheran tradition which dominated German Christianity made a sharp separation between the spiritual Kingdom of God and affairs of State. The Jewish origin of Jesus and his teaching was such an embarrassment to Christian anti-Semites that many denied it entirely. In many quarters it was unacceptable to teach that Jesus and Paul were Jewish, while belief in the incarnation was seen as non-essential.[36] The Jewish spirit was to be purged from all aspects of the Church's life. Not only the Jewish spirit, but the Christian spirit also, for sermons were preached from which all Christian content had been removed: what remained was patriotic paganism. And so on Crystal Night in 1938, when the synagogues were destroyed – as indeed Luther had advocated – there were no protests from church leaders.[37] Indeed the Bishop of Thuringia's response was to reissue Luther's anti-Jewish writings.[38]

Richard Gutteridge, who surveyed with horrifying detail the record of German evangelicals on anti-Semitism concluded:

> During the whole period [1879–1950] there is no evidence whatever of any authoritative statement being issued by the Evangelical Church calling for the earnest consideration of the Jewish problem from the purely biblical standpoint and in the light of the Christian gospel of mercy and love. Nor can we discover any official Church warning against the mounting agitation in certain circles to treat the problem as predominantly one of race . . . Throughout the [Nazi] conflict nobody in a position of authority made a full and plain denunciation of anti-Semitism as such.[39]

Karl Barth, whose theology contributed not a little to the weakness of the Christian resistance, claimed in 1944 that the German tragedy might have been avoided had the Church not accepted the false dualism between spirituality and matters of earthly justice.[40]

I now turn to the question of racial equality in Britain and the Church's response. If, as Tawney held, equality is basic to Christianity, then the assertion of and commitment to equality between races is an acid test of our comprehension of, and fidelity to, that belief. However, the persistence of inequality in Britain, depressingly well-documented, assumes grotesque proportions when the question of racial disadvantage is examined. I stress disadvantage because this is of far greater significance than discrimination alone. Successive census data and other studies have shown the concentration of black communities in areas of high deprivation, while the evidence of racial inequality in employment, housing and other areas is indisputable.[41] All of this was documented long before the uprisings of 1981 and was fully available before Lord Scarman's report. Earlier chapters of this book have drawn attention to many of the studies.

In the early chapters I argued that in order to understand contemporary racism and the position of the black minorities in Britain, we need to go back to the 1950s. The history of attitudes and reactions to recent black immigration in Britain is one which reflects little credit either on the labour movement or on the Church. In the post-war labour shortage, West Indian labour was recruited to help maintain transport and health services in particular. But 'it was their labour that was wanted, not their presence'.[42] And by the early 1960s the cries for control were powerful, leading to the Commonwealth Immigrants Act 1962 by which racism was nationalized. The Labour Party, which under Hugh Gaitskell had opposed the legislation, strengthened it in 1965, and has upheld it consistently ever since.[43] In spite of the clear evidence that the campaign, and the legislation which resulted from it, was concerned to control not immigration but only coloured immigration, within a few years the political parties (and the Church) had accepted the principle of control. The old racism had become the new realism.

Nowhere was the change more obvious than in what was later to be called the 'race relations industry' and its principal spokesman of the mid-1960s, Philip Mason. Mason, who had always insisted on the impartial, fact-gathering role of his Institute of Race Relations was, in January 1965, openly supporting even tighter immigration controls. 'We are determined to cut down sharply the number of fresh entries until this mouthful has been digested.'[44] In the month after the 1965 White Paper, which reinforced and strengthened the racist controls of the 1962 act, Mason was advising the National Committee for Commonwealth Immigrants (NCCI) not to become 'a spokesman or champion for the immigrants as against the rest of the community'.[45] NCCI, which preceded the Community Relations Commission, the Race Relations Board and the Commission for Racial Equality, was chaired by Archbishop Ramsey. It was set up by Harold Wilson within the already existing framework of immigration controls based on colour. Within the framework, the 'problems' of immigrants could be looked at.

So there grew up, in both the major parties and in the

Churches, the view that black people were intrinsically problematic, that it was they, rather than the dominant society, which constituted the problem. Their numbers had to be controlled in the interests of racial harmony; thus racism at the doors of Britain was justified as a means towards overcoming racism within Britain. The ideology behind the demands for tighter and tighter controls was described aptly by Ruth Glass as 'a new doctrine of original sin together with a new faulty political arithmetic.'[46] By the 1971 Immigration Act, the racial aspect of control had been explicitly incorporated into the legislation by the notorious patriality clause. No longer did politicians claim that their concern was with 'numbers, not colour' – as people like Sir Cyril Osborne and Lord Elton had insisted in the late 1950s and early 1960s. It was the number of black people which constituted the problem. Yet the evidence for the number theory of prejudice was weak. There was, and is, no correlation between the number of black people and the manifestation of racism. Indeed, the calls for further restriction served to generate more racial hatred and consequently further demands: after all, if it was the presence of black people which produced racial prejudice and hatred, the solution must be to reduce the numbers and so eliminate racism.

In fact, the theory is dangerous nonsense. Nevertheless, whereas in 1958 Lord Justice Salmon had called the Notting Dale rioters 'a minute and insignificant section of the population',[47] it was clear by the end of the 1960s that support for explicitly racist policies was by no means insignificant. There was little evidence of a consciousness of racial equality in the Survey of Race Relations, which claimed that three-fifths of white British people saw themselves as superior to Africans and Asians.[48] Since then we have seen the influence of Powell (a devout churchman), the rise of the National Front and its satellites, and the incorporation of the essential principles of racism into the assumptions and programmes of the major political parties. In contrast to the speed and efficiency with which immigration controls have been introduced and strengthened, the weakness and half-heartedness of legislation against discrimination and for racial justice has been depressingly obvious. And unlike the situation in the USA, where the Christian leadership of the early Civil Rights Movement was clear, the British Churches have dragged their feet on issues of racial justice until very recently. During the critical years from 1958 to 1971, their role was almost negligible.

Now Tawney and his colleague Richard Titmuss held strongly to the view that one must legislate and take positive action towards equality and social justice. They would not simply happen automatically. Indeed, a fundamental element in the idea of a Welfare State, in their view, was that of redistributive justice. In this they were reiterating a position which was common in Christian writers of the patristic age: that to restore to those who were deprived that which was lawfully theirs was not charity but justice. Thus St Ambrose: 'It is not with your wealth that you give alms to the poor, but with a fraction of their own which you give back: for you are usurping for yourself something meant for the common good of all.'[49] Such statements are repeated throughout the Fathers. In the same vein, but in the twentieth-century context, Titmuss wrote: 'To me the "Welfare State" has no meaning unless it is positively and constructively concerned with redistributive justice.'[50] He used the notion of positive discrimination, a term which has come into prominence recently in relation to black people, with reference to the poor. To discriminate positively in favour of the poor and disadvantaged is to do no more than restore rights which have been taken away. Such a notion has deep roots both in the history of welfare and in the Christian social tradition.

However, when we turn to racial inequality, injustice and disadvantage, there is little evidence that these ideas have played much of a role in the thinking and strategic planning of political and religious groups until recently. Although the evidence of racial inequality is overwhelming, no government has used the Race Relations Act as a campaigning charter for racial justice. Had it not been for the uprisings of 1981, even the very cautious support for positive action in the Scarman Report would never have seen the light of day. British policy on race, with the exception of the fundamental area of immigration control, has been based on what has been termed 'racial inexplicitness' – the view that 'race may be a predicate for positive policy as long as . . . no one takes official notice of the fact'.[51] Church bureaucracies have merely been a pale reflection of their secular counterparts, often lagging behind them, rarely initiating ideas and changes. Indeed, it is interesting that, while Church House, Westminster, follows civil service models in virtually every aspect of its life, the only two areas where it fails to do so are those of ethnic monitoring and equal opportunities policies!

In both the political parties and the Churches there are those who resist any attention to race issues on the grounds that it diverts attention from more fundamental issues, perhaps to do with class or, in Christian circles, with common human sin. Now it is, of course, right to insist that the defence of racial minorities should not be at the cost of the wider defence of the poor and the oppressed of all colours; it is evasive and irresponsible to try to dissolve racial oppression into social and class oppression, or to play one kind of oppression off against another. It is common in church discussions on race or on women's issues for someone to say, 'But shouldn't we really be talking about human liberation?' Such questions frequently come from people who have never shown the slightest interest in any form of oppression until women or black people started to raise issues. The real agenda (not so hidden) behind such questions is that nothing should actually be done about anything. These are standard methods of evasion. Those who claim to combat racism obliquely in the hope that it will disappear before its supporters have noticed are unreliable allies and ineffective fighters.

What, then, can we say about the response of the Church to contemporary racism? With some dramatic exceptions, the British Churches took up no positions on race and racism before the late 1960s. There was virtually no opposition from the Churches to the clearly racist immigration controls of 1962 – though Archbishop Ramsey attacked the legislation as 'lamentable' when it reached the House of Lords[52] – or to the tightening of controls in 1965. Churches played little if any role in campaigning for anti-discrimination legislation.

In recent years, however, there has certainly been an increased willingness by the major Churches to take up explicitly political positions, including positions on race. The Church of England, through its bishops and its General Synod, has undoubtedly moved slightly but significantly to the left on questions of race, while the Catholic Commission for Racial Justice (sadly no longer in existence) led the opposition to the Nationality Bill. The establishment of the Programme to Combat Racism (PCR) of the World Council of Churches (WCC), the work of the Community and Race Relations Unit (CRRU) of the British Council of Churches (BCC), and the appearance of a number of voluntary groups – CARAF (Christians Against Racism and Fascism), ECRJ (Evangelical Christians for Racial Justice), CARJ (Catholic Association for Racial Justice) and the Zebra Project among many – are indications of a new determination to attack racism in the name of the gospel. The Anglican Church internationally presents a more committed face than its English representative. Meeting at Limuru, Kenya, in 1971, the Anglican Consultative Council not only condemned racism and called on Anglicans to examine their life and structures, but specifically commended the PCR and its Special Fund. 'The majority of us find this action of the WCC to be the most important thing it has done in its history.'[53] This was reasserted when the Council met in Dublin in 1973. Fifteen years later the PCR is still not officially supported by the Church of England.

In general it may be said of the Church's response to racism, as Gutteridge said of the German Church's response to the treatment of the Jews: 'It is hard to escape the conclusion that to the great majority of churchmen, this was a matter of no real concern.'[54] The Church in Britain is not in the forefront of the movement for racial justice, despite the fact that some church organizations have been playing vital roles and the institutions have been busy catching up. But in country and suburb and small market town, the anti-racist struggle is simply not on the agenda. The comprehension gap between the Church in the inner city and the Church in the more prosperous suburbs is growing wider by the hour.

What, then, should the future hold for Christians in an age of rising racism? And how does Tawney's thinking throw light on our responsibility? I believe that a prime necessity is for a theologically-based, carefully planned disentanglement of the Church from the capitalist system. Tawney was very clear about the incompatibility between Christian principles and the capitalist spirit: 'Compromise is as impossible between the Church of Christ and the idolatry of wealth, which is the practical religion of capitalist societies, as it was between the

Church and the State idolatry of the Roman Empire.'[55]

The reality, however, is very different, and simply wishing it were not so will not effect change. Many Christians believe that there is a 'third way', a neutral position between capitalism and socialism, from which Christians can work. If by this is meant the impossibility of a simple identification of the Kingdom of God with any specific political system, then one can agree. But for a Church which is deeply implicated in the structures of capitalism to postulate a third way is to assume a situation which in fact has to be created. If racial oppression, internationally and internally, is bound up with the system of investments, profits, labour needs and so on, there can be no real attack on racism without a corresponding attack on the structures of capitalism. Simply to seek racial harmony at the local level, or to place the odd black bishop on the episcopal bench, will not in themselves be adequate. Institutional racism does exist in Britain and it cannot be defeated without a struggle. But, as in the attack on all structural sin, the forces of injustice are very powerful. Christians who enter the anti-racist struggle must expect the most violent and vicious opposition, and they will need all the theological and spiritual resources they can get.

Second, there needs to be a reassertion by the Church – or at least by those members of the Church who believe it! – that equality is of the nature of God and of humankind. To assert this is not only to contradict the fundamental dogma of the present government, and therefore to place the Church firmly in the camp of opposition; it is also to contradict many of the assumptions and trends within authoritarian socialism. Most of all, it is to recognize that the ideology of inequality is most deeply entrenched within the structures of the Church itself. No part of English society is more unequal, more allied to privilege, more culture-bound, more rooted in the private educational system or more alien to working-class people than the Church of England. It is absurd to expect a sustained anti-racist campaign from such a body unless those within it are prepared to combat the social inequality which is so much a part of its own history and life. But this is not to say that we must put the anti-racist struggle into cold storage until we have created a classless society within the Church: the process of radicalization is indivisible. The racial crisis may well be a sieve through which a whole range of impurities in British Christianity will be purged.

Racism in the Church, in its theology, its culture, its institutions and its membership, goes very deep, and the consciousness of its presence remains dim. The attack on church racism must be many-pronged and it has hardly begun. The roots of racism in white society must be penetrated and critiqued, and this ministry of exorcism will not go unresisted. There must be a thorough scrutiny of the spiritual formation of clergy and ministers for work in a multiracial society, for the evidence is that they are not being adequately prepared for their role. The criteria for the choice of bishops in the Church of England remain consistently mysterious, but it seems unlikely that they include evangelical witness against racism. Recently a new bishop was announced for the part of London which includes Notting Hill, where the local churches and community groups are deeply involved with issues of racism, policing, unemployment, housing and so on. Yet all that we were told in the press report (which is the normal way in which Anglicans in England discover who their bishops are to be) about the views of the new bishop on any subject, religious or secular, was that he was opposed to the ordination of women.[56] Is racism so unimportant an issue in Notting Hill that it has no place in the appointment of a bishop for that area, or does not at least merit a mention? Are we not entitled to know something of the commitment of future Christian leaders on such matters? Is it reasonable to have to wait for cases of formal heresy before a bishop's credibility is questioned? 'What did you do in the great war, daddy?' would seem to be a reasonable question for the faithful to ask of their father in God. But all too often the response would be: 'What war?' The war against racism has not entered the consciousness of most churchpeople, even of most bishops, who have promised at their consecration to 'drive away all erroneous and strange doctrine'.

Even in areas where the Church has taken up a formal position, the practice often is in conflict with the rhetoric. Thus in November 1978 the General Synod of the Church of England passed a resolution urging the dioceses to raise £100,000 per year for the Race Relations Projects Fund of the British Council of Churches. The annual contributions have never come remotely near the projected total, while to this day, the response from a number of dioceses remains nil. And this is on the whole not as a result of opposition so much as sheer unawareness of what all the fuss is about.

In a hostile and unfair review of 'the socialism of R. H. Tawney',[57] Alasdair MacIntyre claimed that Tawney never came to terms with the developed nature of capitalism in the era of big corporations and multinationals, and that the moral denunciation of a system is no substitute for efficient attack on it. Testifying to Tawney's essential goodness, MacIntyre asked his readers if they would prefer their shoes to be mended by a good cobbler or a good man. Christians will be unhappy at the simple separation of moral goodness from political action, but MacIntyre's point is that we need to move beyond moral protest to the political attack on structures. This is particularly true of the struggle against racism within the Christian community.

In 1969 the Central Committee of the World Council of Churches stated:

> It is no longer sufficient to deal with the race problem at the level of person to person relationships. It is *institutional racism* as reflected in the economic and political power structures which must be challenged. Combating racism must entail a *redistribution* of social, economic, political and cultural *power* from the powerful to the powerless.[58]

The Church's campaign against racism has to shift from sentiment and moral rhetoric to the confrontation of power, including its own power. And it is at this point that faces begin to drop, sympathizers uneasily edge away, and tolerance changes to implacable opposition. It is at this point that our false friends betray the cause and our true friends are revealed. It is at this point that we may usefully recall Tawney's insistence on 'recourse to principles'. For the Church is not called to compromise with organized injustice, still less to enter into dialogue with it, but to seek to end it.

11

Racism and the Urban Parish

The parish system as we know it in England was devised by Theodore of Tarsus, Archbishop of Canterbury in the seventh century, though he was building upon pre-Christian land arrangements involving pagan religious functionaries. The word 'parish' is derived from the Greek *paroikia* and the Latin *parochia*, meaning 'district'. The parish system was in origin a missionary structure for a network of small agricultural communities, the parish unit being based on agrarian acreage. From early times the English parish has also been a unit of civic administration, and the word has been used throughout history to describe neighbourhood units – what we would now call wards or, in earlier times, entire towns or villages. As a purely territorial notion, it is plainly inadequate for Christian purposes, and Anglicans in the United States (along with other denominations) have abandoned it altogether. There the term 'parish' simply means the congregation, which may be gathered from far and wide and to which the neighbourhood in which the church building is located may be totally irrelevant.

In this chapter I shall use the term to mean the community of faith which meets to worship and serve God and witness to the Kingdom within the framework of a specific neighbourhood. The neighbourhood emphasis is of crucial importance. For the whole concept of the parish witnesses to the impossibility of discipleship in a social vacuum. Our faith, our following of Jesus, our spirituality, our struggle for justice, our resistance to evil, can only occur within the context in which we are placed. It is there that the work of redemption begins and pursues its course. There is something seriously wrong, theologically and ethically, with a Christian community which sees its environment as an irrelevant accident.

The parish church or centre, therefore, should be a place in which the reality of the gospel is lived out in relation to a local neighbourhood, a place to which the needs, frustrations, struggles, joys and sorrows of that neighbourhood are brought and integrated into prayer and struggle. The nature of the parish community was expressed well in a small book from the 1960s by Kilmer Myers, later to become Bishop of California, in which he wrote of his ministry in New York's Lower East Side. Myers described the nature of the parish in this way.

> A parish is made up of a number of redeemed sinners who live in a society which is in large measure unredeemed. The parish is the classical cell whose members are infiltrators into a world mainly hostile to the claims of the Gospel. Its mission is to the sinner. It is a body of people under a divine directive which is to reach out in love to those whose lives are torn and mangled by personal and social sin. It seeks to draw into its fellowship those who do not belong to anything or anyone. It is a center of acceptance and relationships. It therefore does not, cannot, exist for itself . . . The object of the parish in the history of the community which it encompasses is peace, salvation, wholeness, unity, health. This objective is God's who chooses to embody himself in the person, the place and the thing, in order that men may be saved from sin and death.
>
> A parish consists of a group of people who are in relation to each other on the levels of love and forgiveness. And since we never are in such a relationship *in vacuo,* there must be a centre, a point in time and space, where love and forgiveness may have their way. Therefore there is a House about which the life of the parish revolves. It is the parish church which also is a house of hospitality. A parish is, in a real sense, a place. Its physical centre may be a store front or a Gothic structure. It doesn't matter so long as a climate of acceptance and forgiveness is felt to be present and appropriable by all who enter.[1]

The parish, therefore, is one geographically based material point at which the gospel of redemption is proclaimed and realized. It is one point at which evils, including the evil of racism, are encountered and overcome. If that conflict does not take place at the local level, it will have no hope of success at the national or international level.

However, today's parish is a much larger unit than was originally envisaged, and the tendency in urban areas is to merge or group parishes into even bigger units. The effect on the quality, or even the possibility, of pastoral care can be very serious. David Wasdell's work on urban churches has shown that congregations often reach saturation point at around sixty-five members. This figure, according to Wasdell, represents a saturated secondary group just as twelve is a saturated primary group. Wasdell argues that, beyond a certain point, authentic relationships as well as pastoral care cease to exist because the unit has become too large.[2] Wasdell has been accused of 'numerical determinism' and his figures are open to question. But the basic point remains valid: the larger the unit, the less likely it is that pastoral care and grassroots ministry can occur. Urban parishes within multiracial neighbourhoods have an added problem. If they are already stretched to the point where personal care is at a minimum, they are unlikely to have the inner resources and commitment, and therefore are unlikely to be able to devote the time which is needed to reach out towards newcomers, immigrants, people of other faiths or none – indeed to anyone outside the immediate circle of their church. Yet it is precisely at this point that the local faith community has a crucial role to play, for the encounter with race and racism must begin with the smallest urban unit.

Racism manifests itself at the neighbourhood level as well as at the level of national policies and international relations. It is at the neighbourhood level that its effects are most deeply felt: in the Asian family subject to racial violence, in the unemployed white teenager who sees black people as the cause of his or her plight, in the wealthy and influential resident who sees no connection between his or her position in society and the demands of the gospel. The parish church, focused at the point of the local neighbourhood community, is in a position to ignore, or to engage with and seek to combat, racism at this level. Many churches choose the former course. They see themselves as a group of people called to worship and to maintain and develop the life of the church, but they do not engage with the world and its pain. The transformation of such groups into genuinely redemptive cells calls for more than a recognition of specific evils:

it calls for a new attitude towards the world, towards injustice and oppression, towards the purpose of the church itself. It calls for a different theological framework. More will be said about this later.

But if we assume that a parish does wish to take issues of race and racism seriously, how can this manifest itself in concrete forms? How does the urban parish combat racism in its own life and in the life of the surrounding environment?

The parish at worship

It does so, first, in its worship. Worship is at the heart of the church's life. In worship human persons stretch out their hands and hearts towards God. They do so as a community of equals; redeemed sinners bound for glory. In worship all distinctions of race, class, wealth and so on are done away. Worship cannot be Christian if it is not established on this egalitarian basis. Such worship is a subversive act, rooted in the values of equality and community, the very values which the racist philosophies and practices deny. The greatest care needs to be given to the act of worship, for it creates and demonstrates the church's life and character. How worship is offered reveals more about the self-understanding, the theology, the assumptions of the local church than anything else does.

The way in which worship is offered is called liturgy, and liturgy is absolutely central to the struggle against racism. This will be a strange and unfamiliar idea to many, not least to mainstream liturgical scholars. Yet it is in the liturgy that our deepest and most fundamental commitments and aspirations are expressed in symbolic and sacramental forms. Liturgy shapes us at very profound levels of consciousness. The struggles for justice must be incorporated into our liturgical consciousness and embodied in the rites which express them. And here we have a serious problem. In the Church of England, formal liturgical expression is based upon the work of white, mainly male, scholars who are not close to the struggles of the urban parish. Liturgy and social justice have been driven apart. So our official formularies do not at all express what needs to be said and done in this area.

Take the depressing and woefully inadequate Alternative

Service Book, which perpetuates sexist language into the twenty-first century and ignores the existence of racism (and of black people and their spiritual traditions) altogether. The Preface to the book admits that 'any liturgy . . . belongs to a particular period and culture'. However, it goes on to claim that 'those who seek to know the mind of the Church of England in the last quarter of the twentieth century will find it in this book'.[3] If this is true, it serves only to reinforce how distant is the 'mind of the Church of England' from the realities of a multiracial society. While the book contains various forms for use at enthronements, institutions and inductions of prelates and clerics, even including a blessing of an abbot – a fairly rare occasion in the Church of England, one might have thought! – it contains no reference to racial justice or equality, and there is no recognition of the multiracial character of our society. The nearest one gets to any concern with social justice is a form for use 'for social responsibility', one for the peace of the world and one for 'civic occasions'.

So it is important that liturgical renewal takes place at the local parish level. The bureaucrats can catch up later. It is absurd to expect parishes in the thick of the struggle against racial injustice to wait until the consciousness of the Liturgical Commission of the Church of England has been sufficiently raised before we start to incorporate the conflict with social evil into our worship. There needs to be experimentation which is nourished and supported by prayer and action. Liturgy must grow from below and must express the spirituality and the social commitment of the community. Bad liturgy is not likely to inspire and energize a ministry for racial justice. It is very likely to reinforce and perpetuate theologies of oppression. Good liturgy can be a powerful instrument for instilling the vision and values of the Kingdom of God in the hearts, minds and wills of the worshippers.

Take, for example, the liturgy of baptism. The renunciations and the covenant of baptism contain an explicit anti-racist dimension. It is brought out best in the rite of the Episcopal Church of the USA. The candidate is asked, for example:

> Do you renounce Satan and all the spiritual forces of wickedness that rebel against God?

> Do you renounce the evil powers of this world which corrupt and destroy the creatures of God?

A few minutes later, the following questions are asked:

> Will you persevere in resisting evil, and, whenever you fall into sin, repent and return to the Lord? . . .
> Will you seek and serve Christ in all persons, loving your neighbour as yourself?
> Will you strive for justice and peace among all people, and respect the dignity of every human being?

In the teaching which accompanies preparation for baptism, these renunciations and commitments need to be emphasized and related to specific struggles. Racism is one of the spiritual forces of wickedness which is renounced, it is among the 'evil powers of this world which corrupt and destroy the creatures of God'. The renunciation of these evil powers is a condition of becoming a Christian. To serve Christ in all persons, and to respect the dignity of every human being, are clear anti-racist mandates. Racism is a denial of baptism, a regression to the prebaptismal, unregenerate state.

Or take the central act of Christian worship, the Eucharist. In the Eucharist we assert and enact our solidarity in Christ, our *koinonia* or common life in him. The eucharistic action undermines all ideas of hierarchy based on class, wealth or race. It is an essentially egalitarian and communal act, which is one reason why many conservative Anglicans prefer the apparently safer territory of Morning Prayer (although if they listened to the lessons from the Old Testament they would find them equally uncomfortable!) The parish community celebrating the eucharistic memorial of the dying and rising of Christ is performing a fundamental action for humanity and against racism.

The Eucharist is not simply a ritual act which has meaning within its own contours. It is a microcosm of a redeemed society. 'Just as this Eucharistic action is the pattern of all Christian action, the sharing of this bread the sign for the sharing of all bread, so this fellowship is the germ of all society redeemed in Christ.'[4] The parish needs to take very seriously the consequences of being a eucharistic community, of living out the eucharistic principles in an anti-eucharistic, anti-communal world. Racism is one dimension of this basic world view which is rooted in individualism, competition and division. But if worship and prayer shape us fundamentally, at a gut level, then there is no more important act that we can perform than one in which we commit ourselves profoundly and in the depths of our beings to equality and community.

At the Eucharist we are united with the people of God in all ages. The solidarity is not only across geographical, racial and cultural boundaries, but across time and history. John Davies, drawing on years of experience in South Africa, emphasizes the doctrine of the Communion of Saints:

> A Christianity which fails to teach this doctrine can do little about our racial, national or tribal consciousness except tell us to grow out of it, be ashamed of it, or suppress it. Catholicism can recognise that our racial consciousness is indeed part of our created nature: but it also insists that in Christ's descent to Hell he has healed the antagonism which made our ancestors enemies of each other, and that the Christian altar is the meeting place of all the human race, living and departed, in all their ancestral identities.[5]

The sacrifice of Christ, in which we share in each eucharistic celebration, must be recognized, proclaimed and manifested as the healing work in which racial and national limitations are transcended and a new humanity is born. But even where this is not apparent, in churches where there is little awareness of the revolutionary significance of the Eucharist, there is a subversive power which derives from the sacrament itself and which works to undermine the forces of division. A eucharistic sensibility is bound to develop, often in spite of the prejudices, divisions and wishes of the community present, a sensibility which results from the nature of the sacrament. To celebrate the Eucharist is in itself a revolutionary and anti-racist act. It promotes change by its very nature.

In worship it is important that the tradition and gifts of the gathered people are used and expressed. This is part of the meaning of the offertory. Many white-led churches pay no attention to the black Christian heritage even though a sizeable minority, or even a majority, of their members may be black. The black Christian tradition in music is of great historical and theological significance, as the recent rediscovery of gospel music has shown. Martin Luther King used gospel music as a way of rallying his supporters in the Civil Rights Movement of the 1960s. Gospel music grew as the descendants of the slaves moved into urban areas. As the spirituals had developed as the music of communities in captivity, so gospel music developed as the music of the urban black communities seeking the Kingdom. 'It was and is an indispensable support system for the survival, the establishment, growth and continuity, of Black congregations and community as well as Black liberation theology.'[6]

The incorporation of what has been called the 'sublimated outrage' of the spirituals into mainstream white worship would help white Christians to understand the history of slavery, without which there can be no real understanding of racism. Some hymns from the gospel music tradition, such as 'Amazing Grace', written by the former slave-ship captain John Newton in the eighteenth century, have, of course, become popular in the worship of white Christians. Some gospel hymns originated in one way and developed in quite different directions. For example, 'We Shall Overcome' originated in a hymn 'I'll Overcome Someday' by the black pastor Charles Tindley (1856–1933). If we are to create genuinely multiracial worship in our churches, there needs to be an awareness by white Christians of the tremendous gifts and riches of the black Christian community. The recently established network Claiming the Inheritance, set up by black Christians in the Birmingham area, has already brought together large numbers of black Christians to explore what is for many a forgotten history.

An essential element in Christian liturgy is prayer at particular places and at particular times of the day. My experience in Bethnal Green in the 1970s suggests that both are essential in the struggle with racism. Certain places become associated with racial incitement and violence. In our area, a particular stretch of Bethnal Green Road between Brick Lane and Chilton Street was contaminated Sunday by Sunday by the presence of the National Front and its followers. It became essential to pray intensely at this point, to celebrate a rite of decontamination, to reclaim it for the Kingdom of God. On several occasions I sprinkled the area with holy water and prayed that it might be set free from the evil forces which had polluted it.

Moreover, since racial violence and the loneliness and fear associated with it often occur at night, there is a vital place for the praying group which floods the night with intercession and seeks to redeem the night hours for the power of love and gentleness. A network of disciplined systematic intercessors can be of great value in areas infected with racial violence and hatred. It is essential that intercessions are offered regularly for racist groups, their leaders, and those seduced by them; for the perpetrators as well as the victims of racial attacks; and for those in positions to influence the course of events in the field of race relations. Racism is a manifestation of spiritual evil, and it must be fought with the weapons of prayer, fasting and sacrifice.

I have devoted considerable space to the question of worship, because it is in worship most of all that the church expresses its identity and its central focus. If the commitment to a non-racial world and the resistance to the evil of racism is not integrated into this central activity, it will have little hope of success in the peripheral areas of the church's life.

Church, gospel and theology

Second, the parish community confronts racism through its preaching of the gospel. More will be said about this in the next chapter. The gospel proclaims a new humanity, a new creation in Christ. The Son of Man was manifested to destroy the works of the Devil. Racism is clearly a work of the Devil. The critique of racism must be seen as a necessary element in Christian preaching and teaching. Bishops need to bear this in mind when they issue pastoral letters, and parish clergy when they write their parish newsletters and magazines.

The Church is itself an integral part of the gospel. It is a chosen race, a holy nation (1 Peter 2.9). It is a global community. The people to whom Peter addressed his letter, people from Asia, Pontus, Galatia, Cappadocia and Bithynia (1.1), were people of different ethnic origins. The community is seen as a *genos*, a new race. The term *triton genos*, third race, was used derisively of the early Christians. The fact that Christian community transcends nationality is clear from the New Testament (Rom. 1.16; 3.29; Gal. 3.26–8; Col. 3.11). The truth of the gospel must be manifested within the life of this community. The new humanity must be visibly embodied. However, there are Christian groups whose approach helps to reinforce the captivity of the Church to the dominant culture. The American church growth movement, for example, stresses the value of the homogeneous unit. As one of its leaders Donald McGavran has written, 'Men [*sic*] like to become Christians without crossing racial, linguistic or class barriers.'[7] On the other hand, the Chicago theologian James Gustafson has argued that the 'heterogeneous principle' is vital in a church if it is to be protected against a simple reinforcement of cultural norms.[8] A local parish needs to ask itself whether it is merely reinforcing the values of the dominant culture, or witnessing to the new humanity demanded by the gospel.

If the local church is truly living out the character of the gospel, it will be a focal point of welcome for the stranger and the alien, a home for the homeless and unloved, a place of sanctuary for the refugee. It will be a place which opens its doors to the community. Yet very often, even in areas of conflict, the church is remote from what is happening, and is often reduced to being no more than a 'haven of rest for the elderly',[9] a place of refuge rather than of transformation. Churches which see themselves merely as refuges cannot hope to combat the evils of racism. And the way in which they see themselves will be visibly manifested and easily recognizable: a closed church, closed against the community, speaks more powerfully than any number of words. A church which is open and welcoming, warm and inviting, speaks powerfully of Christ who welcomes all.

Third, the parish needs to combat racism theologically. Theology is not an activity for academics, remote in intellectual ghettoes, but an activity for Christian people at street level. It involves a continuous and rigorous process of interrogation and discernment of what God is doing and how the events of the world and of the local community can be understood in relation to the will and purpose of God. It is a process in which mistakes will be made. It has to be a corporate exercise in which there is mutual criticism and correction. It is through the encounter of

Christian truths with the conflicts and issues of the day that the meaning of those truths will be recognized and personalized.

The listening community

Fourth, the local church will only be an effective witness against racism if it is a listening church. All pastoral ministry is based on the ability to listen. Christians need to listen to the voices of the powerless and the neglected, to the voices which are silenced or suppressed beneath the clamour of the streets. Often churches are out of contact with the groups and movements which are at work within their neighbourhoods, and even more out of touch with what Martin Luther King called the voices of the unheard. They do not have their ears to the ground. They have become communities of the deaf. As a result, their words are empty and lifeless, for they do not connect with the reality of human need. All pastoral work and all work for social justice must be rooted in contemplative listening.

This contemplative spirit is particularly important for white clergy and laity in their encounters with the black community. For they will come with their inherited stereotypes, reinforced by the racism of the press and by accumulated ignorance. Such accumulated and reinforced ignorance can only be undone by sustained listening and willingness to learn. And this process cannot be short-circuited or abbreviated. There are centuries, the centuries of slavery and colonialism, to be grappled with at the level of personal encounter. It is high time for white people, who have been vocal for so long, to become silent and let black voices, including black Christian voices, be heard.

The ministry of listening is important also in building relationships with people of other faiths. There was a time when the Church of England lumped them all together as 'Jews, Turks, Infidels and Heretics',[10] and the attitude embodied in that phrase is still widespread. Non-Christians can be seen not as people but as conversion material. So pastoral contact can easily become 'a kind of exploitation, a new religious imperialism, a theological form of racial harassment'.[11] In spite of the great progress made in inter-faith dialogue in recent years, the picture at the local level is often depressing and rooted in ignorant stereotypes. Thus when a plan was launched to build a mosque in Southampton, one local church opposed it, denouncing Islam as 'an evil religion . . . a barbaric and bloodthirsty teaching'.[12]

Listening is a necessary part of the ministry of the parish which, because it contains (or thinks it contains) relatively small numbers of black people, claims that it 'does not have the problem'. When people claim that they 'do not have the problem', they usually mean that they do not have any black people. Behind this claim is a major assumption: that racism only arises when there are black people to produce it. It is essential that such churches recognize their own part in perpetuating racial injustice. Yet this task is normally ignored, because the issue is seen in a grossly simplistic way: no blacks, no race problem, no action needed. Yet there is a whole range of issues which need to be addressed. For example:

> What newspapers do the congregation take? In the present climate, the crudity of the racism expressed in most of the tabloids (not to mention their exploitation of women and general contempt for human dignity) is such that one must face the question of whether to subscribe to such papers is an act of sin for Christian people. Yet how many parish priests raise this question in their teaching and spiritual direction?
>
> How do church members relate to racial issues in their places of work? Do they work for companies which practise discrimination, or which are attempting to initiate equal opportunities policies, or which have not begun to think about the question? Are they, through their work, promoting disadvantage? What position do their companies take on South Africa? If they are teachers, where do they stand on anti-racist education?
>
> How do these members exercise political responsibility through political parties or through their trade unions? Are they helped to exercise such responsibility as Christians?

Once the local church begins to ask questions such as these, a whole new area of connections opens up, and the possibilities for action grow. And this must lead to a recognition of the terrible mass of inaction and apathy which has built up within the white church. The consciousness of its seriousness must bring us to our knees.

Racism and repentance

And so, fifth, racism calls the local parish to repentance. A necessary element in repentance is self-examination. But if the community is to practise self-examination, it must be a corporate discipline. The parish community needs systematically and prayerfully to examine its past and present witness. How far does it reflect the composition of its neighbourhood? Are any groups being excluded? What kind of communication is there with such excluded groups? Are the gifts and insights of groups and individuals within the community being used? Are future ministers being sought from among black Christians? These are only some of the questions which must be asked.

We saw earlier how the churches in Notting Hill in the 1950s failed dismally to offer welcome or support to the new immigrants from the Caribbean. The same story could be repeated for other parts of the country. Local churches need to recognize, and learn from, the failings of their predecessors.

In self-examination and repentance, the church is brought face to face with its own prejudice and hatred. Here is the most difficult and most painful area of the local church's life. For it must be recogized that religious people are often not simply no more loving and open than their neighbours who are outside organized religion; the evidence suggests that they are often less loving, more intolerant and prejudiced, less open to new people and new insights. Churches can be deeply prejudiced and fearful enclaves. In the process of repentance, the pastor needs to teach about the nature of sin and the place of forgiveness and of amendment of life.

Wrestling with the powers

Sixth, the parish is called to struggle against racism as one aspect of the struggle with principalities and powers. We saw earlier how slow the churches in the East End of London were to respond to the threat posed by the National Front and its satellites, and to the growth of racial violence. The local church should be the first place to organize opposition to the racist movements, the first place to offer support and protection to the victims of violence. The sad reality is that the church catches up with the needs years after others have done so. If churches are to become part of the organized struggle against racism, they themselves need to be organized and efficient. The pursuit of righteousness has to be an informed, mobilized pursuit. It calls for discipline and efficiency as well as goodwill and purity of heart.

The local church needs to see itself as part of an international society. Racism is indivisible. It cannot be opposed here and supported elsewhere. Many churches find it easier to support missionaries in Pakistan than to befriend and support an isolated Pakistani in their own parish. Others may respond to incidents of racial discrimination on their own doorstep but fail to make any connection between these incidents and events in South Africa which manifest the same pattern. To recognize that the small parish unit is part of an international community is a valuable way of helping local churches to see their own multiracial and multinational character. The Anglican Church, for instance, is on a world scale a mainly black Church. It is only by seeing it in narrowly English terms that we fail to realize this. It is vital that we learn to think across national and racial boundaries if we are to overcome the racism of our own culture. Anything, including exchange visits and links between parishes, which can help to do this will be valuable.

The parish can only face and overcome racism if it is a community in movement. If the parish sees itself primarily as a preserving body, committed to the defence of the old order, then it is very likely to defend racism as one of the features of that order. The parish needs to see itself as a pilgrim community, constantly on the move, learning new truths, discerning the will of God in the process of movement and struggle towards the Kingdom. If its priorities and its values lie in the new humanity of the future, and not in the preservation of the old order of the past, it will be a force for justice and against racism.

12

Racism and the Proclamation of the Gospel

A gospel of human unity

The Christian faith claims that it is a faith for all nations, a universal faith witnessing to a universal Kingdom. The Jewish and Christian Scriptures, while they contain many examples of ethnic, tribal and localized happenings, are emphatic that Yahweh is the God of all the nations of the earth. Unlike the pagan territorial gods, the God of Abraham, Isaac and Jacob is a God who is known in the process of migration from place to place. The liberation of Israel from Egypt occurred in order to show that the earth is the Lord's (Exod. 9.29). God is identified as Yahweh your God 'from the land of Egypt' (Hos. 12.9; 13.4). Yet the specificity of that act of liberation is complemented by the fact that the God who brought up Israel from Egypt also brought up the Philistines from Caphtor and the Syrians from Kir (Amos 9.7). The community of Israel is seen as one which will in time encompass all humanity and the created order itself, a vision which is brought out most powerfully in Second Isaiah.

> It is too light a thing that you should be my servant to raise up the tribes of Jacob and to restore the preserved of Israel; I will give you as a light to the nations, that my salvation may reach to the end of the earth (Isa. 49.6).

> Behold, I will lift up my hand to the nations, and raise my signal to the peoples; and they shall bring your sons in their bosom, and your daughters shall be carried on their shoulders (49.22).

> And the foreigners who join themselves to the Lord, to minister to him, to live the name of the Lord, and to be his

> servants, every one who keeps the sabbath, and does not profane it, and holds fast my covenant – these I will bring to my holy mountain, and make them joyful in my house of prayer . . . for my house shall be called a house of prayer for all people (56.6–7).

> I am coming to gather all nations and tongues; and they shall come and shall see my glory (66.18).

The books with which the Old Testament concludes contain several visions of universal worship. All nations will come to Jerusalem to worship, according to Zechariah (8.20–3; 14.16), while Malachi prophesies: 'For from the rising of the sun to its setting my name is great among the nations, and in every place incense is offered to my name, and a pure offering; for my name is great among the nations, says the Lord of hosts' (Mal. 1.11). As the Old Testament moves outwards from the particular experience of Israel to the universal vision of the age to come, we find a similar pattern in Jesus' ministry and teaching. Thus while he attacks anti-Samaritan views (Luke. 9.54–5) and holds up the Samaritan as a model (Luke. 10.33), he nevertheless tells his followers not to enter any Samaritan town (Matt. 10.5). Yet we later find him assuring them that when the Holy Spirit comes upon them, they will be ready to go not only to the Samaritans but to all nations (Acts 1.8).

The ministry of Jesus moves between the two poles of Galilee and Jerusalem. Beginning in the despised and rebellious region of 'Galilee of the nations' (Isa. 9.1), he moves towards the city of Jerusalem. In setting his face towards Jerusalem (Luke. 9.51), Jesus heads for a city which was a major multi-ethnic centre, even more so than usual at Passover time. The crowds who came for Passover often stayed until Pentecost, and during this period, according to Jeremias, the city's population grew from 25,000 to 150,000.[1] Jesus' ministry reaches its climax and crisis in Jerusalem, and here he meets his death at Passover time. Jerusalem is portrayed in the Gospels as the city of unbelief and rejection, the city which kills the prophets and does not know the things which make for peace. But it is also the place of resurrection, and from here the risen Jesus moves back to Galilee, and from there to all races and nations (Matt. 28.16ff). In Luke's account, the gospel proclamation is said to begin at Jerusalem (Luke. 24.47) and to move outwards. In John, 'Galilee is the place where the past is recovered in such a way as to make it the foundation for a new and extended identity, the soil on which a redeemed future may grow.'[2] It is an identity and a future which transcends ethnic and tribal limitations, divisions of race and nation; an identity and a future which is not racial; an identity and a future in which humanity is restored to its primal unity.

In the history of the early Church as recorded in the Acts of the Apostles, we can recognize a process of liberation from cultural captivity, a process which the resurrection initiates and energizes. But it is necessary to remember that the resurrection experience occurred within the context created by the faith of Israel. It was the universal thrust of Jewish, not Christian, faith which originally brought together the varied nations listed in Acts 2. Nevertheless, the account is one which has important consequences for Christian identity. For it describes the way in which the experience of Christ's resurrection and the consequent outpouring of the Holy Spirit brought about a transcendence of racial and linguistic barriers.

> Now there were dwelling in Jerusalem Jews, devout men from every nation under heaven. And at this sound the multitude came together, and they were bewildered, because each one heard them speaking in his own language. And they were amazed and wondered, saying, 'Are not all these who are speaking Galileans? And how is it that we hear, each of us in his own native language? Parthians and Medes and Elamites and residents of Mesopotamia, Judea and Cappadocia, Pontus and Asia, Phrygia and Pamphylia, Egypt and the parts of Libya belonging to Cyrene, and visitors from Rome, both Jews and proselytes, Cretans and Arabians, we hear them telling in our own tongues the mighty works of God' (Acts 2.5–11).

The Pentecostal experience here is clearly seen as one which overcomes racial barriers. But this non-racial dimension of the experience, and of the community which grew from it, is one aspect of a more pervasive thrust towards equality and common life. The Pentecostal community was characterized by its sharing of goods and life, and by the fact that it was a community of equals.

Acts goes on to describe the appointment of 'seven men of good repute' (6.3) – usually described as deacons though the word does not occur in the text – as a result of which the movement into Gentile territory began, and a whole new power structure grew up within the Church. Stephen, we are told, went to the 'synagogue of the Freedmen' (6.9), a synagogue which included people from Cyrene in North Africa, Alexandria in Egypt, and Turkey. The great speech of Stephen was a major attack on any ethnocentric understanding of revelation. God, he argued, appeared to Abraham when he was in Mesopotamia (7.2), that is, not in Palestine. He goes on to refer to Joseph in Egypt and to Moses in Midian. It has been said of this speech: 'Stephen's explosive message made Judaism a universal faith. Anyone could come to God and be fully related to him without adopting an ethnocentric Palestinian form of the religion.'[3]

The non-racial character of the gospel is reinforced in the story of Cornelius (Acts 10). Peter is very explicit as to the meaning of the incident. 'You yourselves know how unlawful it is for a Jew to associate with or to visit any one of another nation; but God has shown me that I should not call any man common or unclean' (10.28). It is in Acts 11 that we find a further account by Peter of the significance of this incident for the Gentile mission. In this chapter we find the Church beginning to live in a multicultural way. At first the scattered Christians spoke only to Jews, we are told (11.19). But some, from Cyprus and Cyrene, spoke also to Greeks (11.20). As a result Barnabas, himself a Cypriot (4.36), was sent to Antioch, and it was here that the word 'Christian' came to be used (11.26). Here we find the black man Simeon, the Greek Lucius and the Jew Manaen, as well as Barnabas and Paul. Thus it seems that it is only at the point that the Church becomes recognizably a multiracial and multicultural community that it is described as 'Christian'. And this brings us to a theme which is central to the meaning of the gospel in the New Testament: that of the unity and solidarity of humankind.

According to Paul, while we were alienated from God, he reconciled us by the death of Christ (Rom. 5.10). Our unity is a unity in Christ (12.5). In Christ there is already a new creation (2

Cor. 5.17; Gal. 6.15). Paul tells us that those who have been baptized have 'put on Christ'. As a result of this act of baptism, 'There is neither Jew nor Greek, there is neither slave nor free, there is neither male nor female; for you are all one in Christ Jesus' (Gal. 3.27–8). However, it is the Letter to the Ephesians which most emphatically locates the unity of humanity and of the entire created order within a theological framework. God's will is 'to unite all things in him [Christ], things in heaven and things on earth' (1.10). Paul tells his readers to remember their former condition when they were separate from Christ and strangers to the community of Israel. But now they have been brought near by Christ's blood. Christ has broken down the dividing wall of hostility and created a single new humanity (2.11–22). It is possible that the 'dividing wall of hostility' is a reference to the destruction of the actual wall of Jerusalem,[4] thus endowing the great historical catastrophe with theological significance. The letter goes on to speak of progress towards maturity and fullness, stressing the 'new nature' which Christians share and which has been created 'after God' (4.24).

Other letters also stress the unity which Christ has wrought. Through Christ God has reconciled all things to himself (Col. 1.20). The cosmic dimensions of Christ's work are emphasized in the phrase *ta panta* (all things), repeated six times in Colossians 1. Christians, the letter goes on, share the new nature and so 'there cannot be Greek and Jew, circumcised and uncircumcised, barbarian, Scythian, slave, free man, but Christ is all, and in all' (3.10–11). The phrase 'Jew and Greek' is used by Paul also in the Letter to the Romans (See 1.16; 2.9–10; 3.9, 29–30; 4.11–12, 16; 9.24; 10.11–13; 11.25–6; 15.8–9). Membership of the new community and inheritance of the promises is not based on physical descent but on spiritual renewal. Abraham is the father of us all (4.16). Thus at the heart of the New Testament evangel is the theme of a new humanity, based not on race, colour or ethnic origin, but on the restoration of the human race in Christ. What we now call anti-racism is thus deeply embedded in the very heart of the gospel. To base one's judgements and actions on categories of race is to undermine and renounce the whole meaning of the gospel proclamation, to deny the new creation and the new humanity. Yet the tragic fact remains that racism has, over centuries, deeply infected the Christian body, at times administering to it a near-fatal wound.

A gospel distorted by racism

The history of Christianity is marked by a constant struggle between the original egalitarian dynamic of Christ and the early Church, and the pressures of 'the world' to restore hierarchical, class-based and ethnocentric notions of privilege and power. Some writers, such as Cedric Robinson, see the origins of modern racism in medieval hierarchical notions.[5] The nobles were regarded as being of 'better blood' than the peasants, who were seen as descended from Ham, the cursed son of Noah – a claim which was later explicitly applied to black people. Here the historical details are not our concern. What is clear is that racist ideas have entered into and distorted the proclamation of the gospel and the whole understanding of the new humanity.

One aspect of this distortion goes back to the very early history of the Church, and perhaps to the New Testament itself. It is the anti-Jewish polemic which helped to nourish the soil from which both the persecution of the Jews and later the formulation of anti-Semitic ideology grew. There is no doubt that anti-Semitism owes much to the tradition of anti-Judaism which was promoted by Christian theologians. The idea that the Jews killed Christ, that the Jewish community as a whole is guilty of deicide, is deeply embedded in the Christian tradition. The Bishop of Salisbury has suggested that there may well be a link between this anti-Jewish tradition and the growth of modern racism.

> Christianity must take a major share of the blame for Nazi genocide, and also for the earlier pogroms in Russia. Anti-Judaism did not start out as racist; but in alliance with cultural forces it became racist, and we cannot, I think, be comfortably sure that Christian anti-Semitism did not prepare the ground for the racist troubles we have in respect of other communities in this country today. An act of theological penitence, and a conscious and publicly declared reappraisal of the biblical insights, including a disowning of the distorted features of the New Testament, is essential if the Churches are to address themselves to their part in the racial situation with cleansed consciences.[6]

It is essential that Christians recover their Semitic roots if we are to resist the forces today which are leading to a resurgence of anti-Semitism. We need to recognize that the Christian gospel arose out of Jewish soil. Christianity was in origin a Jewish movement, and apart from the insights and teachings of the Jewish Scriptures it is incomprehensible. The New Testament makes sense only in the context of the Old. Christians need to learn from their Jewish comrades if they are to make sense of the teachings of their own founder, who explicitly claimed to have come to fulfil, and not abrogate, the Jewish law and prophetic tradition.

Yet anti-Semitism is not the only form that Christian racism has taken. There is a long and disreputable – and continuing – tradition of Christian fundamentalism which seeks theological justification for its doctrine of racial superiority in the Bible. According to some fundamentalist Christians, black people are 'pre-Adamic', that is, they are descended not from Adam but from the earlier living creatures created before Adam. Cain established a liaison with a pre-Adamic female, and it was such interbreeding which led to the flood. But it is the curse of Canaan (Gen. 9.18–27) which occurs most frequently in attempts to defend such biblical racism. The curse pronounced by Noah upon Canaan is believed to apply to all black people, who are alleged (without evidence) to be descendants of Canaan. (It is interesting that Noah was suffering from a hangover at the time, though the argument is heard most frequently from teetotallers!) Many liberal-minded Christians in Britain assume that such ideas are discredited and of no religious or political significance. The massive resurgence of the fundamentalist and creationist movements in the United States in recent years should be a powerful warning that such crudities are by no means dead.

Many years ago Thomas Merton, in a perceptive and prophetic article on the growth of a new militant Christian Right, warned that 'a bastard ersatz of Christian faith' was a major factor in the rise of racism in the USA. Linking this phenomenon with the growth of anti-communism, Merton saw the movement as 'a political and social pseudo-religion which also exhibits symptoms of mass paranoia'.[7] Indeed racism exhibits many features of a religious crusade. Recognition of the Christian elements in the origins of racism may lead us to the view that in confronting this evil we are confronting a heresy which has now reached the dimensions of an alternative gospel and an alternative world view. And if this is so, then to examine and confront racism will be to illuminate and strengthen our grasp of the meaning of the gospel and of the Christian view of the world.

The need for white and black liberation

If racism is deeply rooted in Christian history, then a necessary preliminary to the proclamation of the gospel within the context of modern racism is for white Christians to recognize those elements within their tradition and seek to be delivered from them. A process of purification, a *via negativa*, is needed if we are to be set free from these alien elements which have distorted and continue to distort our message. We need to approach our liturgies, our biblical assumptions, our theological systems, with what Segundo calls 'ideological suspicion',[8] that is, with the expectation that these things are very likely to have been distorted by ideological elements, including racism.

We see, for example, the way in which evangelical individualism, combined with a particular interpretation of the Calvinist teaching about election, helped to create the apartheid ideology in South Africa. We see the way in which the Ku Klux Klan in the southern States of the USA grew up in well-nourished Baptist and Methodist soil. But we should not be so quick to condemn such aberrations that we fail to recognize similar features in our own British Christian history. That great Anglican Charles Kingsley, one of the founders of Christian socialism, described the Irish as white chimpanzees, the gypsies as savages, and blacks as 'falling, generation after generation, by the working of original sin'. The black inhabitants of Borneo, he claimed, were not human but apes.[9] While it would be difficult to find theologians expressing similar views today, it is very common for theology, as for Christian teaching and discipleship in general, to accept uncritically the prejudices and governing assumptions of the dominant culture. So the examination of racism raises a larger issue: that of the way in which Christian preaching and living allows itself to succumb to the very captivity to 'the world' which was renounced at baptism, and which is so central a theme of

Paul's writings in the New Testament. To quote the Bishop of Salisbury again:

> Christians have allowed their general world view and scheme of values on all subjects to come adrift from its biblical and doctrinal roots and to be distorted and inverted by the values of the world. We simply shall never be able to exert real force and influence against the evil of racism so long as our total cultural, social and political vision is that of a civilisation in which racism is endemic. If we share the premises of our fellow citizens we need not be surprised if we find it hard work to rebut their conclusions.[10]

Of course, none of this is to deny that Christians have played an important role in overcoming racist ideas and racist practices. There is a close link between the holiness movement, deriving from Wesley's doctrine of perfection, and the ending of slavery, as there is between an incarnational, sacramental Anglicanism and the growth of resistance to apartheid by people of the Michael Scott and Trevor Huddleston generation. But such resistance is not automatic, and most Christians, whether in nineteenth-century America or in twentieth-century South Africa, have accepted racism simply as part of the way things are. A shift in consciousness, involving discernment, prayer, repentence and intellectual wrestling with painful issues, is unavoidable.

However, one result of the racism within the white churches has been the growth of independent black churches. It is very likely that in some British cities the bulk of biblical preaching week by week goes on in such churches, and certainly the growth rate of the newer black-led churches, mainly though not exclusively Pentecostal, is very high. It follows that a major aspect of the relationship between racism and the proclamation of the gospel must focus on what happens to the black churches. What kind of gospel is preached there? What kind of theological reflection takes place there? Can it provide the resources for the struggle against racism among black Christians? Undoubtedly this was the case in the United States in the 1960s, and since then there has been a significant growth of the black liberation theological tradition in that country. But do black churches in

Britain see themselves as part of this movement of black liberation theology? Are they likely to produce thinkers and activists of the calibre and influence of Martin Luther King, James Cone and Cornel West? Cone, the best known of the black theologians, has been critical of the false spirituality of many of the black churches in the USA.

> It is unfortunate that many contemporary black churches have strayed from their liberating heritage. Instead of deepening their commitment to the poor in their community and in the Third World, many have adopted the same attitudes towards the poor as have the white churches from which they separated. Too many black churches are more concerned about buying and building new church structures than they are about feeding, clothing and housing the poor. Too many pastors are more concerned about how to manipulate people for an increase in salary than they are about liberating the oppressed from socio-political bondage. If black churches do not repent by reclaiming their liberating heritage for the empowerment of the poor today, their Christian identity will be no more authentic than that of the white churches that segregated them.[11]

It would be arrogant and presumptuous for a white Christian to judge the future of the black churches in Britain. But my impression, drawn from considerable contact with black pastors and church members over the last ten years, is that Cone's words could be correctly applied to many of them. Nevertheless, the radicalization of the black Church, and its increased willingness to recognize the close link between the gospel and social justice, could be one of the most explosive and powerful forces in British Christian life in the next few decades. For the bigger churches, with their roots and leadership in mainly white North American Churches, this radicalization process would almost certainly involve a break with the American leadership.

For black and white Christians, seeking to examine their past and reconstruct their future together, the importance of careful reflection on the way in which the experience of racism illuminates the meaning of the divine gift of grace cannot be overstressed. Grace is not mediated in some ethereal realm, detached from earthly concerns, but only through and in concrete earthly events. Specifically, as Rowan Williams has pointed out, 'grace is released *only* in confrontation with the victim . . . To hear the good news of salvation, to be converted, is to turn back to the condemned and rejected, acknowledging that there is hope nowhere else.'[12] It may be that it is only through the ministry and testimony of black Christians, with their experience of condemnation and rejection, that grace can be released upon the communities and structures of white racist society.

For both black and white Christians, the memory of their corporate past is vital. To 'claim the inheritance' of the black spiritual tradition involves hearing the forgotten voices of black prayers and songs, of black rebellion and resistance, of the black movements and the black dreams. For white Christians, within Churches warped and twisted by centuries of injustice and racial oppression, the memory of those forces and movements working against the stream are a necessary part of today's spirituality of dissent. Memory is a power which can help us to survive and move beyond the present darkness. 'The cherishing of memory is partly a means of breaking the silence of subordination. The extraordinary resilience of the memory of rebellion can in certain circumstances endure coercion, hardship, ridicule, betrayal, even the sophisticated onslaught of the modern media.'[13] Black and white Christians together need to share each other's memories, dreams, reflections and struggles.

Racism as an alternative gospel

In confronting racism with the prophetic word, we need to realize its own intrinsic power as an alternative world view and an alternative hope. At heart the racist mythology offers a different view of what it is to be human. Historically this mythology has been linked with alleged truths of natural science, in particular the 'truth' of superior and inferior racial types. Today, we have what has been called a 'new racism',[14] which does not use the concepts of superior and inferior but rather those of differences, of the nation as a racial unit, and of an unchanging 'human nature'.

In this way of thinking there are a number of recurring themes. The nation takes precedence over the human race: loyalty, devotion and responsibility can only be to the nation, not to humanity as a whole. The state of nationhood becomes the truly human state. But the sense of unity as a nation is only possible among people of a common racial stock. Thus the Northern Irish and the Falkland Islanders are part of the British nation in the sense that black people born here can never be. And throughout, there is a constant appeal to 'human nature'.

Thus Enoch Powell, speaking at Eastbourne in 1968, described the English as being 'dislodged' from their homeland, a process which he argued could not continue without resistance.

> My judgement then is this: the people of England will not endure it. If so, it is idle to argue whether they ought or ought not to. I do not believe it is in human nature that a country, and a country such as ours, should passively watch the transformation of whole areas which lie at the heart of it into alien territory.[15]

In later speeches, Powell spoke of 'operating with human nature as it is', rather than seeking to alter it.[16]

The theme of 'working with human nature as it is' is a common one among those who seek to defend racial nationalism. Thus Ivor Stanbrook said in a Commons debate: 'I believe that a preference for one's own race is as natural as a preference for one's own family. Therefore it is not racialism if by that one means, as I do, an active hostility to another race. It is simply human nature.'[17] Other writers have not been so concerned to avoid the word 'racialism'. Thus Andrew Alexander, writing in the *Daily Mail* in 1981: 'The time has come to make a stand in favour of racialism . . . racism, racialism, racial discrimination – call it what you will . . . means discerning real and substantial differences between the human races, and maybe their sub-divisions too, and to act on the basis of that discernment.'[18]

This kind of language, and the view of 'human nature' which underlies it, is in fundamental conflict with traditional Christian theology. Biblical language contains no word for race in the modern sense: *ho genos ton anthropon* refers to the human race, as distinct from animals and plants. There is a solidarity and kinship among human beings by virtue of their humanity. Human beings are the offspring of God: *tou gar kai genos esmen* (Acts 17.28). This solidarity of all humankind in God is emphasized particularly within the Eastern Orthodox tradition as being a solidarity which is rooted in human nature as created. The contemporary Orthodox theologian John Meyendorff expresses the doctrine in this way: 'Man is truly man when he participates in God's life. This participation therefore is not a supernatural gift but the very core of man's nature.'[19] Human nature is thus fundamentally open to God and to the activity of grace. Orthodox theologians sometimes express this doctrine by saying that humanity as created is deiform, made in the image and likeness of God. In the West the fourteenth-century mystic Julian of Norwich expressed the same idea: 'our nature is wholly in God . . . for our nature . . . is joined to God in its creation'.[20] This openness to God is not something added to humanity at a later stage: it expresses what human beings are in their essential nature.

There is thus, according to Christian theology, a radical openness to God and to our sisters and brothers who share God's image. Human nature is not fixed and static, irredeemably narrow and tribal. It is open to change and transformation. 'You can't change human nature' is so profoundly anti-Christian that, if taken seriously, it would undermine the whole of Christian faith, which is based on the assumption that human nature can be, and has been, changed. In racist doctrine, what matters most about human beings is their birth and ethnic origin: in Christian doctrine, what matters is that they are made in the divine image and shine with the divine light.

It is this image and glory which Christ in the incarnation both shared and further transformed, introducing a new phase in the divine–human relationship. Christian faith is rooted and grounded in the doctrine of the incarnation, the belief that in Christ God took human nature to himself, raising it up to share the divine nature. In Mascall's words:

> Human existence and human history can never be the same again since the moment when God the Son united human nature to himself in a union which will never be dissolved. It will be one of the tasks of the theology of the future to work out the implications of this amazing truth, for, apart from occasional adumbrations in such fathers as St Irenaeus, the

theology of the past, especially in the west, has paid little attention to it.[21]

If we are to preach effectively against racism, we need to grasp the two basic truths of creation and incarnation, and their consequences for our view of human nature. It was orthodox Christology which formed the heart of the anti-Nazi movement in the churches. Bonhoeffer was writing his book on Christology at the very point at which Hitler came to power, and it was out of this book that the Confessing Church was to draw much of its material in the resistance to Nazism.

As racism offers an alternative view of human nature, so it offers an alternative view of human love, care and relationship. In Powell's view, a successful multiracial society is impossible. Such ideas of intrinsically limited human love and care are not new. They occur, for example, in Hume's *Treatise of Human Nature*. Altruism, Hume argues, is natural to humankind, but only within limits.[22] In recent New Right thinking we find the same idea. What we call racism is no more than a 'feeling of loyalty to people of one's own kind'.[23] As one journalist wrote: 'It's in our genes. It is part of every person's nature, black or white.'[24] The war in the Falkland Islands reinforced such notions of 'kith and kin'. The war was defended on the grounds that the inhabitants were 'our own people', genuinely British.

Those who hold such ideas of the impossibility of loving people beyond limited kinship boundaries have in recent years looked for scientific support in the new discipline of sociobiology. This is not to say that sociobiology is in itself racist, but that those who seek a scientific basis for their racist ideas have, rightly or wrongly, found sociobiology a convenient source. They have been impressed by claims from within this discipline which appear to support their views. Thus the popular writer Desmond Morris has described the idea of 'a worldwide brotherhood of man' as 'a naive utopian dream. Man is a tribal animal and the great supertribes will always be in competition with one another.'[25] According to Edward Wilson, 'nationalism and racism . . . are the culturally nurtured outgrowths of simple tribalism'.[26] Such simple tribalism is in fact kin altruism in action, the extension of love of family. Richard Lynn sees a line of succession from Darwin through the psychologist William MacDougall to contemporary sociobiology.

> The first stage was initiated by Charles Darwin and reached its apogee in the second decade of this century in the work of William MacDougall who listed a dozen or so instincts which motivated most of human behaviour . . . The third phase can be dated from around the mid-1960s and has resurrected the older doctrine of instincts. This swing back to the Darwin–MacDougall position is represented, among others, by Konrad Lorenz, Lionel Tiger, Robin Fox and Edward O. Wilson.[27]

According to MacDougall, racism is no more than preference for one's own kind, and he sees it as a necessary part of 'conservatism'.

> The essential expressions of conservatism are respect for the ancestors, price in their achievements, and reverence for the traditions which they have handed down: all of which means what is now fashionable to call 'race prejudice' and 'national prejudice', but may more justly be described as preference for, and belief in the merits of, a man's own tribe, race or nation, with its peculiar customs and institutions – its ethos in short.[28]

MacDougall saw black people as 'a race which never yet has shown itself capable of raising or maintaining itself unaided above a barbaric level of culture'.[29]

Again, such ideas of essentially limited love and concern are in conflict with Christian faith, which stands or falls on the belief that love is possible among people of differing races and nations, that love is more fundamental to the nature of the human person than is selfishness, and that such love is rooted in our own openness to the love of God. That self-giving love represents that which is most true to human nature as created, that it is in fact most natural, is basic to the Christian understanding of God as love and of humanity as made to reflect that love. If human beings are incapable of transcending the limits of tribal and national boundaries, then we must revert to the 'culture religions' of paganism. And indeed it is significant that many racist and fascist movements show a strong preference for the pagan gods, the gods of race and nation.

Fundamentally, what is at issue here is the potential and scope of the grace of God in the work of redemption. By focusing on a fixed and unchangeable 'human nature', the racist doctrine ignores or rejects the Christian view that human nature has been transformed, that a new humanity has been created, and that therefore humanity is greater than its most limited and most base and corrupt aspects. By appealing always to these base and corrupt aspects as the rationale for policy, racism reinforces the notion of irredeemable human degeneracy. In theological terms, fallenness comes to dominate and to obscure the gift and power of grace. If grace is seen to operate, it is only within a restricted field.

And here we encounter a more pervasive problem which affects many Christians: the fact that the transforming power of the grace of God is widely seen as only operative within a closed realm, identified as the sacred, the sacramental world, the realm of the personal, or whatever. Transformation is not seen as affecting the way in which life in the real world goes on. So lip service is paid to themes such as liberation, sanctification, transformation, but they are all seen as making no effective difference to reality. The spiritual world is carefully insulated from the world of concrete social and political action.

This dualistic theology is not new. Martin Luther responded to the peasants who demanded an end to serfdom in the name of the redemption wrought by Christ with precisely this kind of theology: 'It is a malicious and evil idea that serfdom should be abolished because Christ has made us free. This refers only to the spiritual freedom given to us by Christ in order to enable us to withstand the devil.'[30] Two hundred years later an eighteenth-century Bishop of London made the same point:

> The freedom which Christianity gives is a freedom from the bondage of sin and Satan and from the dominion of men's lusts and passions and inordinate desires: but as to their *outward* condition, whatever that was before, whether bond or free, their being baptized and becoming Christian makes no matter of change in it.[31]

Against such false spiritualizing, Christian preaching needs to assert that redemption is not limited to the realm of the inward or contained within a protected area, but affects all social, economic and political relationships. Unless redemption is total, it does not occur at all.

Since racism offers an alternative understanding of the gospel, its view of the nature and function of the Church is different. The Church comes to be seen as a religious arm of the nation, a unifying force for national pride and identity, a community of common stock and of the like-minded. So the Union Jack (or its equivalent elsewhere) is flown over the church. Its role is to reinforce the national character and aspirations. But Christian theology sees the Church as the social aspect of Christ's humanity, incomplete until all humanity is redeemed. It is therefore potentially as inclusive as creation itself. The Church is, by its very nature, international, non-racial, cosmic in its range and scope. In the New Testament, the terms race (*genos*) and nation (*ethnos*) are used of the Church itself, that is, not of an ethnic community but of a spiritual community into which entrance is by repentance and baptism (1 Peter 2.9). So the doctrine of the Church becomes a subversive doctrine in relation to ideologies of race and nation. John Davies has written, with the South African Church struggle in mind:

> The most powerful weapon in Catholicism's armoury of imagery in the struggle against injustice is the doctrine of the Body of Christ . . . There has been nothing radical or intellectually daring about this: the South African situation has required Catholicism to be thoroughly conservative and oppose the moral nonsense of upstart racism with a traditional orthodoxy which insists that there must be a visible fellowship of believers and that Christian love must be acted out in visible terms.[32]

The apartheid theology, Davies claims, involves a version of the old Eutychian heresy, which denies that the love and fellowship of the gospel needs to be structurally embodied.

Thus on the four central questions of the nature of humanity, the potential for human love, the nature and scope of grace and the character of the Church itself, racism offers a different and incompatible gospel and world view. The conflict between the Christian gospel and racism is therefore not a mere side-show, an incidental aspect of Christian action, but is deeply theological, a conflict which touches the very heart of the gospel message.

In the twentieth century the most dramatic point at which these two theologies came into collision was the Nazi period, and Christians today need to learn from the witness, and the failure to witness, of the Church in Nazi Germany. Most of the features which we have considered in this chapter as distortions of, or alternatives to, the gospel were present there: the neglect of the Old Testament and the Jewish prophetic tradition; the false dualism of social and spiritual; the neglect of Christology and its ethical dimensions, and of discipleship; and the close link between Christianity and national identity. Richard Gutteridge, who studied anti-Semitism in the evangelical churches from 1870 to 1950, found virtually no evidence of theologically based critique of the treatment of the Jews or of the anti-Semitic ideology which was so pervasive within the Church. What he did find was a prevailing tendency to identify the Church with race and nation. 'The Protestant tendency to anti-Semitism was part and parcel of the well-established tradition of close identification between Christianity and a mystical interpretation of nationality in manifestly untranslatable terms such as *Deutschtum* and *Volkstum*.'[33] And this identification had disastrous consequences for the understanding of the nature of the Christian community, as Bonhoeffer saw in 1935: 'Under the onslaught of new nationalism, the fact that the Church of Christ does not stop at national and racial boundaries, so powerfully attested in the New Testament and in the confessional writings, has been far too easily forgotten.'[34]

Yet Bonhoeffer's voice was a lonely one. More typical was that of the distinguished theologian Gerhard Kittel, an enthusiastic Nazi, who contrasted the internationalism of Jewish faith with the racial nationalism of Hitler – making his own preference very clear.

> At the cradle of modern Judaism stands the idea of humanity as superior to the concept of the race . . . To him [the Jew] racial culture is but a preparation for a culture embracing all humanity.

However, Kittel assured his readers:

> A new movement full of life has broken out in our midst, to which not world citizenship and universal culture is the ideal, but a culture bound up with the people . . . What it can contribute in spiritual values, it can give best by developing its own inherent culture which springs from blood and soil, and by killing as poison all that opposes it.[35]

We know only too well the terrible consequences of this view. It was a reduced and watered-down gospel which helped it to flourish, while its effects on the preaching of the gospel were that many sermons were preached from which all Christian references had been removed.

Reinhold Niebuhr and others have argued that Germany's plight was in part the result of the theology of the Lutheran Reformation, with its dualism of 'two kingdoms' and its lack of interest in issues of justice.[36] Certainly one major factor in the capitulation of the churches to Hitler was the fact that the proclamation of the gospel had gone seriously astray. It is equally clear that out of the terrible experience of Nazism came a thorough and continuing critique and reappraisal of Christian theology itself.

Today, the experience of racism can act as a force for the renewal of the wholeness of Christian proclamation. We shall need to hear the voices from the Third World, the theologies of liberation, which are seeking to end the identification of the Church with oppressive power structures and false spiritualities. We shall need to recover neglected emphases – on the creation, on incarnation, on the social and political dimensions of redemption, on the meaning of the Kingdom of God. The experience of racism, much of it based upon, or feeding upon, defects and distortions of Christian faith, should lead us to renew our theology and our preaching. It should, more than anything else, lead us to see that the gospel is not merely about certain truths: it is about the truth which makes us free, truth in action, truth in concrete struggle with the forces of evil. As J. H. Oldham wrote in 1924:

> Christianity is not primarily a philosophy but a crusade. As Christ was sent by the Father, so he sends his disciples to set up in the world the Kingdom of God . . . He was manifested to

destroy the works of the devil. Hence when Christians find in the world a state of things which is not in accord with the truths which they have learned from Christ, their concern is not that it should be explained, but that it should be ended.[37]

Epilogue

'The Sky is Red and Threatening'

The following is the text of a sermon which I preached at Christ Church Cathedral, Oxford, on 30 April 1968, at a Memorial Service for Martin Luther King. I reprint it here, on the twentieth anniversary of King's death, essentially unchanged, though I have updated some of the language. (For example, the term 'coloured', which was acceptable usage in 1968, is no longer so: I have replaced it with 'black'. And I have tried to get rid of the exclusive language, which was also common at that time.) But the main points I made twenty years ago are still valid. That I did not see the need to alter anything of substance is depressing, but it is also a reminder that so much remains to be done.

'The sky is red and threatening' (Matthew 16.3).

The American folk singer Paul Simon, in a song called 'A Church is Burning', tells of the setting alight by the Ku Klux Klan of a black church in 1964.

> The flames rise higher,
> Like hands that are praying,
> Aglow in the sky.

Each verse ends:

> Like hands that are praying,
> The fire is saying,
> You can burn down my churches,
> But I shall be free.

Today we think of fire and of freedom.

The sky is red and threatening. Red is the colour both of fire and of freedom, and on the eve of May Day our minds are on the unity of the human race. Red, in theological as well as in political mythology, is the colour of unity, of the blood which unites humankind in solidarity. To Christians, the blood-red banner of the Son of Man is the banner of justice and freedom.

But red, too, is the colour of the blood of the martyrs which unites the freedom fighters in a red stream of sacrifice, and we have come together to remember one such martyr. Martin Luther King died, as he lived, for the unity and freedom of the children of God. His blood flowing in death symbolizes his life's witness to the gospel that God 'has made of one blood all nations'. We celebrate his living and dying with gratitude and joy, and yet with a sense of apprehension.

Apprehension because the sky is red and threatening. We know only too well that red symbolizes also the blood shed in race riots, which do not unite but divide humanity. The fire which set the church alight is not the fire of justice but the fire of hell, the red agony of the racial nightmare of which James Baldwin speaks in the frightening last paragraph of *The Fire Next Time*. And in England, too, the murder of Martin Luther King should scream at us that the sky is red and threatening.

There was a cynical irony in the fact that so soon after the American freedom fighters marched with Martin Luther King, a section of British dockers marched for Enoch Powell with placards saying 'Back Britain Not Black Britain'. The march to freedom is followed by the march to hatred and slavery. It was horribly significant that so soon after the death of Martin Luther King, we should see in Britain the kindling of the fires of racial hatred. To us, then, the central message of his death is that the sky is red and threatening.

First, because Martin Luther King lived and died for a non-racial society. He fought for the liberation of an oppressed minority from the slavery of the ghetto. We applaud him, and the establishments and governments of the West applaud him now. But if ghettoes are wrong in the USA, they cannot be right here. Racism is indivisible. You cannot fight segregation and discrimination abroad and condone it here. Equally, you cannot accept discrimination at the doors of Britain and pretend to oppose it within Britain. Once the principle of racism is incorporated into legislation – as it now has been incorporated in this country – we have created a situation where all talk of conciliation and Race Relations Acts will seem suspiciously like window dressing.

For this country has in recent years witnessed a growing movement of racism under the name of realism. Sentiments which were regarded as fanatical and the fruits of prejudice in 1958 are now expressed by the pillars of liberal opinion. The Commonwealth Immigrants Act, the 1965 White Paper, the Kenyan Asian episode, Enoch Powell – these are only facets of a pervasive disease. Black people, it is now argued, are undesirable *per se*. A few years ago even the 'extremists' were at pains to stress that 'this is not a question of colour': now nobody bothers to deny the fact. So now we have what Ruth Glass has called 'a new doctrine of original sin combined with a faulty political arithmetic'. For racism is a vicious doctrine which cuts at the heart of the gospel and of catholic Christianity. The true opposite of catholic is not Protestant but racist, for catholicism proclaims the unity of humankind while racism divides people and returns us to a fallen world, the dominion of the demons.

Second, Martin Luther King lived and died for nonviolence. Racial hatred breeds violence and thrives upon it. The sentiments expressed in this past week are in essence no different from those which led to the shootings at Sharpeville and the tragedies revealed at the Eichmann trial. To counteract violence by more violence generates still more of the same; but to compromise by making more and more concessions to prejudice and hatred under the name of liberal opinion sets us on the typically British slide to respectable racism. Nonviolent resistance, Martin Luther King argued, is not just the only practicable alternative to race war, it *is* the Christian gospel of love and justice expressed in terms of conflict with evil and injustice.

Third, Martin Luther King lived and died for social justice. He did not see race relations as a special sphere isolated from the social structure. As long as there is poverty and squalor, there will be scapegoats. As long as there are twilight zones, acres of desperation, stagnant decaying districts without hope of renewal, as long as these remain, people will continue to blame the new minorities for the long-standing evils of the social order. Mr Powell speaks the same language as that used by the sons of

Irish immigrants against the Jews in East London in 1902, language which had in its turn been used against their parents in the 1840s. The point is not that these are evil people driven forward by evil doctrines (though they may be), but that the whole social order, based on the concentration of power and profit and geared to organized violence, *does* corrupt and degrade human beings. Martin Luther King saw that racial goodwill could not be separated from housing exploitation, poverty and capital, or from the Vietnam war where black conscripts are sent to defend a liberty which they do not enjoy at home.

The sky is red and threatening. No amount of compromise and no amount of reformist tinkering with the status quo will avert a racial holocaust. Only the rise of a new generation dedicated to freedom and justice will cut through the vicious reality of racism which threatens to engulf the cosmos in a baptism of blood. Martin Luther King saw that a new world order based on love and justice and the rejection of war, poverty and inequality was a possibility, and he was wild enough to see the Church as the vanguard of this new world.

But not the Church as it stands, a ritual re-enactment of the old order, riddled through and through with racial and class divisions, tamed and compromised by the establishment. The old decaying structures must be burnt down in the furnace of God's love and justice. While the sky is red and threatening, the Sun of Justice must arise in the Church like fire in the heavens, for the liberation of humankind for which Martin Luther King lived and fought and still prays.

> Like hands that are praying,
> The fire is saying,
> You can burn down my churches,
> But I shall be free.

Notes

Chapter One – Race, Class and the Church of England

1 I owe the title, as some readers will recognize, to the ongoing debate on the connections between race, class and other formations, as in the journal *Race and Class*, in Selma James' *Sex, Race and Class* (Race Today 1975) and in many other articles.
2 For a general background to the debate see, for example, Gareth Stedman Jones, *Language of Class: Studies in English Working Class History 1832–1982* (Cambridge University Press 1984); Basil Bernstein, *Class, Codes and Control*, vol. 1 (Routledge and Kegal Paul 1971); Ralf Dahrendorf, *Class and Class Structure in Industrial Society* (Routledge and Kegan Paul 1959); and Frank Parkin, *Marxism and Class Theory* (Tavistock 1979).
3 See E. P. Thompson, 'Eighteenth-Century English Society: Class Struggle Without Class?' in *Social History*, 3.1 1978, pp. 133–65. For more detailed studies see Thompson's *The Making of the English Working Class* (Penguin 1963) and T. B. Bottomore, *Classes in Modern Society* (Allen and Unwin, 1966 edn.).
4 Richard Hoggart, *The Uses of Literacy* (Penguin 1958 edn.), p. 13.
5 See F. A. Hayek, *The Road to Serfdom* (Routledge and Kegan Paul 1944). On the New Right see Ruth Levitas (ed.), *The Ideology of the New Right* (Polity Press 1986), and Nick Bosanquet, *After the New Right* (Heinemann 1983).
6 C. A. R. Crosland, *The Future of Socialism* (Cape 1956) and *Socialism Now and Other Essays* (Cape 1974). See also David Lipsey and Dick Leonard (eds.), *The Socialist Agenda: Crosland's Legacy* (Cape 1981). For a Conservative critique of Crosland see Ian Gilmour, 'Why Social Democrats are Wrong' in *The Sunday Times*, 2 October 1977.
7 Douglas Jay, *Socialism in the New Society* (Longmans 1962).
8 Ferdinand Zweig, *The Worker in an Affluent Society* (Heinemann 1961).
9 J. H. Goldthorpe *et al.*, *The Affluent Worker in the Class Structure* (Cambridge University Press 1969).
10 See Daniel Bell, *The End of Ideology* (Glencoe, Free Press, 1960).

11 Stuart Hall, 'The Sense of Classlessness' in *Universities and Left Review*, Autumn 1958; Raphael Samuel, 'Class and classlessness', ibid., Spring 1959.
12 E. J. Hobsbawm, 'The Forward March of Labour Halted' in *Marxism Today*, September 1979, pp. 265–8. The essay is reprinted in Martin Jacques and Frances Mulhern (eds), *The Forward March of Labour Halted?* (Verso 1981). For a critique see Ben Fine *et al.*, *Class Politics: An Answer to its Critics* (Central Books 1984).
13 I. Crewe, 'The Labour Party and the Election' in Denis Kavanagh (ed.), *The Politics of the Labour Party* (Allen and Unwin 1982), pp. 10ff. See also Mark N. Franklin, *The Decline of Class Voting in Britain: Changes in the Basis of Electoral Choice 1964–1983* (Clarendon Press 1985).
14 Jeremy Seabrook, *The Idea of Neighbourhood: What Local Politics Should be About* (Pluto 1984).
15 See André Gorz, *Farewell to the Working Class* (Pluto 1982).
16 Richard Hyman and Robert Price (eds.), *The New Working Class: White Collar Workers and their Organisations* (Macmillan 1983); Raphael Samuel, 'The SDP and the New Political Class' in *New Society*, 22 April 1982, pp. 124–7, and 'The SDP and the Working Class', op. cit., 29 April 1982, pp. 169–71.
17 Raphael Samuel, 'Benn past and Benn present' in *New Socialist*, 28 September 1984, p. 13.
18 For a critique of such notions see John Westergaard, 'Class of 84' in *New Socialist*, January–February 1984, pp. 30–6, and 'Sociology: The Myth of Classlessness' in Robin Blackburn (ed.), *Ideology in Social Science* (Fontana 1977 edn.), pp. 119–63; and, for a more detailed account, John Westergaard and Henrietta Resler, *Class in a Capitalist Society* (Penguin 1976).
19 Royal Commission on the Distribution of Income and Wealth, Report No. 4, *Second Report on the Standing Reference* (HMSO Cmnd 6626, 1976); *The A to Z of Income and Wealth* (HMSO 1980).
20 Inland Revenue, *Survey of Personal Incomes* (HMSO 1984).
21 *New Earnings Survey* (Department of Employment, October 1982).
22 *Inland Revenue Statistics* (HMSO, October 1983).
23 The literature on poverty is enormous and is in inverse relationship to the attack on poverty. See A. B. Atkinson, *The Economics of Inequality* (Oxford University Press 1975); Frank Field, *Inequality in Britain* (Fontana 1981); Peter Townsend, *Poverty in the United Kingdom* (Penguin 1979); Joanna Mack and Stuart Lansley, *Poor Britain* (Allen and Unwin 1985); and the regular publications of the Low Pay Unit and the Child Poverty Action Group.

24 See Bruce Coleman, *The Church of England in the Mid Nineteenth Century: A Social Geography* (Historical Association 1980); A. D. Gilbert, *Religion and Society in Industrial England: Church, Chapel and Social Change 1740–1914* (Longmans 1976); K. S. Inglis, *Churches and the Working Classes in Victorian England* (Routledge and Kegan Paul 1963); Hugh McLeod, *Church and Class in Late Victorian England* (Croom Helm 1974); R. F. Wearmouth, *Methodism and the Working Class Movement in England 1800–1850* (Epworth 1937), etc.
25 cited in Inglis, op. cit.
26 Benjamin Disraeli, *Church and Queen* (1865), p. 18.
27 cited in Inglis op. cit. p. 60.
28 R. A. Solway, *Prelates and People: Ecclesiastical Social Thought in England 1783–1852* (Routledge and Kegan Paul 1969).
29 On Christian Socialism see Peter d'A. Jones, *The Christian Socialist Revival 1877–1914* (Princeton University Press 1968); John R. Orens, *Politics and the Kingdom* (Jubilee Group 1981).
30 Inglis, op. cit., p. 323.
31 F. E. E. Bell, *At the Works: A Study of a Manufacturing Town* (David and Charles 1969 edn.).
32 cited in Frederick How, *Bishop Walsham How* (Isbister 1898), p. 129.
33 *South London Mail*, 11 February 1888.
34 *John Bull*, 12 July 1879.
35 Charles Booth, *Life and Labour of the People in London*, 7 vols., (Macmillan 1892–7); Richard Mudie Smith, *The Religious Life of London* (Hodder and Stoughton 1904).
36 See Stanley G. Evans, *The Church in the Back Streets* (Mowbray 1963).
37 S. A. and H. O. Barnett, *Towards Social Reform* (T. Fisher Unwin 1909), p. 26.
38 George Lansbury, *My Life* (1928), pp. 129–30.
39 Letter dated 3 February 1859 in Church Commissioners' file 28529.
40 Bryan King, *Sacrilege and its Encouragement* (Joseph Masters 1860), p. 7.
41 cited in St John B. Groser, *Politics and Persons* (SCM Press 1949), p. 21.
42 Kathleen Jones, 'The House of Laity in the General Synod: A Membership Analysis' in *Crucible*, July–August 1971, pp. 104–8.
43 George Moyser, 'The Political Organisation of the Middle Class: The Case of the Church of England' in John Garrard (ed.), *The Middle Class in Politics* (Saxon House 1978).
44 George Moyser, 'The 1980 General Synod: Patterns and Trends' in *Crucible*, April–June 1982, pp. 75–86.
45 Details are given annually in *The Church of England Yearbook*.
46 Kit and Frederica Konolige, *The Power of Their Glory: America's Ruling*

Class, The Episcopalians (New York, Wyden Books, 1978), pp. 26–33.

47 *Mission for the Church in East London*, Report of the Bishop of Stepney's Commission (1974).

48 Paddington Community Consortium, *False Profits?* (May 1984). See also the Bishop of Stepney's letter in the *Church Times*, 18 January 1985.

49 Robert Runcie, *Racial Attitudes in Britain: The Way Forward* (Church Information Office 1982), pp. 10–11.

50 *Faith in the City: A Call to Action by Church and Nation*, Report of the Archbishop's Commission on Urban Priority Areas (ACUPA) (Church House Publishing 1985), p. 31.

51 See Michael LeRoy, *Riots in Liverpool 8: Some Christian Responses* (Evangelical Coalition for Urban Mission 1983) and 'A voice Still Unheard' in *Third Way*, July–August 1984, p. 12.

52 Renate Wilkinson in *Inheritors Together: Black People in the Church of England* (Board for Social Responsibility 1985), pp. 20–33.

53 'Race and Theological Education: A Discussion Paper', MS, 1983.

54 Clifford Hill, *Renewal in the Inner City* (Methodist Church Home Mission Division, undated) and *Mission in the Urban Jungle* (Evangelical Race Relations Group, January 1975.)

55 Gavin Stamp, 'The Vanishing Church of Bishop Jim' in the *Spectator*, 8 March 1986, pp. 9–12.

56 John Rowe in Christopher Lind and Terry Brown (eds.), *Justice as Mission: An Agenda for the Church* (Burlington, Ontario, Trinity Press, 1985), pp. 39–40.

Chapter Two – The Roots of Urban Conflict

1 Ernest de Selincourt and Helen Darbishire (eds.), *Preface to Lyrical Ballads: Prospectus to The Excursion, Poetical Works of William Wordsworth* (Oxford University Press 1949), p. 5.

2 cited in Ebenezer Howard, *Garden Cities of Tomorrow* (1902 edn), p. 42.

3 cited in Paul Johnson, *The Offshore Islanders* (Weidenfeld and Nicolson 1972), p. 367n; Keith Robbins, *Sir Edward Grey* (Cassells 1971), p. 372.

4 Asa Briggs, *A Social History of England* (Weidenfeld and Nicolson 1983), p. 40.

5 *Elements of Success* cited in 'Society Today' in *New Society*, 15 February 1979.

6 Ruth Glass, 'The Alarming but Tired Clichés about Urban Doom' in *The Times*, 4 August 1976.

7 M. J. Dyos and M. Wolff, *The Victorian City in Image and Reality*, 2 vols. (Routledge and Kegan Paul 1973).
8 Faber and Faber 1954 edn.
9 cited in 'Society Today', op. cit.
10 See Robert E. L. Farris, *Chicago Sociology 1920–1932* (University of Chicago Press 1967).
11 Louis Wirth, *The Ghetto* (University of Chicago Press 1928); 'Urbanism as a Way of Life' in Paul K. Hatt and Albert J. Reiss, Jr, *A Reader in Urban Sociology* (Glencoe, Free Press, 1951), pp. 32–49. The original essay appeared in the *American Journal of Sociology*, 44 (1938), pp. 1–44.
12 Peter Willmott and Michael Young, *Family and Kinship in East London* (Routledge and Kegan Paul 1957).
13 David Donnison, 'What is the "Good City"?' in *New Society*, 13 December 1973, pp. 647–8.
14 Ruth Glass, 'London on the Move' in *The Times*, 18 and 19 June 1956.
15 A. C. L. Day and Ralph Turvey, 'The Parking Problem in Central London' in *The Times*, 7 June 1954.
16 'Business Moving Out of Town' in *The Times*, 14 October 1958.
17 Ruth Glass and John Westergaard, *London's Housing Needs* (Centre for Urban Studies 1965), p. x.
18 *Faith in the City: A Call to Action by Church and Nation*, Report of the Archbishop's Commission on Urban Priority Areas (ACUPA) (Church House Publishing 1985), p. 23. Cited below as ACUPA.
19 Glass and Westergaard, op. cit., pp. 4–5.
20 ACUPA, p. 23. See also Chris Hamnett, 'Housing in the Two Nations: Socio-Tenurial Polarisation in England and Wales 1961–81' in *Urban Studies*, 43 (1984), pp. 384–405.
21 On Newham see David White, 'Newham: An Example of Urban Decline' in *New Society*, 23 October 1975, pp. 201–4. On Hackney see *An Interim Report on Social Trends in the London Borough of Hackney* (START 1976); *Needs and Resources in Hackney* (Hackney Inner City Partnership Unit, October 1983); and Paul Harrison, *Inside the Inner City* (Penguin 1983). For documentation on the other parts of London see the references in Chapter Three.
22 See Chapters Three and Five for further details.
23 See R. Nabarro, 'The Impact on Workers from the Inner City of Liverpool's Economic Decline' in A. Evans and D. Evans (eds.), *The Inner City* (Heinemann 1980).
24 Gabrielle Cox in *Letters from Seven Churches* (Jubilee Group 1983), p. 9. See also *Social Information Study* (City of Manchester, City Planning Department and Social Services Department, September 1975), p. 25.

25 Sir J. P. Dickson-Poynder, Chair of LCC Housing of the Working Classes Committee in *The Times*, 26 November 1883.

26 Glass and Westergaard, op. cit., p. 24.

27 *Capital Decay: An Analysis of London's Housing* (SHAC 1985, 2nd edn.).

28 *Inner City Crisis: Manchester Hulme* (Hulme People's Rights Centre 1977).

29 Philip Tunley *et al.*, *Depriving the Deprived* (Centre for Institutional Studies, North East London Polytechnic, and Kogan Page 1979).

30 The term was first used by Julian Tudor Hart, 'The Inverse Care Law' in *The Lancet*, 27 February 1971, pp. 405–12.

31 On urban health issues see: Peter Townsend, 'Inequality and the Health Service' in *The Lancet*, 15 June 1974, pp. 1179–90; Peter Townsend *et al.*, *Health and Deprivation: Inequality and the North* (Croom Helm 1987); Thomas Arie, 'Class and Disease', in *New Society*, 27 January 1966, pp. 8–11; Julian Le Grand, *Inequalities in Health and Health Care*, (Nuffield Provincial Hospitals Trust 1984); Jocelyn Cornwell, *Hard Earned Lives: Accounts of Health and Illness from East London* (Tavistock 1984); John Robson *et al*. 'Quality, inequality and Health Care: Notes on Medicine, Capital and the State' in *Medicine in Society*, April 1977; Bethnal Green and Stepney Trades Council, *A People's Health Service for Tower Hamlets*, undated; Psychiatric Rehabilitation Association, *The Mental Health of East London* (1966) and *Mental Illness in City and Suburb* (1970); Protasia Torkington, *The Racial Politics of Health: A Liverpool Profile* (Merseyside Area Profile Group 1983); 'Grim Health Report Reveals Bristol's Poverty Trap' in *Venue* (Bristol), 8–12 July 1983, pp. 6–7; W. W. Holland and D. P. Reid, 'The Urban Factor in Chronic Bronchitis' in *The Lancet*, 1965, p. 445.

32 *Inequalities in Health* (HMSO 1980); *The Health Service in England*, Annual Report (HMSO 1985).

33 *Evening News*, 3 October 1972.

34 *The Recurrent Crisis of London*, CIS Anti-Report on Property Developers, undated.

35 *Urban Wasteland* (Civic Trust 1977).

36 David Donnison, *Urban Policy: A New Approach* (Fabian Tract 487, 1983), p. 4.

37 *Tower Hamlets: The Fight for Jobs* (Bethnal Green and Stepney Trades Council 1975).

38 Cited in Andrew Friend and Andy Metcalf, *Slump City: The Politics of Mass Unemployment* (Pluto Press 1981), p. 10.

39 Stephen Holley, cited in *New Society*, 23 May 1986, p. 26.

40 ACUPA, op. cit., p. xiv.

41 Margaret Simey, *Government by Consent* (Bedford Square Press 1985), pp. 1ff.
42 K. Coates and R. Silberman, *Poverty: the Forgotten Englishmen* (Penguin 1970), p. 21.
43 *The Observer*, 11 May 1986.
44 Marplan Poll, BBC TV, 16 October 1984.
45 The *Guardian*, 8 June 1984.
46 Cmnd 6848 (1977), para 22.
47 *New Society*, 13 September 1985.

Chapter Three – London's Racial Crisis: The Early Years

1 Hamza Alavi, 'Immigrants and the Housing Problem' in *Tribune*, 10 September 1965.
2 *London: Employment, Housing, Land* (HMSO, Cmnd 1952, 1963), pp. 2, 4.
3 D. V. Donnison, Christine Cockburn and T. Corlett, *Housing since the Rent Act*, Rowntree Trust Housing Study Report (Codicote Press 1962), p. 12.
4 *Report of the Committee on Housing in Greater London* (HMSO, Cmnd 2605, 1965).
5 Ruth Glass and John Westergaard, *London's Housing Needs* (Centre for Urban Studies 1965), p. 10.
6 ibid., p. 44.
7 John Rex, 'Integration – the reality' in *New Society*, 12 August 1965.
8 Michael Banton, *The Coloured Quarter* (Cape 1955).
9 *Report of the Committee on Housing*, op. cit., p. 203.
10 See Ruth Glass's letter, 'The Technique of Powellism' in the *Guardian*, 9 January 1969.
11 'Health by Act of Parliament' in *Household Words I* (1850), p. 463.
12 Cited in Edward Pilkington, 'The 1958 Notting Hill Race Riots', MS, 1984, p. 6. See also F. M. Gladstone, *Notting Hill in Bygone Days* (1924).
13 *Kensington Post*, 23 May 1958.
14 Pearl Jephcott, *A Troubled Area* (Faber and Faber 1964), p. 14.
15 cited in *Portobello Project Annual Report*, 1967.
16 Rachel Powell, 'Mosley and Notting Hill', MS, 1959.
17 Centre for Urban Studies, North Kensington Survey, MS, 1961. See Ruth Glass's letter in the *Guardian*, 10 May 1969.
18 Jephcott, op. cit., pp. 93–5.
19 *Empire News*, cited in Shirley Green, *Rachman* (Michael Joseph 1979), p. 59.

20 See Michael Abdul Malik, *From Michael de Freitas to Michael X* (André Deutsch 1968), p. 93. For a contemporary assessment of 'Rachmanism' see Peter Kemp, 'The Ghost of Rachman' in *New Society*, 6 November 1987, pp. 13–15.
21 Green, op. cit.
22 21 November 1956.
23 Cited in *Tribune*, 10 April 1964.
24 South Kensington Tenants Association Report, October 1957, p. 2.
25 Report of the Committee of Inquiry into Homelessness (LCC Agenda Paper No. 4171, 17 July 1962), paras. 8 and 176.
26 The phrase comes from George Austin, 'The Tough Life in Notting Hill' in the *Church Times*, 26 June 1959.
27 All Saints Church in Clydesdale Road stands at the heart of Notting Hill's black community. Throughout the key period of immigration, its congregation remained wholly white. It was a classic example of the precious and pietist side of Anglo-Catholicism.
28 *Church of England Newspaper*, 2 August 1963.
29 Ian Nairn, *The Daily Telegraph*, 19 August 1963.
30 William Hale, *Observations on the Distress Peculiar to the Poor of Spitalfields Arising from their Local Situation*, 17 November 1806, 2nd edn. 1807; W. C. Johnson, letter in the *East London Observer*, February 1906.
31 From Edith Ramsey's papers, now deposited in Tower Halmets Central Library, Bancroft Road, London E1, archive accession no. TH/8260. For a valuable study of Edith Ramsey's role in the East End at this time see Bertha Sokoloff, *Edith and Stepney* (Stepney Books, 19 Tomlins Grove, London E3, 1987).
32 Ashley Smith, *The East Enders* (Secker and Warburg 1961), pp. 75, 162.
33 Banton, op. cit.
34 *East London Advertiser*, 26 August 1962.
35 Norman Pritchard, answer to Question 27 to Chair of Housing Committee, LCC Meeting, 16 May 1961; the *Daily Mail*, 17 May 1961.
36 *Stratford Express*, 6 July 1962.
37 Christopher Bonham-Carter, letter on behalf of the Duke of Edinburgh to the Revd J. Williamson, 16 July 1962.
38 Sir Keith Joseph, answer to Gilbert Longden, MP, House of Commons, 16 July 1961.
39 Sir Keith Joseph, House of Commons, 31 July 1962, col. 327.
40 *Evening Standard*, 13 July 1964.
41 I have quoted extensively from Williamson's correspondence in a forthcoming study of the Cable Street area in the 1950s and 1960s.

Chapter Four – Racism and Violence

1 The *Guardian*, 19 June 1984.

2 For discussions of the State, the police and racism see such studies as Phil Scraton, *The State of the Police* (Pluto 1985); *The Empire Strikes Back: Race and Racism in 70s Britain* (Centre for Contemporary Cultural Studies/Hutchinson 1982); A. Sivanandan, 'Race, Class and the State' in *Race and Class*, 17.4 (1976), pp. 347–68; Lee Bridges and Liz Fekete, 'Victims, the "Urban Jungle" and the New Racism', op. cit., 27.1 (1985), pp. 45–62; and other issues of that journal.

3 See *Taking Liberties* (Sheffield Policewatch 1984); Brian Jenner, *The Coal Strike: Christian Reflections on the Miners' Struggle* (New City 1986); Jim Coulter, Susan Miller and Martin Walker, *A State of Siege* (Canary Press 1984).

4 On Nazi anti-Semitism see Peter Pulzer, *The Rise of Political Anti-Semitism in Germany and Austria* (New York 1964); George L. Mosse, *Toward the Final Solution* (Dent 1979); and, on the Churches' involvement, Richard Gutteridge, *Open Thy Mouth for the Dumb: The German Evangelical Church and the Jews 1879–1950* (Blackwell 1976).

5 On the roots of anti-Semitism in Christian theology see Rosemary Ruether, *Faith and Fratricide: The Theological Roots of anti-Semitism* (New York, Seabury Press, 1974); Michael B. McGarry, *Christology after Auschwitz* (New York, Paulist Press, 1977); Robert P. Ericksen, *Theologians under Hitler* (Yale University Press 1985).

6 On the definition of racism see Michael Banton, 'What do we Mean by "Racism"?' in *New Society*, 10 April 1969, pp. 551–4; and Kenneth Leech, '*Diverse Reports* and the meaning of "racism" in *Race and Class*, 28.2 (1986), pp. 82–6.

7 See 'Violence Wave Scares Ladbroke Grove' in *Kensington News*, 15 August 1958.

8 Ruth Glass, *Newcomers* (Allen and Unwin 1960), pp. 133–4.

9 ibid., p. 140.

10 *Manchester Guardian*, 25 September 1958; *Kensington News*, 5 September 1958; *Kensington Post*, 12 September 1958.

11 Glass, op. cit.

12 The Revd David Mason, cited in Edward Pilkington, 'The 1958 Notting Hill Race Riots', MS, 1984, p. 86.

13 *Daily Mail*, 2 September 1958.

14 ibid., 3 September 1958.

15 Paul Gilroy, *There Ain't No Black in the Union Jack: The Cultural Politics of Race and Nation* (Hutchinson 1987), p. 11.

16 *Racial Attacks* (Home Office 1981).

17 Francesca Klug, *Racist Attacks* (Runnymede Trust 1982); Paul Gordon, *Racial Violence and Harassment* (Runnymede Trust 1986); *Racial Attacks and Harassment* (3rd Report of the Home Affairs Committee, HMSO 1986); *Racial Harassment in London* (Report of the GLC Panel of Inquiry, Greater London Council 1984); *CAPA Annual Report* (December 1982); *Racial Harassment in Manchester and the Response of the Police 1980–85* (Manchester Council for Community Relations 1986); *Self-Defence Is No Offence: How the Bradford 12 Won their Freedom* (Leeds Other Paper 1982); *Racial Harassment in Glasgow* (Scottish Ethnic Minorities Research Unit., Glasgow College of Technology 1986); Andy Sils *et al.*, *Fear and Crime in the Inner City* (Leicester Community Consultants 1987); and many other studies.

18 Gabrielle Cox in *Letters from Seven Churches* (Jubilee Group 1984), p. 10.

Chapter Five – Brick Lane and the Local Growth of Fascism

1 Daniel Defoe, *A Tour Thro' the Whole Island of Great Britain by a Gentleman* (1748), p. 105.

2 Cited in Henry Walker, *East London* (Religious Tract Society 1896), pp. 61–2.

3 *East London Observer*, 25 June 1892.

4 See L. P. Garner, *The Jewish Immigrant in England 1870–1914* (Allen and Unwin 1960); V. D. Lipman, *Social History of the Jews in England 1850–1950* (Watts 1954); J. A. Garrard, *The English and Immigration* (Institute of Race Relations/Oxford University Press 1971).

5 Alamgir Kabir, 'The Growing Campaign against Pakistanis in Britain' in *Peace News*, 19 March 1965.

6 Louise London, 'The East End of London: Paki-Bashing in 1970' in *Race Today*, December 1973.

7 See Derek Cox, *A Community Approach to Youth Work in East London* (YWCA 1970), pp. 117–18; Susie Daniel and Pete McGuire, *The Paint House: Words of an East End Gang* (Penguin 1972); Derek Humphrey in *The Sunday Times*, 2 July 1978.

8 Cox, op. cit.

9 *Race Today*, June 1976.

10 ibid., May 1977.

11 *East London Advertiser*, 3 June 1977.

12 *The Sunday Times*, 5 June 1977.

13 The *Guardian*, 9 December 1977; *East Ender*, 17 December 1977. Ten years later, Hackney Council set up special squads to clean off slogans! (*Daily Mail*, 30 March 1977).

14 *The Times*, 23 December 1977.
15 See Arnold White, *The Truth about the Russian Jew* (reprinted from Contemporary Review, 1897); *The Destitute Alien in Great Britain* (Swan, Sonnenschein and Co. 1892); W. Evans Gordon, *The Alien Immigrant* (Heinemann 1903). For a critique of the White and Evans Gordon positions see M. J. Landa, *The Alien Problem and its Remedy* (P. S. King and Son 1911).
16 See Caroline Adams, *They Sell Cheaper and They Live Very Odd* (British Council of Churches 1976).
17 On Mosley see R. M. Benewick, *The Fascist Movement in Britain* (Allen Lane 1972); W. F. Mandle, *Anti-Semitism and the British Union of Fascists* (Barnes and Noble 1968); Robert Skidelsky, *Oswald Mosley* (MacMillan 1975), ch. 21 'The Campaign in East London', pp. 393–410.
18 J. H. Robb, *Working Class Anti-Semite* (Tavistock 1945).
19 On the anti-Holocaust movement of 'revisionist historians' see Gill Seidel, *The Holocaust Denial: Anti-Semitism, Racism and the New Right* (Beyond the Pale Collective 1986).
20 The best source for information on fascist and far right groups is the monthly magazine *Searchlight* (37b New Cavendish Street, London W1M 8JR).
21 *Spearhead*, May–June 1979. See also G. Weightman and S. Weir, 'The National Front and the Young: A Special Survey' in *New Society*, 27 April 1978, pp. 186–93. For the current attraction of fascist groups for alienated young people see Harry McGurk (ed.), *What Next?* (Economic and Social Research Council 1987).
22 For a detailed study of the NF support in the East End see C. T. Husbands, *Racial Exclusionism and the City: The Urban Support for the National Front* (Allen and Unwin 1982).
23 On the 'Rock Against Racism' movement see David Widgery, *Beating Time* (Chatto and Windus 1986).
24 *East London Advertiser*, 12 May 1978.
25 *Blood on the Streets* (Bethnal Green and Stepney Trades Council, September 1978), p. 56.
26 *New Statesman*, 19 May 1978.
27 *East London Advertizer*, 18 August 1978.
28 *The Asian*, 1.4 (August 1978).
29 Hackney and Tower Hamlets Defence Committee leaflet, *They Shall Not Pass*, 24 September 1978.
30 *Is the Police Force Racist*? (leaflet issued prior to 24 September 1978).
31 *No Holocaust in East London* (ANL leaflet of 1 October 1978).
32 Spartacist League, *Break with the ANL: For Militant Union/Black Defence of the East End* (leaflet of 24 September 1978).

33 David Pallister and Lindsey Mackie, the *Guardian*, 13 June 1978.
34 *Evening News*, 14 June 1978.
35 The *Guardian*, 14 June 1978.
36 *Asians and Housing: The Bengali Housing Action Group Statement* (June 1978).
37 A. Sivanandan in *Race and Class*, 26.4 (1985), p. 9.
38 From the interview with Gordon Burns on *World in Action*, Granada TV, 30 January 1978.
39 Z. Layton Henry, *The Politics of Race in Britain*, Allen and Unwin 1984, p. 106.
40 For a detailed critique of this publication see my *Brick Lane 1978: The Events and Their Significance* (Birmingham AFFOR 1980), pp. 18–23.
41 *Brick Lane and Beyond* (Commission for Racial Equality, April 1979), p. 25.
42 For a period there were two bodies in Tower Hamlets, the Tower Hamlets Council for Racial Equality (THCRE), the former Council of Citizens of Tower Hamlets (CCTH) and the new Tower Hamlets Association for Racial Justice (THARJ). Eventually they merged to form the Tower Hamlets Association for Racial Equality (THARE).
43 Cited in *Searchlight*, 93 (March 1983), p. 2.
44 *Hackney Gazette*, 7 July 1978.
45 Caroline Adams, 'The Spitalfields Bengali Action Group and the Kobi Nazrul Centre 1974–78', MS, Avenues Unlimited, 1979. For the early history see her *Across Seven Seas and Thirteen Rivers* (THAP Books 1987).
46 St John B. Groser, *Politics and Persons* (SCM Press).

Chapter Six – After Scarman: The Events of 1981 in Retrospect

1 *The Brixton Disorders, 10–12th April 1981*, the Scarman Report (Cmnd 8427, HMSO November 1981), 4.93; 4.63; 2.38. Cited below as Scarman.
2 Elinor Harbridge, 'Toxteth: The Price of Neglect' in *Community Care*, 23 July 1981.
3 Cited in the *Church Times*, 12 July 1981.
4 Margaret Simey, *Government by Consent* (Bedford Square Press/ NCVO 1985), p. 10.
5 *The Sunday Times*, 12 July 1981.
6 *The Times*, 8 August 1981; the *Guardian*, 8 June 1984.
7 Cited in *New Statesman*, 17 July 1981.
8 Cited in the *Guardian*, 6 October 1981.
9 *The Times*, 11 July 1981.

10 Scarman, 9.5.
11 Press conference, 14 June 1979.
12 Cited in the *Guardian*, 25 September 1979.
13 Sir Kenneth Newman, cited in *Emergency*, 2 (1984), p. 56.
14 Sir Kenneth Newman, cited in *The Times*, 17 October 1985.
15 *Daily Mail*, editorial, 21 March 1987.
16 See Frank Reeves, *British Racial Discourse* (Cambridge University Press 1983).
17 *The Financial Times*, 12 October 1985.
18 The *Guardian*, 23 September 1985.
19 Letter to Douglas Hurd from nineteen Anglican clergy, cited in the *Church Times*, 25 October 1985; Douglas Hurd, letter to the Revd R. W. Shaw, January 1986.
20 Statement from the Brixton Council of Churches, 1981.
21 Cited in *The Times*, 14 July 1981.
22 Eldon Griffiths, MP in the *Guardian*, 25 May 1984; Chief Constable James Anderton in *The Times*, 11 December 1979; Sir Kenneth Newman, cited by Tony Benn in the *Guardian*, 4 July 1983.
23 *Report of the Moss Side Enquiry Panel to the Leader of the Greater Manchester Council*, 30 September 1981, cited in Sarah Benton and Patrick Wintour, 'The Backlash to Scarman' in *New Statesman*, 26 March 1982, p. 6.
24 Colonel Sir Eric St Johnston in the *Guardian*, 10 August 1981.
25 John Newman of the Police Federation, cited in *The Times*, 17 October 1985.
26 *Daily Mail* and *Daily Telegraph*, 20 March 1987.
27 *The Times*, editorial, 13 September 1986; *Western Daily Press*, 15 September 1986.
28 The documentation on Alinsky is enormous. See his own books *Reveille for Radicals* (New York, Random House, 1969 edn.) and *Rules for Radicals* (New York, Random House, 1971). See also Arthur M. Brazier, *Black Self-Determination: The Story of the Woodlawn Organisation* (Eerdmans 1969); *The Report of the Bishop's Committee for the Re-evaluation of the Alinsky Community Project* (Kansas City, Mo., 19 October 1965); P. David Finks, *The Radical Vision of Saul Alinsky* (Paulist Press 1984). According to a report in *The Daily Telegraph* on 29 January 1983, 'Alinsky . . . was a Marxist revolutionary.' In fact, there was virtually no Marxist influence on Alinsky. 'I guess you could call me an urban populist,' he once said. 'My philosophy is rooted in an American radical tradition, not in a Marxist tradition' (Marion K. Sanders, 'The Professional Radical: Conversations with Saul Alinsky' in *Harper's Magazine*, June 1965, p. 47). According to

Finks: 'Saul Alinsky was never a revolutionary. He called himself an American "radical". By that he meant he was a political descendant of a long line of American activists . . . His ideological mentors were not Marx and Lenin but Thomas Jefferson and James Madison' (op. cit., pp. 31–2).

This is all well known. However, it has not deterred right-wing groups from linking Alinsky both with Marxism and with violent military-type urban warfare. In 1981 I had a bizarre correspondence with the Parochial Church Council of St Thomas à Becket, Box, Bath, in which it was suggested that Alinsky's work had influenced the Liverpool riots. 'We see nothing puzzling about the possible connection between events in Chicago and those in Liverpool' (letter from Mrs. E. Slade, 24 November 1981). The sudden appearance of Alinsky's name in the literature of right-wing groups in 1981 – his work was well-known among Roman Catholics in the USA and community workers generally long before – seems to have a common origin in a discovery of a line connecting Alinsky mistakenly with the Blackstone Rangers, a well-known Chicago gang which later regrouped into the notorious El Ruken. (Milton Kotler in *Radical Sociology*, ed. by J. David Colfax and Jack L. Roach (New York, Basic Books, 1971), p. 366.)

29 *The Times*, 18 March 1982.

30 Cited in *New Standard*, 9 July 1981.

31 Jones also accused the British Council of Churches of promoting anarchy (*The Times*, 27 August 1981) and attacked the police authority for interfering (ibid., 13 November 1981).

32 William Whitelaw, speech at Warrington, 10 July 1981. For media use of 'outside agitators' themes, cf. 'Search for the Masked Men', *Daily Mail*, 9 July 1981; 'Four Behind the Riots' (*Standard*, 10 July 1981; 'Riots: Four Men Hunted', *Standard*, 12 July 1981; 'Extremists' Master Plan for Chaos' *Daily Mail*, 12 July 1981.

33 Scarman, 3.101; 2.26.

34 John Alderson, lecture to the Royal United Services Institution, cited in Paul Gilroy, *The Empire Strikes Back: Race and Racism in 70s Britain* (Hutchinson/Centre for Contemporary Cultural Studies 1982), p. 167.

35 Sir David McNee, LWT, *The London Programme*, 3 April 1981; *The Times*, 4 April 1981.

36 The *Guardian*, 16 September 1985.

37 *Police/Immigrant Relations* (Cmnd 5438, HMSO 1973).

38 Metropolitan Police evidence to the House of Commons Select Committee, 25 March 1976, cited in Gilroy, op. cit., p. 159.

39 *The Times*, 13 April 1981; the *Guardian*, 19 August 1981.
40 David Webb in *New Democrat*, 3.5 (1985), p. 24.
41 Radio 4, 10 July 1981; *The Times*, 22 January 1977 (speech at Stretford); speech at Ashton-under-Lyne, 30 March 1981; House of Commons, 16 July 1981; speech at Cobham, 25 September 1981, etc.
42 *The Sunday Times*, 15 September 1985.
43 Scarman, 6.4.
44 cf. Martin Kettle, 'The March of Black Outcast London' in *New Society*, 12 March 1981, pp. 456–7.
45 See Clare Demuth, *SUS: A Report on Section 4 of the Vagrancy Act 1824* (Runnymede Trust 1978).
46 *Police Against Black People* (Institute of Race Relations 1979).
47 Gabrielle Cox, *The Church of England and Racism – and Beyond* (Race, Pluralism and Community Group, Board for Social Responsibility 1982), p. 23.
48 Scarman, 9.1.
49 *The Times*, 13 April 1981.
50 Cited in Derek Humphry, *Police Power and Black People* (Panther 1972), p. 13.
51 Colin McGlashan, 'Inside England's Oldest Ghetto' in *The Observer*, 13 August 1972.
52 *Sick City: A Report on Community Relations in Liverpool* (NW Area Young Conservatives 1974).
53 *The Times*, 3 September 1981.
54 ITN, 13 April 1981.
55 John Alderson, Ditchley Conference on Preventative Policing 1977. See also his *Policing Freedom* (Macdonald and Evans 1979).
56 *The Times*, 27 November 1981.
57 *The Times*, 18 June 1981.
58 Sir Kenneth Newman, 'Why I Back the Scarman Line' in *The Times*, 14 June 1982.
59 West Midlands Police, *Handsworth/Lozells September 1985* (1985), p. 71.
60 *Diverse Reports*, Channel 4 TV, 17 October 1984.
61 See Jim Coulter, Susan Miller and Martin Walker, *A State of Siege* (Canary Press 1984).
62 Brian Jenner, *The Coal Strike: Christian Reflections on the Miners' Struggle* (New City 1986), pp. 39, 41.
63 Sir John Biggs-Davison, MP, 'The Role of the Armed Forces in Peace Keeping in the 1970s', Royal United Services Institution seminar, 4 April 1973.
64 Peregrine Worsthorne in *Police Review*, 91.4699 (March 1984), p. 422.

65 Steve Wright, 'New Police Technologies' in *Journal of Peace Research*, 15.4 (1978), pp. 305–22.
66 City of Birmingham, *Independent Inquiry into the Handsworth Disturbances September 1985, Report by Julius Silverman*, p. 11. Cited below as Silverman.
67 Scarman, 6.6
68 Joan Higgins *et al. Government and Urban Poverty* (Blackwell 1983), p. 11.
69 Scarman, 6.4.
70 Silverman, p. 48.
71 Scarman, 4.63.
72 Andrew M. Coleman and L. Paul Gorman, 'Conservatism, dogmatism and Authoritarianism in British Police Officers' in *Sociology*, 16 (1982), pp. 1–11.
73 D. J. Smith and J. Gray, *Police and People in London*, vol. 4 (*The Police in Action* (Policy Studies Institute 1983); George Gaskell, 'The Young, the Black and the Police' in *New Society*, 24 November 1983, pp. 317–18.
74 Metropolitan Police advert in the press, 1975.
75 *150 Years Policing in Bristol* (Avon and Somerset Constabulary 1986), p. 39.
76 Gabrielle Cox, cited in the *Guardian*, 11 August 1984.
77 *National Advisory Commission on Civil Disorders, The Kerner Report* (Washington, DC, 1968), pp. 110–11. Cited below as Kerner.
78 ibid., p. 304.
79 George Gaskell and Patten Smith, 'Are Young Blacks Really Alienated?' in *New Society*, 14 May 1981, pp. 260–1; Scarman, 2.23.
80 Kerner, pp. 110–11.
81 *The Times*, 12 April 1980.
82 Cited in Kerner, p. 485.

Chapter Seven – The Church in a Plural Society

1 Alasdair MacIntyre in D. L. Edwards (ed.), *The Honest to God Debate* (SCM Press 1963), p. 228.
2 'A Society Without a Metaphysics' in *The Listener*, 13 September 1956, pp. 375–6.
3 T. S. Eliot, *The Idea of a Christian Society* (Faber and Faber 1939).
4 The *Guardian* and *The Times*, 21 September 1978. The report referred to was the *National Survey of Religious Attitudes of Young People* (Bible Society 1978).
5 Andrew Greeley, *The Persistence of Religion* (SPCK 1973).

6 R. H. Tawney, *The Western Political Tradition* (SCM 1949), pp. 18–19.
7 *UK Protestant Missionary Handbook* (Evangelical Alliance 1977).
8 W. J. Hollenweger, 'After Twenty Years Research on Pentecostalism' in *Theology*, 87.720. (November 1984), pp. 403–12.
9 *UK Protestant Missions Handbook.*
10 Kenneth Cracknell and Christopher Lamb, *Theology on Full Alert* (British Council of Churches 1986 rev. edn.), p. 9.
11 Report of the National Association of Evangelicals, October 1978.
12 Kenneth Leech, *Youthquake: The Growth of a Counter Culture Through Two Decades* (Sheldon Press 1973).
13 See L. D. Strieker, *The Jesus Trip* (Nashville, Abingdon Press, 1971); and R. M. Enroth, E.E. Ericson and C. B. Peters, *The Jesus People* (Eerdmans 1972).
14 See Jean Holm, 'Religious Education in Britain and the Study of Religion' in *Religion*, 10.2 (Autumn 1980), pp. 209–21.
15 See Kenneth Cracknell, David Jennings and Christine Trethowan, *Blind Leaders for the Blind? Theological Training in Today's Plural Society* (Birmingham AFFOR 1982); Cracknell and Lamb, op. cit.
16 See *Learning in Diversity: A Challenge to Catholic Education* (Catholic Media Office 1984), pp. 55–60.
17 Alasdair MacIntyre, 'A society without a metaphysics', op. cit.
18 See Kenneth Leech, *The Liverpool 8 Defence Committee* (Race, Pluralism and Community Group, Board for Social Responsibility 1981).
19 E. R. Norman, *Christianity and the World Order* (Oxford University Press 1978). See Kenneth Leech (ed.), *Christianity Reinterpreted?* (Jubilee Group 1979).
20 See P. H. Connell, 'Ether Drinking in Ulster' in the *Quarterly Journal of Studies in Alcoholism*, vol. 26 (1965), pp. 629–53.
21 Cain Felder, 'Racial Ambiguities in the Biblical Narratives' in Gregory Baum and John Coleman (eds.), *The Church and Racism* (*Concilium*, T. and T. Clark 1982), p. 23.

Chapter Eight – The Archbishop's Commission and Beyond

1 *Faith in the City: A call to Action by Church and Nation*, Report of the Archbishop's Commission on Urban Priority Areas (Church House Publishing 1985). Cited below as ACUPA.
2 ibid., pp. 361–6.
3 ibid., p. 9.
4 ibid., p. 13.

5 For a survey of government inner-city initiatives see Joan Higgins *et al.*, *Government and Urban Poverty* (Blackwell 1983).
6 Scarman, 6.6
7 Cited in St John B. Groser, *Politics and Persons* (SCM Press 1949), p. 25.
8 ACUPA, p. xiv.
9 *The Daily Telegraph*, 2 December 1985.
10 Auberon Waugh, 'Runcieballs Revisited or What To Do with the Beveridge Boys' in the *Spectator*, 21–8 December 1985.
11 Digby Anderson (ed.), *The Kindness that Kills: The Church's Simplistic Response to Complex Social Issues* (SPCK 1984). For a critique of this book see David Edgar, Kenneth Leech and Paul Weller, *The New Right and the Church* (Jubilee Group 1985).
12 *The Times*, 10 December 1985.
13 Paul Johnson in the *Daily Mail*, 3 December 1985.
14 Ronald Butt, *The Times*, 16 October 1975.
15 Eric James, 'The Church's Position in Cities' in *New Christian*, 30 May 1968, p. 12.
16 ACUPA, p. 10.
17 ibid., p. 9.
18 ibid., p. 205.
19 ibid., p. 23.
20 ibid., p. xv.
21 ibid., p. 57.
22 ibid., pp. 95–100.
23 ibid., p. 96.
24 John Tiller, *A Strategy for the Church's Ministry* (Church Information Office 1983), pp. 37–8.
25 ACUPA, p. 36.
26 Mark R. D. Johnson in *Ethnic and Racial Studies*, 8.3 (July 1985), p. 427.
27 *Journal of the Evangelical Race Relations Group*, Autumn 1984, pp. 3–6.
28 Valerie Pitt, 'Memorandum of Dissent' to *Church and State: Report of the Archbishop's Commission*, The Chadwick Report (Church Information Office 1970), pp. 68–79.
29 For the Board for Social Responsibility's thinking on race issues, see the following General Synod papers: *Britain as a multi-racial and multi-cultural society* (GS 328, 1977); *Pluralism and Community* (GS 450, 1980); *Faith in the City: The Church and Minority Ethnic Groups*, A Report by the Standing Committee (GS 753, 1986). For a critical assessment of the first six years of race relations work within the BSR, see Kenneth Leech, *The Fields of Charity and Sin: Reflections on Combating Racism in the Church of England* (Board for Social Responsibility 1986).

30 ACUPA, p. 75.
31 ibid., p. 109.
32 ibid., p. 114.
33 ibid., p. 119. The whole text is published in *Christian Action Journal*, Autumn 1984.
34 George Moyser, 'The 1980 General Synod: Patterns and Trends' in *Crucible*, April/June 1982, pp. 75–86.
35 ACUPA, p. 313.
36 ibid., p. 55.
37 ibid., p. 25.
38 ibid.
39 ibid., p. 208.
40 ibid., p. 56.
41 ibid., p. 351.
42 John Rex and Robert Moore, *Race, Community and Conflict* (Oxford University Press/Institute of Race Relations 1967), p. 273.
43 R. H. Tawney, *Poverty as an Industrial Problem* (William Morris Press 1913).
44 *The Times*, 21 December 1985.
45 J. N. Figgis, *Churches in the Modern State* (Longmans 1913), pp. 133f.
46 Karl Marx, Preface to *Capital* (ET Moscow, Foreign Languages Publishing House, 1958), vol. 1, p. 10.
47 ACUPA, p. 261.
48 The *Guardian*, 6 December 1985.
49 ACUPA, p. xiv.
50 ibid., pp. 47, 57.
51 ibid., p. 57.
52 ibid., p. 47; *Weekend World*, London Weekend TV, 6 January 1980; *The Times*, 12 January 1980 (Thatcher); *Panorama*, BBC TV, 8 October 1984 (Tebbit).
53 ibid., p. 48.
54 A. E. Harvey, '*Faith in the City*: The Theologian's View' in *Encyclical*, 49 (Autumn 1986), pp. 15–18.
55 ACUPA, p. 48.
56 ibid., p. 59.
57 ibid., p. 55.
58 Stanley Hauerwas, *Vision and Virtue: Essays in Christian Ethical Reflection* (Notre Dame, Fides, 1974), p. 7.
59 'Church and State Agree on Inner Cities' in the *Guardian*, 29 January 1986.
60 Jim Wallis, *Agenda for Biblical People* (Harper and Row 1976), p. 54. Rev. edn. reissued by Triangle 1986.

Chapter Nine – The Urban Church in Retreat: Some Lessons from Chicago

1 Giuseppe Giacosa, 'A City of Smoke' in Bessie Louise Pierce (ed.), *As Others See Us* (University of Chicago Press 1933), p. 276.
2 Lyman Abbott, cited in Josiah Strong, *The Challenge of the City* (New York, Young People's Missionary Movement, 1907), p. v.
3 See George D. Younger, 'The Mission of Christ and the Work of the Church in Chicago' in *International Review of Mission*, 63.250 (April 1974), pp. 256–63.
4 *The City Church*, 14.4 (September/October 1963).
5 I have used the offensive term 'Negroes' when referring to historical documents where the term is used. It is rightly resented and rejected by the black community and by many white people today in the USA.
6 See Melvin G. Halli and Peter d'A. Jones (eds.), *The Ethnic Frontier: Essays on the History of Group Survival in Chicago and the Midwest* (Grand Rapids, Eerdmans, 1977); and Edward R. Kantowicz, *Polish American Politics in Chicago 1888–1940* (Chicago 1975).
7 See *The Negro in Chicago: A Study of Race Relations and a Race Riot* by a Chicago Commission on Race Relations (University of Chicago Press 1922).
8 Allan H. Spear, *Black Chicago: The Making of a Negro Ghetto 1890–1920* (University of Chicago Press 1967).
9 T. L. Philpott, *The Slum and the Ghetto: Neighbourhood Deterioration and Middle Class Reform, Chicago 1880–1930* (New York, Oxford University Press, 1978), p. xvii.
10 St Clair Drake and Horace R. Cayton, *Black Metropolis: A Study of Negro Life in a Northern City* (New York, Harcourt Brace, 1945).
11 ibid., p. xx.
12 Cited in Thomas V. Millea, *Ghetto Fever* (Milwaukee, Bruce, 1968).
13 Evelyn M. Kitagawa and Karl E. Taeuber (eds.), *Local Community Fact Book, Chicago Metropolitan Area* (University of Chicago Community Inventory 1967 edn.).
14 See Pierre de Vise, 'The Wasting of Chicago' in *Focus/Midwest*, 9.58 (1973), pp. 7–9; and 'The Future of Chicago: A Profile of Social Change', op. cit., 11.73 (1977), pp. 16–22.
15 Tom Brune and Eduardo Camacho, *Race and Poverty in Chicago* (Chicago, Community Renewal Society, 1984).
16 William Julius Wilson, *The Declining Significance of Race* (University of Chicago Press 1978). For some of the ensuing debate see Joseph R. Washington, Jr (ed.), *The Declining Significance of Race? A Dialogue among Black and White Social Scientists* (New York, SCI Press, 1979).

17 P. J. Stackhouse, *Chicago and the Baptists* (University of Chicago Press 1933), pp. 200–7.
18 See Gibson Winter, *The Suburban Captivity of the Churches* (Doubleday 1961).
19 Howard Hageman, 'The Theology of the Urban Church' in *The Church Herald*, 7 November 1958.
20 Ross W. Sanderson, *The Strategy of City Church Planning* (New York, Institute of Social and Religious Research, 1932), p. 13.
21 W. C. Hallenbeck, *Minneapolis Churches and their Community Problem* (New York, Institute of Social and Religious Research, 1929).
22 Robert Lee Sutherland, 'An Analysis of Negro Churches in Chicago', Ph.D. thesis, University of Chicago 1930.
23 New York, Seabury Press, 1964.
24 See Kit and Frederica Konolige, *The Power and their Glory: America's Ruling Class, the Episcopalians* (New York, Wyden Books, 1978).
25 See George D. Younger, *The Church and the Urban Power Structure* (Philadelphia, Westminster Press, 1963) and *The Church and Urban Renewal* (Philadelphia, J. B. Lippincott, 1965).
26 On East Harlem see George W. Webber, *The Congregation in Mission* (Nashville, Abingdon Press, 1964).
27 Harvey Cox, *The Secular City* (SCM Press 1963); Gibson Winter, *The New Creation as Metropolis* (New York, Macmillan, 1963).
28 Norman Faramelli, 'The Next Step: The End to Utopian Visions' in *Inside*, June 1976, pp. 17–19.
29 Report to the General Convention by the Standing Commission on the Church in Metropolitan Areas (1982), p. 3.
30 *To Hear and to Heed: The Episcopal Church Listens and Acts in the City* (Forward Movement and Urban Bishops' Coalition, Chicago 1978), p. 4.
31 See Saul Alinsky, *Reveille for Radicals* (University of Chicago Press 1946; New York, Random House, 1969 edn.) and *Rules for Radicals* (New York, Random House, 1971); and John Hall Fish, *Black Power/White Control: The Struggle of the Woodlawn Organisation in Chicago* (Princeton University Press 1961).
32 Walter Kloetzli, *The Church and the Urban Challenge* (Philadelphia, Muhlenberg, 1961).
33 See John R. Fry, *Locked Out Americans* (Harper and Row 1973).
34 Walter E. Ziegenhals, 'Churches in Transition', MS, (Chicago, Community Renewal Society, June 1971), p. 4.
35 Millea, op. cit.
36 *The Edge of the Ghetto: A Study of Church Involvement in Community Organisation* (University of Chicago Divinity School 1966), p. 137.

37 The Ecumenical Institute also called itself the Institute of Cultural Affairs and Fifth City, and for a while worked in the Isle of Dogs in East London.
38 Younger, op. cit., p. 257.
39 Preface to Richard H. Luecke, *Perchings* (Chicago Urban Training Centre Press 1972), pp. 5–6.
40 John Atherton, *Chicago Sermons and Papers* (Manchester William Temple Foundation 1963), p. 2.
41 Martin Marty, *Second Chance for American Protestants* (Harper and Row 1963), p. 65.
42 Younger, op. cit., pp. 261–2.
43 See Marjaleena Repo, 'Organising "the poor" against the Working Class' in *Transformation* [Toronto], 1.2 (1972), p. 4–15, 42–4.
44 Younger, op. cit., p. 261.

Chapter Ten – Religion and the Rise of Racism

1 A. Sivanandan, *Race, Class and the State: The Black Experience in Britain* (Institute of Race Relations 1976), p. 367. This and other papers are included in his book *A Different Hunger* (Pluto Press 1982).
2 Max Weber, *The Protestant Ethic and the Spirit of Capitalism* (1920; Unwin University Books, 1976 edn.).
3 R. H. Tawney, *Religion and the Rise of Capitalism* (1926; Penguin 1969 edn.), Cited below as RRC.
4 R. H. Preston, *Religion and the Persistence of Capitalism* (SCM Press 1979).
5 R. H. Tawney, *Land and Labour in China* (Allen and Unwin 1932) and *The Condition of China* (Newcastle, Earl Grey Memorial Lecture 1933).
6 Partha Sarathi Gupta, *Imperialism and the British Labour Movement 1914–1964* (Macmillan 1975), p. 337. Those who are in any doubt as to how racist some of the early Fabians were should read the accounts of China in Beatrice Webb's diaries. The Webbs were crudely racist in their accounts of the Chinese people, and used language which makes the National Front seem quite restrained. They argued that the moral defects of the Chinese as a race, demonstrated particularly in their homosexuality, made them incapable of orderly government. Beatrice Webb wrote in her unpublished diaries: 'It is this rottenness of physical and moral character that makes one despair of China – their constitution seems devastated by drugs and abnormal sexual indulgence. They are essentially an unclean race.' (*Diaries*, vol. 30, 6 November 1911, cited in J. M. Winter, *Socialism and the Challenge of War* (Routledge and Kegan Paul 1974), p. 43). They had

'horrid expressions' on their faces, and were a 'horrid race'. Sidney Webb, too, saw the Chinese as a 'striking example of arrested development', and based his conclusion on what appears to be a crude early form of sociobiology.

7 Ross Terrill, *R. H. Tawney and his Times: Socialism as Fellowship* (Harvard University Press 1973), p. 276.

8 *International Review of Mission*, 31.51 (July 1924), reviewing J. H. Oldham, *Christianity and the Race Problem* (SCM Press 1924).

9 Foreword to Max Weber, op. cit., p. 2.

10 RRC, pp. 195–6.

11 See Jeremy Rifkin and Ted Howard, *The Emerging Order: God in an Age of Scarcity* (New York, G. P. Putnams Sons, 1979); and their article 'Hope for a Second Reformation' in *Sojourners*, September 1979, p. 11.

12 R. H. Tawney, *Equality* (Allen and Unwin 1964 edn.), p. 197.

13 J. M. Winter and D. M. Joslin (eds.), *R. H. Tawney's Commonplace Book* (*Economic History Review* Supplement 5, Cambridge University Press 1972), p. 53.

14 ibid., p. 67.

15 See John Hall and Joan Higgins, 'What Influences Today's Labour MPs?' in *New Society*, 2 December 1976, pp. 457–9; and George Moyser, 'Voting on Moral Issues in the House of Common, in *Papers in Religion and Politics*, no. 10, Spring Term 1980, University of Manchester, Faculty of Theology and Department of Government.

16 *The Times*, 9 June 1978.

17 Prebendary John Pearce in *Third Way*, June 1980, pp. 31–2, reviewing Keith Joseph and Jonathan Sumpton, *Equality* (John Murray 1979).

18 *The Times*, 17 December 1975.

19 Peter Walker, *The Ascent of Britain* (Sidgwick and Jackson 1977), pp. 20–2.

20 George Gale in Maurice Cowling (ed.), *Conservative Essays* (Cassell 1978), p. 190.

21 Peter Townsend, *Poverty in the United Kingdom* (Penguin 1979).

22 RRC, p. 265.

23 The *Guardian*, 3 July 1978.

24 R. H. Tawney, *Commonplace Book*, (Cambridge University Press, 1972) p. 18.

25 Ruth Glass and John Westergaard, *London's Housing Needs* (Centre for Urban Studies 1965), p. xi.

26 Tawney, op. cit., p. 51.

27 See Charles Gore, *The Sermon on the Mount* (1896) and *The Social Doctrine of the Sermon on the Mount* (1904).

28 R. H. Tawney, *The Acquisitive Society* (1921) p. 239.
29 RRC, pp. 17–74.
30 Trevor Huddleston, *Naught for Your Comfort* (Fontana 1971 edn.), p. 50.
31 For the application of Tawney's thesis to the South African situation, see A. Sivanandan, 'Race, Class and Caste in South Africa – An Open Letter to No Sizwe' in *Race and Class*, 22.3 (Winter 1981), pp. 293–300; and Ken Jordaan, 'Iberian and Anglo-Saxon Racism: A Study of Portuguese Angola and South Africa', op. cit., 20.4 (Spring 1979), pp. 391–412.
32 See the works of Frantz Fanon, especially *Black Skin, White Masks* (MacGibbon and Kee 1968).
33 See S. M. Lipset and Earl Raab, *The Politics of Unreason: Right-Wing Extremism in America 1790–1970* (Heinemann 1971), pp. 117–23; Kennett T. Jackson, *The Ku Klux Klan in the City 1915–1930* (New York, Oxford University Press, 1967), p. 63. For more up-to-date information on the recent resurgence of the Ku Klux Klan contact KlanWatch, PO Box 548, Montgomery, Alabama 36101.
34 See Charles Y. Glock and Rodney Stark, *Christian Beliefs and Anti-Semitism* (Harper and Row 1966).
35 See Kenneth Leech, 'Is There a New Religious Fascism?' in *The Social God* (Sheldon Press 1981), pp. 97–115.
36 A. S. Duncan-Jones, *The Struggle for Religious Freedom in Germany* (Gollancz 1938), pp. 299f.
37 William Shirer, *The Rise and Fall of the Third Reich* (Secker and Warburg 1960), p. 435.
38 Richard Gutteridge, *Open Thy Mouth for the Dumb: The German Evangelical Church and the Jews 1879–1950* (Blackwell 1976), p. 191.
39 ibid., pp. 41, 268.
40 ibid., p. 282.
41 Sally Holterman, 'Areas of Urban Deprivation in Great Britain: An Analysis of the 1971 Census' in *Social Trends*, 6 (1975).
42 A. Sivanandan, 'From Resistance to Rebellion: Asian and Afro-Caribbean Struggles in Britain' in *Race and Class*, 23.3 (1981–2), p. 112.
43 On Gaitskell's role see Philip M. Williams, *Hugh Gaitskell: A Political Biography* (Cape 1979), pp. 676–9. However, it should be remembered that the earliest calls for control of black immigration came from Labour members – John Hynd (House of Commons, 5 November 1954) and Patrick Gordon Walker (*News Chronicle* and *Smethwick Telephone*, 12 November 1954) – and others followed after the Notting Hill riots, including the local Member, George Rogers (*Daily Herald*, 2 September 1958).

44 The *Guardian*, 23 January 1965.
45 Address to NCCI, 2 September 1965.
46 *The Times*, 5th August 1967.
47 *The Times*, Law Report, 16 September 1958.
48 Nicholas Deakin, *Colour, Citizenship and British Society* (Panther 1970), p. 325.
49 Migne, *Patrologia Graeca*, 14.747.
50 R. M. Titmuss, 'Goals of Today's Welfare State' in Perry Anderson and Robin Blackburn (eds.), *Towards Socialism* (Fontana 1964), p. 354. See also his *Commitment to Welfare* (Allen and Unwin 1968), pp. 113–14.
51 David L. Kirp, *Doing Good by Doing Little: Race and Schooling in Britain* (University of California Press 1981), p. 2.
52 House of Lords, 12 March 1962; *Church Times*, 16 March 1962.
53 *The Time Is Now* (SPCK 1971), p. 18.
54 Gutteridge, op. cit., p. 96.
55 RRC, p. 280.
56 *Church Times*, 14 August 1987.
57 Reprinted in Alasdair MacIntyre, *Against the Self-Images of the Age* (Duckworth 1971), pp. 38–42.
58 Statement of the Central Committee of the WCC, Canterbury, August 1969.

Chapter Eleven – Racism and the Urban Parish

1 C. Kilmer Myers, *Light the Dark Streets* (Dolphin 1961), pp. 141–2.
2 See the reports from Wasdell's Unit for Research into Changing Institutions (URCHIN), formerly called the Urban Church Project (St Matthias Vicarage, Poplar High Street, London E14 0AE). Examples include *Divide and Conquer: Toward the Multi-Centre Parish* (1974); *Let My People Grow* (1974) and *Long Range Planning and the Church* (1979).
3 The Alternative Service Book (Clowes, SPCK and Cambridge University Press 1980), p. 10.
4 J. A. T. Robinson, *On Being the Church in the World* (SCM Press 1964), p. 71.
5 John Davies in Kenneth Leech and Rowan Williams (eds.), *Essays Catholic and Radical* (Bowerdean Press 1983), p. 192.
6 Rose C. Jackson, 'The Nature and Role of Black Gospel Music in the Black Pentecostal Worship Service, D.Min.thesis, University of Chicago 1986, p. 1. See also J. H. Cone, *The Spirituals and the Blues* (Seabury Press 1972), and Viv Broughton, *Black Gospel* (Blandford 1985).

7 Donald McGavran, *Understanding Church Growth* (Grand Rapids, Eerdmans, 1970), p. 86. For a critique of this view see Greg Smith, *Christian Ethnics: Church Growth in Multi-Cultural Britain* (British Church Growth Association 1983).
8 J. M. Gustafson, *The Church as Moral Decision Maker* (Philadelphia, Pilgrim Press, 1970), pp. 122–3.
9 Roderick Hewitt, 'Reflections on the Handsworth Riot: An Agenda for Action by the Churches', MS, 1985.
10 Book of Common Prayer, Collect for Good Friday.
11 Roger Hooker and Christopher Lamb, *Love the Stranger: Ministry in Multi-Faith Areas* (SPCK 1986), p. 11.
12 *Southampton Advertiser*, 24 July 1986.

Chapter Twelve – Racism and the Proclamation of the Gospel

1 J. Jeremias, *Jerusalem at the Time of Jesus* (Philadelphia, Fortress Press, 1969), pp. 77–84.
2 Rowan Williams, *Resurrection* (Darton, Longman and Todd 1982), p. 35.
3 Thom Hopler, *A World of Difference* (Downers Grove, Illinois, Inter-Varsity Press, 1981), p. 97.
4 Markus Barth, *The Broken Wall* (Collins 1960), p. 34.
5 Cedric Robinson, 'The Emergence and Limitations of European Radicalism' in *Race and Class*, 21.2 (1979), p. 158.
6 J. A. Baker in *Theology and Racism No. 1: The Bible, Racism and Anti-Semitism* (Board for Social Reponsibility 1985), pp. 12–13.
7 Thomas Merton, 'A Mystique of Violence' in *Peace News*, 18 September 1964, p. 6.
8 J. L. Segundo, *The Liberation of Theology* (Maryknoll, Orbis, 1976), *passim*.
9 Edward Norman, *The Victorian Christian Socialists* (Cambridge University Press 1986), p. 56. See also L. P. Curtis, *Apes and Angels: The Irishman in Victorian Caricature* (David and Charles 1971) and *Anglo-Saxons and Celts* (New York University Press 1968).
10 Baker, op. cit., p. 13.
11 J. H. Cone, *Speaking the Truth: Ecumenism, Liberation and Black Theology* (Grand Rapids, Eerdmans, 1986), p. 122.
12 Williams, op. cit., pp. 10–11.
13 Sheila Rowbotham, *Dreams and Dilemmas: Collected Writings* (Virago 1983), p. 217.
14 See Martin Barker, *The New Racism* (Junction Books 1981) and Paul

Gordon and Francesca Klug, *New Right, New Racism* (Searchlight Publications 1986).

15 *The Times*, 18 November 1968; Bill Smithies and Peter Fiddick, *Enoch Powell on Immigration* (Sphere 1969), pp. 73–4.

16 *The Daily Telegraph*, 22 January 1977.

17 House of Commons, *Hansard*, 914.137 (5 July 1976), p. 1409.

18 *Daily Mail*, 9 November 1981.

19 John Meyendorff, *Christ in Eastern Christian Thought* (New York, St Vladimir's Seminary Press, 1975), p. 11.

20 E. Colledge and J. Walsh (trs. and eds.), *Julian of Norwich: Showings*, (SPCK, Paulist 1978), ch. 57, p. 291.

21 E. L. Mascall, *Theology and the Future* (Darton, Longman and Todd 1968), p. 133.

22 David Hume, *A Treatise of Human Nature*, ed. by P. Ardal (Fontana 1972 edn), pp. 73, 219.

23 John Casey, 'One Nation: The Politics of Race' in *Salisbury Review*, 1 (Autumn 1982), pp. 14ff.

24 Robert McNeill in the *Daily Star*, 18 April 1984.

25 Desmond Morris, *The Human Zoo* (Corgi 1971), p. 126.

26 E. O. Wilson, *On Human Nature* (Harvard University Press 1978), p. 92.

27 Richard Lynn, 'The Sociobiology of Nationalism' in *New Society*, 1 July 1976, cited by Barker, op. cit., p. 108.

28 William MacDougall, *Ethics and Some Modern World Problems* (Methuen 1924).

29 ibid., p. 15.

30 Cited in Reinhold Niebuhr, *The Nature and Destiny of Man* (New York, Scribners, 1964 edn.), vol. 2, p. 194.

31 Cited in Charles Jones, *The Religious Instruction of Negroes in the United States* (Savannah, T. Purse Co., 1842), p. 20.

32 John Davies in Kenneth Leech and Rowan Williams (eds), *Essays Catholic and Radical* (Bowerdean Press 1983), pp. 188f.

33 Richard Gutteridge, *Open Thy Mouth for the Dumb: The German Evangelical Church and the Jews 1879–1950* (Blackwell 1976), p. 2.

34 Dietrich Bonhoeffer, *No Rusty Swords* (Collins 1965), p. 326.

35 Gerhard Kittel, *Die Judenfrage* (1933), cited in Olga Levertoff, *The Jews in a Christian Social Order* (Sheldon Press 1942), pp. 13, 14.

36 Reinhold Niebuhr, 'Christianity and Political Justice' in *Christian Newsletter*, supplement no. 11 (10 January 1940).See also Niebuhr's comments on the period in his various works.

37 J. H. Oldham, *Christianity and the Race Problem* (SCM Press 1925 edn.), p. 26.

Acknowledgements

Acknowledgements are due to the following for permission to quote from their material:

Central Board of Finance of the Church of England, for excerpts from *Faith in the City: A Call to Action by Church and Nation*, the Report of the Archbishop's Commission on Urban Priority Areas (Church House Publishing,1985).

Faber and Faber, for an excerpt from *A Troubled Area*, by Pearl Jephcott, published in 1964.

London Borough of Tower Hamlets Local History Library and Archives, for excerpts from the papers of Edith Ramsey.

Lyrics from Paul Simon's song *A Church is Burning* are reproduced by kind permission of Pattern Music Ltd.

Bible quotations in this book are from the Revised Standard Version of the Bible, copyright 1946, 1952, 1957, 1971, by the Division of Christian Education of the National Council of the Churches of Christ in the USA, and are used by permission.

Index

SOUL FRIEND

A Study of Spirituality

Kenneth Leech

Soul Friend examines the concept of spiritual guidance in the Christian tradition from the Desert Fathers to the more recent thinking of the Roman Catholic Church, and relates it to the contemporary quest for spirituality.

'A book which is practical, packed with information, and completely successful in its aim – to provide some nourishment for the ministry of spiritual direction by bringing together the teachings of the great spiritual guides, and to help anyone who wishes to know more about the Christian tradition of prayer.' – *Church Times*

'I do hope that no one is going to miss *Soul Friend* . . . This book really is a "must".' – *The Tablet*

'This is an amazing compendium, in fact, a prodigy.' – *Methodist Recorder*

'This superbly unitive study, which is sympathetic to all traditions, aware of psychology without making theology its slave, strikes a proper balance between the mystical and the prophetic, and above all, is radiant with the gentleness of Christ.' – *Expository Times*

'Enormously learned but never loaded with learning; the learning illuminates, but the theme, the texture are sweet and loving and tender; it is a wise work.' – *The Friend*

ISBN 0 85699 133 6

True Prayer

An Introduction to Christian Spirituality

Kenneth Leech

'Why should I pray' and 'How should I pray?' These questions are comprehensively answered in *True Prayer*. It is written for the thinking, lay Christian who, although lacking a theological background, feels the need for a deeper spiritual life. 'This widespreading introduction to prayer finds space to range from the nature of prayer to personal relationship with God; from prayer and politics to Eucharistic worship. Ken Leech calls on many writers, ancient and modern, to back and illumine his thesis. He is lucid and compelling.' – *Fr Michael Hollings*. It is essential material for theological college students, parish training, Lent courses and for individuals.

'This is an admirable resource book of the teaching programme of the parish priest, and as full a study of Christian belief and practice in the spiritual life as the enquiring lay person will need. With its informativeness and imaginative grasp it may well come to be regarded as the current textbook of the subject.' – *Church Times*

'In *True Prayer* we have a rare peak among the plains . . . It is clear that Kenneth Leech is now a foremost writer on late 20th century Western spirituality.' – *Church of England Newspaper*

'Lucid and compelling . . . I recommend it to parish priests and others who are called upon to teach about the life of prayer to congregations and individuals; and to anyone setting out on the Christian life.' – *The Tablet*

'This is a book well worth reading and should prove a great help for prayer.' – *Catholic Herald*

ISBN 0 85969 255 8

TRUE GOD

An Exploration in Spiritual Theology

Kenneth Leech

True God completes the acclaimed trilogy Kenneth Leech began with *Soul Friend* and *True Prayer*. It draws together spirituality and social concern, and relates theology to the practice of prayer. It is not simply *about* God, but aims to help people move towards union *with* God.

The book begins by examining the experience of God in the Old and New Testaments, and considers some of the key symbols and themes which people have used to try and describe their own experience of God – desert, darkness, water, fire and incarnation. It reasserts the central position of the Eucharist and throws new light on the important themes of sexuality and of the motherhood of God, and the God of justice. Finally all these diverse strands are gathered together, to present a challenging manifesto for a renewed spirituality.

'In *True God* Ken Leech, the most angry and prophetic writer in British theology, has produced a truly magnificent book.'
– *Church Times*

ISBN 0 85969 462 3 Price: £9·95 net

Spirituality and Pastoral Care

Kenneth Leech

This book examines the rich Christian tradition of personal spiritual disciplines, and considers the ministry of spiritual direction – its links with counselling and therapy and its prophetic dimension.

Through his portraits of four very different priests – Brother Nevill SSF, Canon Stanley Evans, Fr Hugh Maycock and Bishop Colin Winter – he shows spirituality in action, and gives a fascinating insight into the different spiritual and pastoral influences that shaped his thinking and his spiritual growth.

'Funny, touching and disturbing.' – *Church Times*

'A wealth of perceptive comment on the fundamental theme of spirituality.' – *Church of England News*

'. . . Will provoke deep thought and call you to a more robust spirituality.' – *Baptist Times*

'This is a practical book rooted in scripture, and the author draws from a wide range of different traditions of spiritual writers, and conveys with real conviction his belief that spiritual direction is a deeply personal ministry with the Body of Christ.' – *Expository Times*

ISBN 0 85969 520 4

Price: £4·95 net